Mastering Swift 4

Fourth Edition

An in-depth and comprehensive guide to
modern programming techniques with Swift

Jon Hoffman

BIRMINGHAM - MUMBAI

Mastering Swift 4

Fourth Edition

First published: June 2015

Second edition: November 2015

Third edition: October 2016

Fourth edition: September 2017

Production reference: 1250917

Published by Packt Publishing Ltd.
Livery Place
35 Livery Street
Birmingham
B3 2PB, UK.
ISBN 978-1-78847-780-2

www.packtpub.com

Credits

Author

Jon Hoffman

Reviewer

Arthur Ariel Sabintsev

Commissioning Editor

Ashwin Nair

Acquisition Editor

Reshma Raman

Content Development Editor

Vikas Tiwari

Technical Editor

Subhalaxmi Nadar

Copy Editor

Safis Editing

Project Coordinator

Ulhas Kambali

Proofreader

Safis Editing

Indexer

Rekha Nair

Graphics

Abhinash Sahu

Production Coordinator

Melwyn D'sa

About the Author

Jon Hoffman has over 25 years of experience in the field of information technology. Over these years, Jon has worked in the areas of system administration, network administration, network security, application development, and architecture. Currently, Jon works as a senior software engineer for Syn-Tech Systems.

Jon has developed extensively for the iOS platform since 2008. This includes several apps that he has published in the App Store, apps that he has written for third parties, and numerous enterprise applications. He has also developed mobile applications for the Android and Windows platforms. What really drives Jon is the challenges that the field of information technology provides, and there is nothing more exhilarating to him than overcoming a challenge.

Some of Jon's other interests are spending time with his family, robotic projects, and 3D printing. Jon also really enjoys Tae Kwon Do, where he and his oldest daughter, Kailey, earned their black belts together early in 2014, Kim (his wife), earned her black belt in December 2014, and his youngest daughter, Kara, is currently working toward her black belt.

About the Reviewer

Arthur Ariel Sabintsev is one of the lead iOS engineers at The Washington Post. His mobile engineering career includes working for a U.S. government-funded digital identity startup (ID.me), a Techstars-funded video startup (Shelby.tv), and an award winning mobile development agency (Fueled). He's spent the last 4 years teaching Swift and Objective-C for General Assembly and Betamore. He also maintains over a dozen open source iOS libraries and has made contributions to the Swift language and to the Swift Source Compatibility Suite. Before leaving his PhD program, he was an experimental nuclear physicist who worked underground colliding subatomic and subnuclear particles.

www.PacktPub.com

For support files and downloads related to your book, please visit `www.PacktPub.com`.

Did you know that Packt offers eBook versions of every book published, with PDF and ePub files available? You can upgrade to the eBook version at `www.PacktPub.com` and as a print book customer, you are entitled to a discount on the eBook copy. Get in touch with us at `service@packtpub.com` for more details.

At `www.PacktPub.com`, you can also read a collection of free technical articles, sign up for a range of free newsletters and receive exclusive discounts and offers on Packt books and eBooks.

`https://www.packtpub.com/mapt`

Get the most in-demand software skills with Mapt. Mapt gives you full access to all Packt books and video courses, as well as industry-leading tools to help you plan your personal development and advance your career.

Why subscribe?

- Fully searchable across every book published by Packt
- Copy and paste, print, and bookmark content
- On demand and accessible via a web browser

Customer Feedback

Thanks for purchasing this Packt book. At Packt, quality is at the heart of our editorial process. To help us improve, please leave us an honest review on this book's Amazon page at https://www.amazon.com/dp/1788477804.

If you'd like to join our team of regular reviewers, you can email us at customerreviews@packtpub.com. We award our regular reviewers with free eBooks and videos in exchange for their valuable feedback. Help us be relentless in improving our products!

Table of Contents

Preface   1

Chapter 1: Taking the First Steps with Swift   7

  What is Swift?   7

    Swift features   9

  Playgrounds   11

    Getting started with Playgrounds   11

    iOS, tvOS, and macOS Playgrounds   15

    Showing images in a Playground   16

    Creating and displaying graphs in Playgrounds   21

    What Playgrounds are not   22

    Swift language syntax   23

    Comments   23

    Semicolons   26

    Parentheses   27

    Curly brackets   28

    An assignment operator does not return a value   29

    Spaces are optional in conditional and assignment statements   30

  Hello World   30

  Summary   32

Chapter 2: Learning about Variables, Constants, Strings, and Operators   33

  Constants and variables   34

    Defining constants and variables   35

    Type safety   37

    Type inference   38

    Explicit types   38

    Numeric types   39

      Integer types   39

      Floating-point and Double values   42

    The Boolean type   43

    The string type   44

    Optional variables   48

    Optional binding   51

    Optional chaining   52

    Enumerations   54

Operators 58
The assignment operator 58
Comparison operators 59
Arithmetic operators 59
The remainder operator 60
Compound assignment operators 60
The ternary conditional operator 61
The logical NOT operator 61
The logical AND operator 61
The logical OR operator 62
Summary 62
Chapter 3: Using Swift Collections and the Tuple Type 63
Swift collection types 64
Mutability 64
Arrays 65
Creating and initializing arrays 65
Accessing the array elements 67
Counting the elements of an array 68
Is the array empty? 69
Appending to an array 69
Inserting a value into an array 70
Replacing elements in an array 70
Removing elements from an array 70
Merging two arrays 71
Retrieving a subarray from an array 71
Making bulk changes to an array 72
Algorithms for arrays 73
Sort 73
Sorted 74
Filter 74
Map 75
forEach 76
Iterating over an array 76
Dictionaries 77
Creating and initializing dictionaries 78
Accessing dictionary values 78
Counting the key or values in a dictionary 79
Is the dictionary empty? 79
Updating the value of a key 79
Adding a key-value pair 80

Removing a key-value pair	80
Set	81
Initializing a set	81
Inserting items into a set	82
Determining the number of items in a set	82
Checking whether a set contains an item	83
Iterating over a set	83
Removing items in a set	83
Set operations	84
Tuples	86
Summary	87
Chapter 4: Control Flow and Functions	89
What have we learned so far?	89
Curly brackets	90
Parentheses	90
Control flow	91
Conditional statements	91
The if statement	91
Conditional code execution with the if...else statement	92
The guard statement	93
The for-in loop	95
Using the for...in loop	95
The while loop	96
Using the while loop	97
Using the repeat-while loop	97
The switch statement	98
Using case and where statements with conditional statements	102
Filtering with the where statement	103
Filtering with the for-case statement	103
Using the if-case statement	106
Control transfer statements	107
The continue statement	107
The break statement	108
The fallthrough statement	108
Functions	109
Using a single parameter function	109
Using a multi-parameter function	111
Defining a parameter's default values	111
Returning multiple values from a function	112
Returning optional values	114
Adding external parameter names	115

Using variadic parameters	116
Inout parameters	117
Putting it all together	118
Summary	119

Chapter 5: Classes and Structures — 121

What are classes and structures?	122
Similarities between classes and structures	122
Differences between classes and structures	122
Value versus reference types	123
Creating a class or structure	124
Properties	124
Stored properties	125
Computed properties	127
Property observers	130
Methods	131
Custom initializers	133
Internal and external parameter names	135
Failable initializers	136
Access controls	137
Inheritance	139
Overriding methods and properties	141
Overriding methods	142
Overriding properties	144
Preventing overrides	144
Protocols	145
Protocol syntax	145
Property requirements	146
Method requirements	147
Extensions	148
Memory management	150
How ARC works	150
Strong reference cycles	152
Summary	157

Chapter 6: Using Protocols and Protocol Extensions — 159

Protocols as types	160
Polymorphism with protocols	162
Type casting with protocols	162
Protocol extensions	164

Do I need to use protocols?	173
Swift's standard library	173
Summary	174
Chapter 7: Protocol-Oriented Design	175
Requirements	176
Object-oriented design	176
Protocol-oriented design	182
Protocol inheritance	183
Protocol composition	184
Protocol-oriented design	185
Using the where statement with protocols	188
Structures versus classes	189
The array structure	190
Summary	191
Chapter 8: Writing Safer Code with Availability and Error Handling	193
Native error handling	194
Representing errors	194
Throwing errors	195
Catching errors	198
The availability attribute	202
Summary	204
Chapter 9: Custom Subscripting	205
Introducing subscripts	205
Subscripts with Swift arrays	206
Creating and using custom subscripts	207
Read-only custom subscripts	208
Calculated subscripts	209
Subscript values	209
External names for subscripts	209
Multidimensional subscripts	211
When not to use a custom subscript	213
Summary	214
Chapter 10: Using Optional Types	215
Introducing optionals	215
The need for optional types in Swift	217
Defining an optional	218
Using optionals	218

Forced unwrapping of an optional 219
Optional binding 220
Returning optionals from functions and methods 221
Using an optional as a parameter in a function or method 222
Optional binding with the guard statement 223
Optional types with tuples 223
Optional chaining 224
The nil coalescing operator 226
Summary 227

Chapter 11: Working with Generics 229
An introduction to generics 229
Generic functions 230
Generic types 234
Generic subscripts 237
Associated types 238
Summary 241

Chapter 12: Working with Closures 243
An introduction to closures 243
Simple closures 244
Shorthand syntax for closures 247
Using closures with Swift's array algorithms 250
Standalone closures and good style guidelines 254
Changing functionality 257
Selecting a closure based on results 259
Creating strong reference cycles with closures 261
Summary 265

Chapter 13: Using Mix and Match 267
What is mix and match? 267
When to use mix and match 268
Using Swift and Objective-C together in the same project 269
Creating the project 269
Adding Swift files to the Objective-C project 272
The Objective-C bridging header file - part 1 275
Adding the Objective-C file to the project 276
The Messages Objective-C class 278
The Objective-C bridging header file - part 2 280
The MessageBuilder Swift class - accessing Objective-C code from Swift 280
The Objective-C class - accessing Swift code from Objective-C 281

Summary	282
Chapter 14: Concurrency and Parallelism in Swift	283
Concurrency and parallelism	284
Grand Central Dispatch	285
Calculation type	287
Creating queues	287
Creating and using a concurrent queue	288
Creating and using a serial queue	290
async versus sync	292
Executing code on the main queue function	292
Using asyncAfter	293
Using the Operation and OperationQueue types	293
Using BlockOperation	294
Using the addOperation() method of the operation queue	296
Subclassing the Operation class	297
Summary	300
Chapter 15: Swift Formatting and Style Guide	301
What is a programming style guide?	301
Your style guide	302
Do not use semicolons at the end of statements	303
Do not use parentheses for conditional statements	303
Naming	303
Custom types	304
Functions and methods	304
Constants and variables	304
Indenting	305
Comments	306
Using the self keyword	307
Constants and variables	307
Optional types	307
Using optional binding	307
Using optional chaining instead of optional binding for multiple unwrapping	308
Using type inference	309
Using shorthand declaration for collections	310
Using switch rather than multiple if statements	310
Don't leave commented-out code in your application	311
Summary	311
Chapter 16: Swift Core Libraries	313
Apple's URL loading system	314
URLSession	314

URLSessionConfiguration 315
URLSessionTask 316
URL 316
URLRequest 316
HTTPURLResponse 316
REST web services 317
Making an HTTP GET Request 317
Making an HTTP POST request 320
Formatter 323
DateFormatter 323
NumberFormatter 326
FileManager 327
Encoding and Decoding JSON Data 330
Using JSONEncoder 331
Using JSONDecoder 333
Summary 334
Chapter 17: Adopting Design Patterns in Swift 335
What are design patterns? 336
Creational patterns 337
The singleton design pattern 338
Understanding the problem 339
Understanding the solution 339
Implementing the singleton pattern 340
The builder design pattern 341
Understanding the problem 342
Understanding the solution 342
Implementing the builder pattern 342
Structural design patterns 347
The bridge pattern 348
Understanding the problem 348
Understanding the solution 348
Implementing the bridge pattern 348
The façade pattern 353
Understanding the problem 353
Understanding the solution 353
Implementing the façade pattern 353
The proxy design pattern 356
Understanding the problem 356
Understanding the solution 356
Implementing the proxy pattern 357
Behavioral design patterns 359

The command design pattern   360
    Understanding the problem   360
    Understanding the solution   360
    Implementing the command pattern   360
The strategy pattern   363
    Understanding the problem   363
    Understanding the solution   363
    Implementing the strategy pattern   363
Summary   365
Index   367

Preface

Swift is a programming language that was first introduced by Apple at the World Wide Developers Conference (WWDC) in 2014. Each year since that initial announcement, Apple has announced a new version of Swift. At the WWDC in 2017, Apple announced Swift 4.

Swift 4 offers some exciting changes, such as Strings, which are once again a collection of Generic subscripts and one-side range operators. In this book, we will look at these and other changes in Swift.

What this book covers

Chapter 1, *Taking the First Steps with Swift*, introduces you to the the Swift programming language and discusses what inspired Apple to create Swift. We'll also go over the basic syntax of Swift and how to use Playgrounds to experiment and test the Swift code.

Chapter 2, *Learning about Variables, Constants, Strings, and Operators*, introduces you to variables and constants in Swift and when to use them. We will also look at the most common operators in the Swift language.

Chapter 3, *Using Swift Collections and the Tuple Type*, explains Swift's array, set, and dictionary collection types and shows examples of how to use them. We'll also show how to use the Tuple type in Swift.

Chapter 4, *Control Flow and Functions*, shows you how to use Swift's control flow statements. These include loops, conditional, and control transfer statements. The second half of the chapter is all about functions.

Chapter 5, *Classes and Structures*, dedicates itself to Swift's classes and structures. We'll look at what makes them similar and what makes them different. We'll also look at access controls. We will conclude this chapter by looking at memory management in Swift, so you will understand how ARC works and how to avoid strong reference cycles.

Chapter 6, *Using Protocols and Protocol Extensions*, covers both protocols and protocol extensions in detail because protocols are very important to the Swift language, and having a solid understanding of them will help us write flexible and reusable code.

Chapter 7, *Protocol-Oriented Design*, covers the best practices of protocol-oriented design with Swift. This will be a brief overview of what is covered in the protocol-oriented programming book.

Chapter 8, *Writing Safer Code with Availability and Error Handling*, covers error handling in depth as well as the new availability feature. This feature is really important for writing safe code.

Chapter 9, *Custom Subscripting*, discusses how we can use custom subscripts in our classes, structures, and enumerations.

Chapter 10, *Using Optional Types*, explains what optional types really are and what are the various ways to unwrap them. For a developer who is just learning Swift, optional types can be one of the most confusing items to learn.

Chapter 11, *Working with Generics*, explains how Swift implements generics. Generics are a very important part of the Swift language and it is essential to understand them.

Chapter 12, *Working with Closures*, teaches you how to define and use closures in our code. Closures in Swift are similar to blocks in Objective-C except that they have a much cleaner and easier way of using syntax.

Chapter 13, *Using Mix and Match*, explains mix and match and demonstrates how you can include Swift code in your Objective-C projects and Objective-C code in your Swift projects.

Chapter 14, *Concurrency and Parallelism in Swift*, shows you how to use both grand central dispatch and operation queues to add concurrency and parallelism to your applications. Understanding and knowing how to add concurrency and parallelism to your apps can significantly enhance the user experience.

Chapter 15, *Swift Formatting and Style Guide*, defines a style guide for the Swift language that can be used as a template for enterprise developers who need to create a style guide.

Chapter 16, *Swift Core Libraries*, explores some of the functionality in the Swift core library. This will include accessing REST services working with JSON data and the formatting framework.

Chapter 17, *Adopting Design Patterns in Swift*, shows you how to implement some of the more common design patterns in Swift. A design pattern identifies a common software development problem and provides a strategy for dealing with it.

What you need for this book

To follow along with the examples in this book, you'll need to have an Apple computer with OS X 10.13 or higher installed. You'll also need to install Xcode version 9.0 or higher with Swift version 4 or higher.

Who this book is for

This book is for developers who want to dive into the newest version of Swift. If you are a developer who learns best by looking at and working with code, then this book is for you. A basic understanding of Apple's tools is beneficial, but not mandatory.

Conventions

In this book, you will find a number of text styles that distinguish between different kinds of information. Here are some examples of these styles and an explanation of their meaning. Code words in text, database table names, folder names, filenames, file extensions, pathnames, dummy URLs, user input, and Twitter handles are shown as follows: "The class will be named `TestClassOne`."

A block of code is set as follows:

```
var name1 = "Jon"
var name2 = "Kim"
var name3 = "Kailey"
var name4 = "Kara"
```

Any command-line input or output is written as follows:

```
TestClassOne deinitialized
testClassOne is gone
TestClassTwo deinitialized
testClassTwo is gone
```

New terms and **important words** are shown in bold. Words that you see on the screen, for example, in menus or dialog boxes, appear in the text like this: "We will be using the **Blank** template for all of our code."

Warnings or important notes appear like this.

Tips and tricks appear like this.

Reader feedback

Feedback from our readers is always welcome. Let us know what you think about this book-what you liked or disliked. Reader feedback is important for us as it helps us develop titles that you will really get the most out of. To send us general feedback, simply email feedback@packtpub.com, and mention the book's title in the subject of your message. If there is a topic that you have expertise in and you are interested in either writing or contributing to a book, see our author guide at www.packtpub.com/authors.

Customer support

Now that you are the proud owner of a Packt book, we have a number of things to help you to get the most from your purchase.

Downloading the example code

You can download the example code files for this book from your account at http://www.packtpub.com. If you purchased this book elsewhere, you can visit http://www.packtpub.com/support and register to have the files emailed directly to you. You can download the code files by following these steps:

1. Log in or register to our website using your email address and password.
2. Hover the mouse pointer on the **SUPPORT** tab at the top.
3. Click on **Code Downloads & Errata**.
4. Enter the name of the book in the **Search** box.
5. Select the book for which you're looking to download the code files.
6. Choose from the drop-down menu where you purchased this book from.
7. Click on **Code Download**.

Once the file is downloaded, please make sure that you unzip or extract the folder using the latest version of:

- WinRAR / 7-Zip for Windows
- Zipeg / iZip / UnRarX for Mac
- 7-Zip / PeaZip for Linux

The code bundle for the book is also hosted on GitHub at
`https://github.com/PacktPublishing/Mastering-Swift-4-Fourth-Edition`. We also
have other code bundles from our rich catalog of books and videos available at
`https://github.com/PacktPublishing/`. Check them out!

Downloading the color images of this book

We also provide you with a PDF file that has color images of the screenshots/diagrams used
in this book. The color images will help you better understand the changes in the output.
You can download this file from `http://www.packtpub.com/sites/default/files/
downloads/MasteringSwift4FourthEdition_ColorImages.pdf`.

Errata

Although we have taken every care to ensure the accuracy of our content, mistakes do
happen. If you find a mistake in one of our books-maybe a mistake in the text or the code-
we would be grateful if you could report this to us. By doing so, you can save other readers
from frustration and help us improve subsequent versions of this book. If you find any
errata, please report them by visiting `http://www.packtpub.com/submit-errata`, selecting
your book, clicking on the **Errata Submission Form** link, and entering the details of your
errata. Once your errata are verified, your submission will be accepted and the errata will
be uploaded to our website or added to any list of existing errata under the Errata section of
that title. To view the previously submitted errata, go to
`https://www.packtpub.com/books/content/support` and enter the name of the book in the
search field. The required information will appear under the **Errata** section.

Piracy

Piracy of copyrighted material on the internet is an ongoing problem across all media. At
Packt, we take the protection of our copyright and licenses very seriously. If you come
across any illegal copies of our works in any form on the internet, please provide us with
the location address or website name immediately so that we can pursue a remedy. Please
contact us at `copyright@packtpub.com` with a link to the suspected pirated material. We
appreciate your help in protecting our authors and our ability to bring you valuable
content.

Questions

If you have a problem with any aspect of this book, you can contact us at
`questions@packtpub.com`, and we will do our best to address the problem.

1

Taking the First Steps with Swift

Ever since I was 12 years old and wrote my first program in the BASIC programming language, programming has been a passion for me. Even as I became a professional programmer, programming remained more of a passion than a job, but in the years preceding the first release of Swift, that passion had waned. I was unsure why I was losing that passion. I attempted to recapture that passion with some of my side projects, but nothing really brought back the excitement that I used to have. Then Apple announced Swift in 2014. Swift is such an exciting and progressive language that it has brought a lot of that passion back and made programming fun again. Now that official versions of Swift are available for the Linux platform, and un-official versions for Windows and the ARM platform, learning and using Swift is becoming available to people outside the Apple ecosystem. This is really an exciting time to be learning the Swift language.

In this chapter, you will learn:

- What is Swift?
- What are some of the features of Swift?
- What are Playgrounds?
- How to use Playgrounds?
- What the basic syntaxes of the Swift language are?

What is Swift?

Swift is a programming language that was introduced, by Apple, at the **World Wide Developers Conference (WWDC)** in 2014. Swift was arguably the most significant announcement at WWDC 2014 and very few people, including Apple insiders, were aware of the project's existence prior to it being announced.

It was amazing, even by Apple's standards, that they could keep Swift a secret for as long as they did and that no one suspected they were going to announce a new development language. At WWDC 2015, Apple made another big splash when they announced Swift 2. Swift 2 was a major enhancement to the Swift language. During that conference, Chris Lattner said that a lot of the enhancements were based on direct feedback that Apple received from the development community. It was also announced that Swift would become an open source project. In my opinion, this was the most exciting announcement of the WWDC 2015.

In December of 2015, Apple officially released Swift as open source with the `https://swift.org/` site dedicated to the open source Swift community. The Swift repository is located on Apple's GitHub page (`http://github.com/apple`). The Swift evolution repository (`https://github.com/apple/swift-evolution`) tracks the evolution of Swift by documenting the proposed changes. A list of which proposals were accepted and which were rejected can be found in the evolution repository.

Swift 3, which was released in 2016, was a major enhancement to the Swift language that was not source-compatible with previous releases of the Swift language. It contained fundamental changes to the language itself and to the Swift standard library. One of the main goals of Swift 3 was to be source-compatible across all platforms so the code that was written for one platform would be compatible with all other platforms. This means that the code we develop for macOS should work on Linux.

Now, Apple has released Swift 4. One of the primary goals of the Swift 4 compiler is to be source-compatible with Swift 3. This will allow us to compile both Swift 3 and Swift 4 projects with the Swift 4 compiler. Apple has established a community-owned source compatibility test suite that will be used to regression-test changes to the compiler. Projects that are added to the test suite will be periodically built against the latest development version of Swift to help understand the impact of the changes being made to Swift. You can find the Swift source compatibility page here: `https://swift.org/source-compatibility/`.

One of the original goals of Swift 4 was to stabilize the Swift **ABI (Application Binary Interface)**. The main benefit of a stable ABI is to allow us to distribute frameworks in a binary format across multiple versions of Swift. If a stable ABI were in place, we would be able to build a framework with the Swift 4 compiler and have it work with applications that were written in future versions of Swift. This feature ended up being deferred for now. Hopefully, Apple will be able to stabilize the ABI in future versions of Swift.

The development of Swift was started in 2010 by Chris Lattner. He implemented much of the basic language structure with only a few people being aware of its existence. It wasn't until late 2011 that other developers began to contribute to Swift. In July of 2013, it became a major focus of the Apple Developer Tools group.

Chris started working at Apple in the summer of 2005. He has held several positions in the Developer Tools group, and was the director and architect of that group when he left Apple in 2017. On his home page (http://www.nondot.org/sabre/), he notes that Xcode's Playground (read more on Playgrounds a little later in this chapter) became a personal passion of his because it makes programming more interactive and approachable. If you are using Swift on the Apple platform, you will be using Playgrounds a lot as a test and experimentation platform. You can also use Swift Playgrounds on the iPad.

There are a lot of similarities between Swift and Objective-C. Swift adopts the readability of Objective-C's named parameters and dynamic object model. When we refer to Swift as having a dynamic object model, we are referring to the ability for types to change at runtime. This includes adding new (custom) types and changing/extending the existing types.

While there are a lot of similarities between Swift and Objective-C, there are significant differences between them as well. Swift's syntax and formatting are a lot closer to Python than Objective-C, but Apple did keep the curly braces. I know Python people would disagree with me, and that is all right because we all have different opinions, but I like the curly braces. Swift actually makes the curly braces required for control statements, such as `if` and `while`, which eliminates bugs, such as the `goto fail`, in Apple's SSL library.

Swift features

When Apple first introduced Swift, it said that *Swift is Objective-C without the C*. This really only tells us half of the story. Objective-C is a superset of C and provides object-oriented capabilities and a dynamic runtime to the C language. This meant that with Objective-C, Apple needed to maintain compatibility with C, which limited the enhancements it could make to the Objective-C language. As an example, Apple could not change how the `switch` statement functioned and has still maintained compatibility with the C language.

Since Swift does not need to maintain the same C compatibility as Objective-C, Apple was free to add any feature/enhancement to the language. This allowed Apple to include the best features from many of today's most popular and modern languages, such as Objective-C, Python, Java, Ruby, C#, Haskell, and many others.

The following chart shows a list of some of the most exciting enhancements that Swift offers as compared to the Objective-C language:

Swift feature	Description
Type inference	Swift can automatically deduce the type of a variable or constant, based on the initial value.
Generics	Generics allow us to write code only once to perform identical tasks for different types of object.
Collection mutability	Swift does not have separate objects for mutable or non-mutable containers. Instead, you define mutability by defining the container as a constant or variable.
Closure syntax	Closures are self-contained blocks of functionality that can be passed around and used in our code.
Optionals	Optionals define a variable that might not have a value.
Switch statement	The Switch statement has been drastically improved. This is one of my favorite improvements.
Tuples	Functions can have multiple return types using tuples.
Operator overloading	Classes can provide their own implementation of existing operators.
Enumerations with associated values	In Swift, we can do a lot more than just define a group of related values with enumerations.
Protocols and Protocol-oriented Design	Apple introduced the Protocol-oriented Programming paradigm with Swift version 2. This is a new way of not only writing applications but also changes how we think about programming.

There is one feature that I did not mention in the preceding chart because it is technically not a feature of Swift; it is a feature of Xcode and the compiler. This is also a feature that is specific to the Apple platform with Xcode. This feature is **Mix and Match**, which allows us to create applications that contain both Objective-C and Swift files. This allows us to systematically update our existing Objective-C applications with Swift classes and use Objective-C libraries/frameworks in our Swift applications.

Before we begin our journey into the wonderful world of Swift development, let's take a detour and visit a place that I have loved ever since I was a kid: the Playground.

Playgrounds

When I was a kid, the best part of the school day was going to the playground. It really did not matter what we were playing as long as we were on the playground. When Apple introduced Playgrounds as part of Xcode 6, I was excited just by the name, but I wondered if Apple would be able to make its Playground as fun as the playgrounds of my youth. While Apple's Playgrounds might not be as fun as playing kickball when I was 9-years old, it definitely brings a lot of fun back to experimenting and playing with code.

Getting started with Playgrounds

Playgrounds are interactive work environments that let us write code and see the results immediately as changes are made to the code. This means that Playgrounds are a great way to learn and experiment with Swift. Now that we can use Swift Playgrounds on the iPad, we do not even need to have a computer in front of us to experiment with Swift.

 If you are using Swift on the Linux platform you will not have Playgrounds available, but you can use the **REPL (Read-Evaluate-Print-Loop)** shell to experiment with Swift without compiling your code. If you are using Swift on something other than a macOS computer or an iPad, you can safely skip this section.

Playgrounds also make it incredibly easy to try out new APIs, prototype new algorithms, and demonstrate how code works. We will be using Playgrounds throughout this book to show how our sample code works. Therefore, before we really get into Swift development, let's spend some time learning about, and getting comfortable with, Playgrounds.

Do not worry if the Swift code does not make a lot of sense right now; as we proceed through the book, the code we use in the following examples will begin to make sense. We are simply trying to get a feel for Playgrounds right now.

A Playground can have several sections, but the three that we will be using extensively in this book are:

- **Coding Area**: This is where you enter your Swift code.
- **Results Sidebar**: This is where the results of your code are shown. Each time you type in a new line of code, the results are re-evaluated and the results sidebar is updated with the new results.
- **Debug Area**: This area displays the output of the code, and it can be very useful for debugging.

The following screenshot shows how the sections are arranged in a Playground:

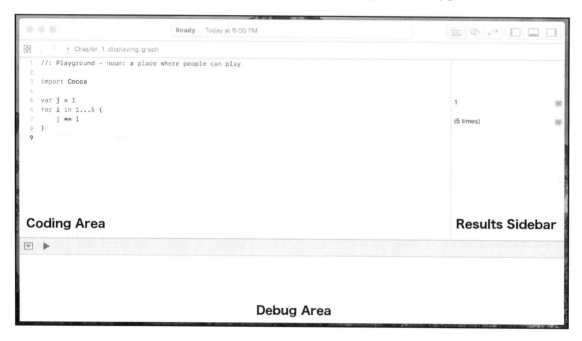

Let's start a new Playground. The first thing we need to do is to start Xcode. Once Xcode has started, we can select the **Get started with a playground** option, as shown in the following screenshot:

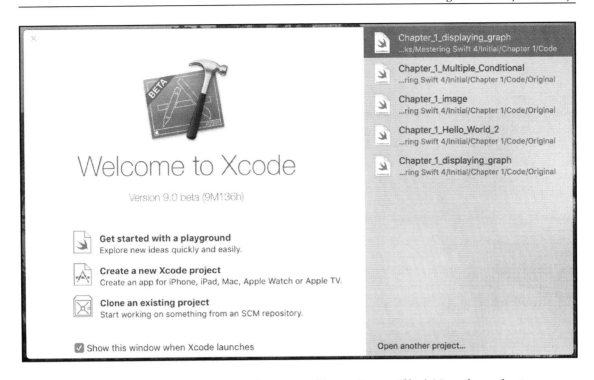

Alternatively, we can navigate to the Playground by going to **File** | **New** from the top menu bar, as shown in the following screenshot:

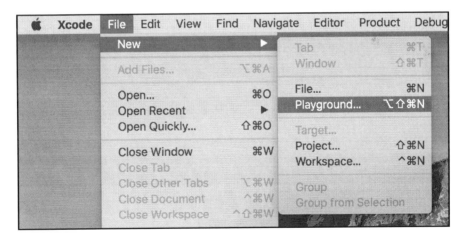

Next, we should see a screen similar to the following screenshot. This screen lets us name our Playground and select whether the Playground is an *iOS, tvOS,* or *macOS* Playground. For most of the examples in this chapter, it is safe to assume that you can select any of the OS options unless it is otherwise noted. You can also select a template to use. For the examples in this book, we will be using the **Blank** template for all of our code:

Finally, we are asked for the location in which to save our Playground. After we select the location, the Playground will open and look similar to the following screenshot:

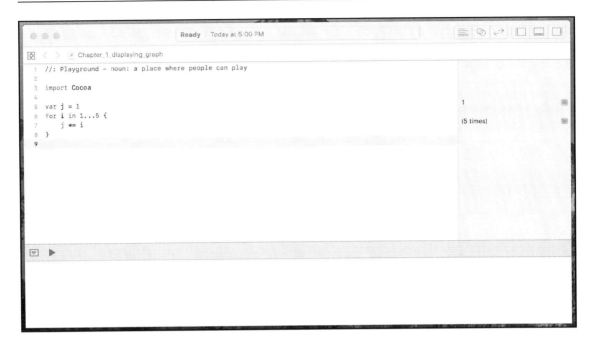

In the preceding screenshot, we can see that the coding area of the Playground looks similar to the coding area for an Xcode project. What is different here is the sidebar on the right-hand side. This sidebar is where the results of our code are shown. The code in the previous screenshot imports the Cocoa framework since it is a macOS playground. If it was an iOS playground it would import the UIKit framework instead.

If your new Playground does not open the debug area, you can open it manually by pressing the *shift* + *command* + *Y* keys together. You can also close the debug area by pressing *shift* + *command* + *Y* again. Later in the chapter, we will see why the debug area is so useful. Another way to open or close the debug area is to click on the button that looks like an upside-down triangle in a box that is in the border between the debug area and the coding area.

iOS, tvOS, and macOS Playgrounds

When you start a new iOS or tvOS Playground, the Playground imports the UIKit framework. This gives us access to the UIKit framework that provides the core infrastructure for iOS and tvOS applications. When we start a new macOS Playground, the Playground imports the Cocoa framework.

What the last paragraph means is that, if we want to experiment with specific features of either UIKit or Cocoa, we will need to open the correct Playground. As an example, if we have an iOS Playground open and we want to create an object that represents a color, we would use a UIColor object. If we had a macOS playground open, we would use an NSColor object to represent a color.

Showing images in a Playground

Playgrounds are great at showing the results of code as text in the results sidebar; however; they can also do a lot more than just work with text. We can display other items such as images and graphs. Let's look at how we would show an image in a Playground. The first thing we need to do is to load the image into the resource directory of our Playground.

The following steps show how to load an image into the resource directory:

1. Let's begin by showing the project navigator sidebar. To do this, in the top menu bar, navigate to **View** | **Navigators** | **Show Project Navigator** or use the *command + 1* keyboard shortcut. The project navigator looks similar to this:

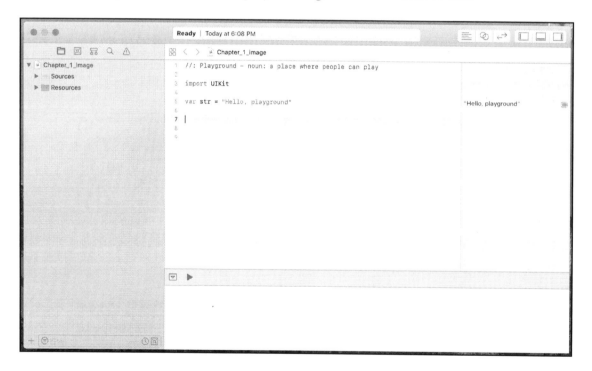

2. Once we have the **Project Navigator** open, we can drag the image into the Resources folder so that we can access it from our code. Once we drag the image file over it and drop it, it will appear in the Resources folder, as shown here:

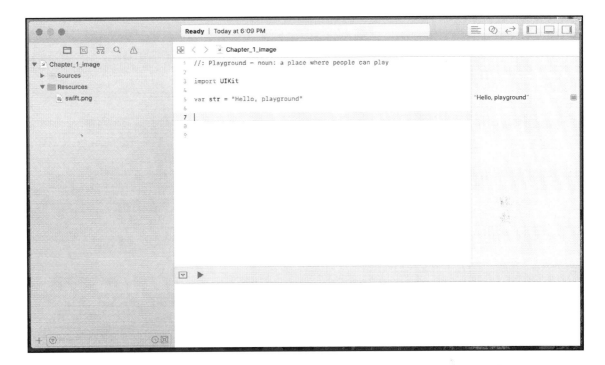

3. Now, we can access the image that is in our `Resources` folder within our code. The following screenshot shows how we would do this. At this time, the code used to access the image is not as important as knowing how to access resources within a Playground:

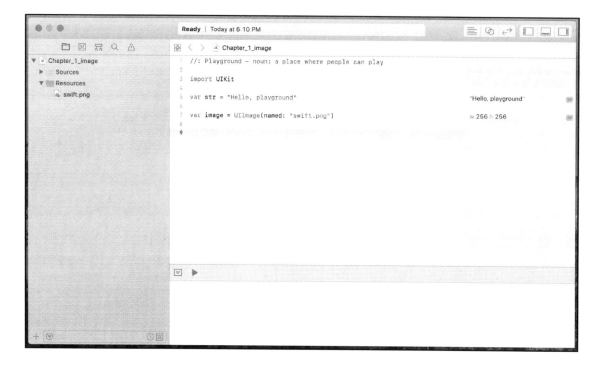

4. To view the image, we need to hover our cursor in the results sidebar over the section that shows the width and height of the image. In our example, the width and height section shows **w 256 h 256**. Once we hover the mouse pointer over the width and height, we should see two symbols, as shown in the following screenshot:

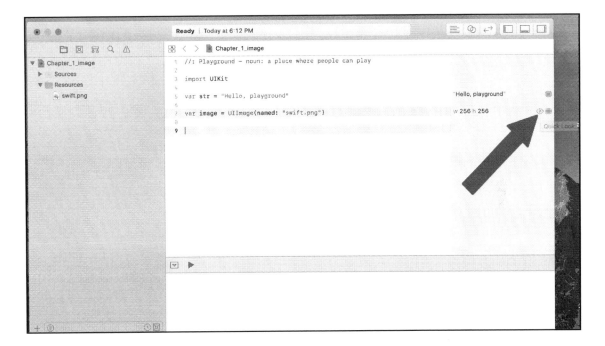

5. We can press either of the symbols to show the image. The one that looks like a box within a box will display the image within the playground's code section, while the one that looks like an eye will pop the image up outside the playground. The following screenshot shows what it looks like if we display the image within the playground:

Having the ability to create and display graphs can be very useful when we want to see the progression of our code. Let's look at how we can create and display graphs in a playground.

Creating and displaying graphs in Playgrounds

Creating and displaying graphs is really useful when we are prototyping new algorithms because it allows us to see the value of a variable throughout the course of the calculations. To see how graphing works, look at the following Playground:

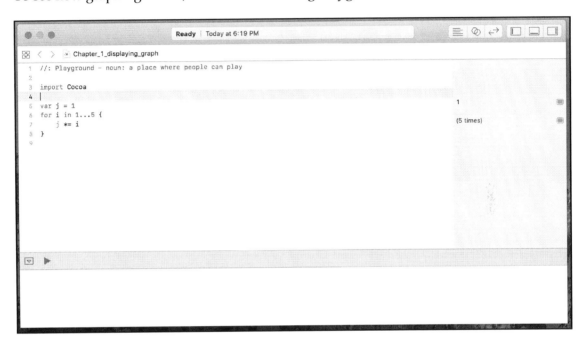

In this Playground, we set the variable j to 1. Next, we create a for loop that assigns numbers 1 through 5 to the variable i. At each step in the for loop, we set the value of the variable j to the current value of j multiplied by i. The graph shows the values of the variable j at each step of the for loop. We will be covering for loops in detail later in this book.

To bring up the graph, click on the symbol that is shaped like a circle with a dot in it. We can then move the timeline slider to see the values of variable j at each step of the for loop. The following Playground shows what the graph should look like:

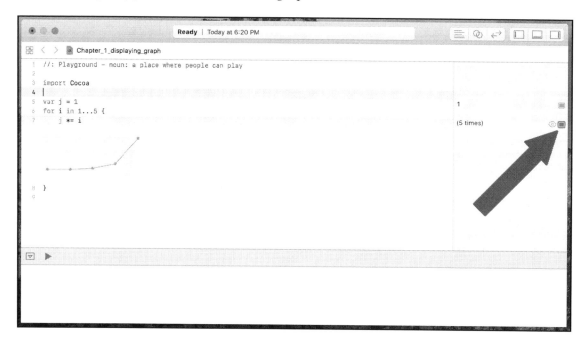

What Playgrounds are not

There is a lot more that we can do with Playgrounds, and we have only scratched the surface in our quick introduction here. Before we leave this brief introduction, let's take a look at what Playgrounds are not so that we can better understand when not to use Playgrounds:

- Playgrounds should not be used for performance testing: The performance you see from any code that is run in a Playground is not representative of how fast the code will run when it is in your project.
- Playgrounds do not support on-device execution. You cannot run the code that is present in a Playground as an external application or on an external device.

Swift language syntax

If you are an Objective-C developer, and you are not familiar with modern languages such as Python or Ruby, the code in the previous screenshots may have looked pretty strange. The Swift language syntax is a huge departure from Objective-C, which was based largely on Smalltalk and C.

The Swift language uses modern concepts and syntax to create very concise and readable code. There is also a heavy emphasis on eliminating common programming mistakes. Before we get into the Swift language itself, let's look at some of the basic syntax of the Swift language.

Comments

Writing comments in Swift code is a little different from writing comments in Objective-C code. We can still use the double slash `//` for single-line comments and the `/*` and `*/` for multiline comments; however, if we want to use the comments to also document our code, we need to use the triple slash `///`.

Xcode will also auto-generate a comment template based on your signature of the method/function by highlighting it and pushing *command + option + /* together.

To document our code we generally use fields that Xcode recognizes. These fields are:

- **Parameter**: When we start a line with `- parameter {param name}:` Xcode recognizes this as the description of a parameter
- **Return**: When we start a line with `- return:` Xcode recognizes this as the description of the return value
- **Throws**: When we start a line with `- throws:` Xcode recognizes this as the description of any errors that this method may throw

The following Playground shows examples of both single-line and multiline comments and how to use the comment fields:

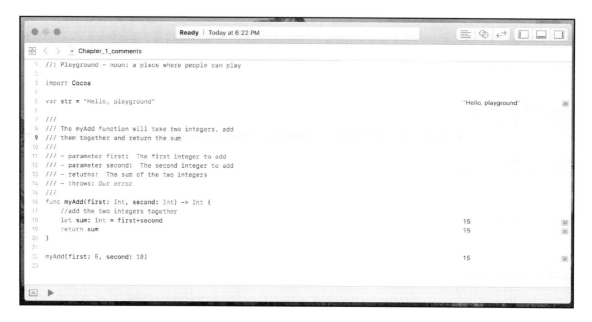

```
//: Playground - noun: a place where people can play

import Cocoa

var str = "Hello, playground"                                    "Hello, playground"

///
/// The myAdd function will take two integers, add
/// them together and return the sum
///
/// - parameter first:  The first integer to add
/// - parameter second:  The second integer to add
/// - returns:  The sum of the two integers
/// - throws: Our error
///
func myAdd(first: Int, second: Int) -> Int {
    //add the two integers together
    let sum: Int = first+second                                  15
    return sum                                                   15
}

myAdd(first: 5, second: 10)                                      15
```

To write good comments, I would recommend using single-line comments within a function to give quick one-line explanations of your code. We then use multiline comments outside functions and classes to explain what the function and class do. The preceding Playground shows a good way to use comments. By using proper documentation, as we did in the preceding screenshot, we can use the documentation feature within Xcode. If we hold down the *option* key and then click on the function name anywhere in our code, Xcode will display a pop-up with the description of the function.

This next screenshot shows what that pop-up would look like:

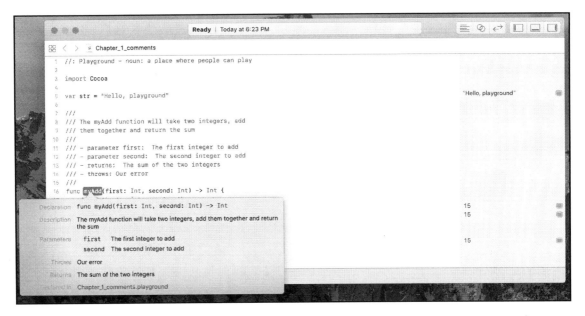

We can see that the documentation contains six fields. These fields are:

- **Declaration**: This is the function's declaration
- **Description**: This is the description of the function as it appears in the comments
- **Parameters**: The parameter descriptions are prefixed with the `Parameters:` tag in the comment section
- **Throws**: The throws description is prefixed with the `throws:` tag and describes what errors are thrown by the methods
- **Returns**: The return description is prefixed with the `returns:` tag in the comment section
- **Declared In**: This is the file that the function is declared in so that we can easily find it

There are significantly more fields that we can add to our comments. You can find the complete list on Apple's site here:

`https://developer.apple.com/library/content/documentation/Xcode/Reference/xcode_markup_formatting_ref/MarkupFunctionality.html`

If you are developing for the Linux platform, I would still recommend using Apple's documentation guidelines because as other Swift IDEs are developed, I believe they will support the same guidelines.

Semicolons

You may have noticed, from the code samples so far, that we are not using semicolons at the end of lines. The semicolons are optional in Swift; therefore, both lines in the following Playground are valid in Swift:

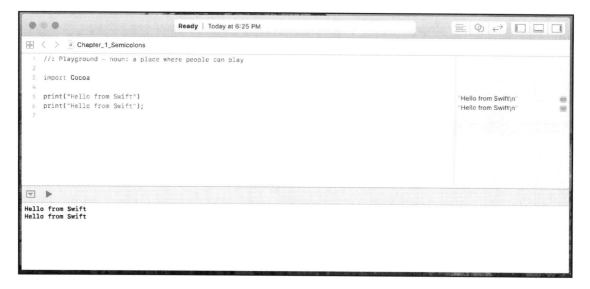

For style purposes, it is strongly recommended that you do not use semicolons in your Swift code. If you are really set on using semicolons, then be consistent and use them on every line of code; however, there is no warning if you forget them. I will stress again, that it is recommended that you do not use semicolons in Swift.

Parentheses

In Swift, parentheses around conditional statements are optional; for example, both `if` statements in the following Playground are valid:

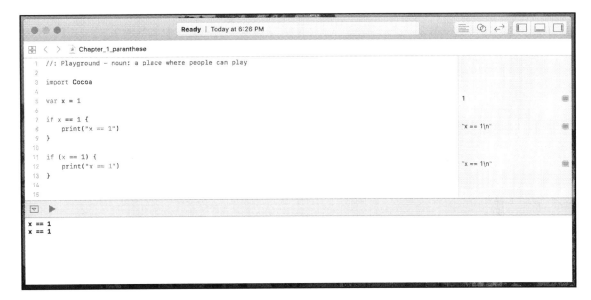

For style purposes, it is recommended that you do not include parentheses in your code unless you have multiple conditional statements on the same line. For readability purposes, it is good practice to put parentheses around the individual conditional statements that are on the same line.

Curly brackets

In Swift, unlike most other languages, the curly bracket is required after conditional or loop statements. This is one of the safety features that are built into Swift. Arguably, there have been numerous security bugs that may have been prevented if the developer would have used curly braces. These bugs could also have been prevented by other means such as unit testing and code reviews, but requiring developers to use curly braces, in my opinion, is a good security standard.

The following Playground shows you the error you get if you forget to include curly braces:

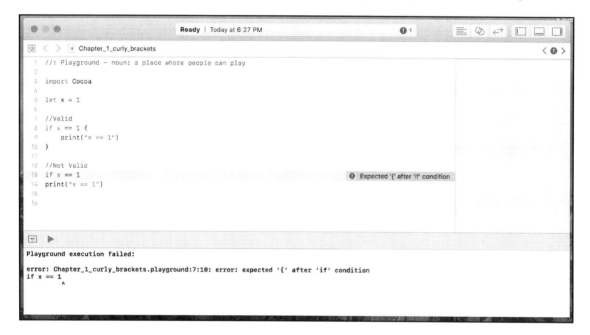

An assignment operator does not return a value

In most other languages, the following line of code is valid, but it probably is not what the developer meant to do:

```
if (x = 1) {}
```

In Swift, this statement is not valid. Using an assignment operator (=) in a conditional statement (if, while, and guard) will throw an error. This is another safety feature built into Swift. It prevents the developer from forgetting the second equals sign (=) in a comparison statement. This error is shown in the following Playground:

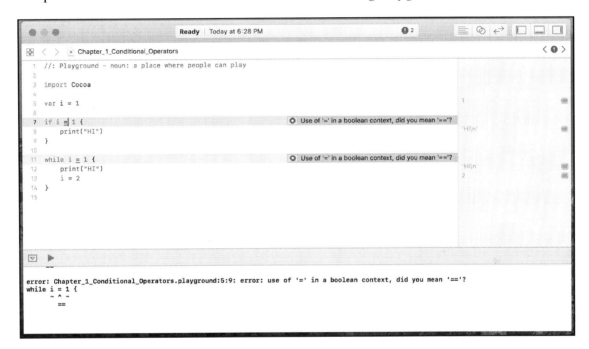

Spaces are optional in conditional and assignment statements

For both conditional (`if` and `while`) and assignment (=) statements, the white spaces are optional. Therefore, in the following Playground, both the `i block` and the `j block` of code are valid:

For style purposes, I would recommend adding the white spaces as the `j block` shows (for readability purposes) but, as long as you pick one style and are consistent, either style should be acceptable.

Hello World

All good computer books that are written to teach a computer language have a section that shows a user how to write a Hello World application. This book is no exception. In this section, we will show you how to write two different Hello World applications.

Our first Hello World application will be a traditional Hello World application that simply prints Hello World to the console. Let's begin by creating a new Playground and naming it `Chapter_1_Hello_World`.

In Swift, to print a message to the console, we use the `print()` function. In its most basic form, we would use the `print` function to print out a single message, as shown in the following code:

```
print("Hello World")
```

Usually, when we use the `print()` function, we want to print more than just static text. We can include the value of variables and/or constants by using string interpolation or by separating the values within the `print()` function with commas. String interpolation uses a special sequence of characters, \( ), to include the value of variables and/or constants in the string. The following code shows how to do this:

```
var name = "Jon"
var language = "Swift"

var message1 = " Welcome to the wonderful world of "
var message2 = "\(name), Welcome to the wonderful world of \(language)!"

print(message2)
print(name, message1, language, "!")
```

We can also define two parameters in the print function that change how the message is displayed in the console. These parameters are the **separator** and **terminator** parameters. The separator parameter defines a string that is used to separate the values of the variables/constants in the `print()` function. By default, the `print()` function separates each variable/constant with a space. The terminator parameter defines what character is put at the end of the line. By default, the newline character is added at the end of the line.

The following code shows how we would create a comma-separated list that does not have a newline character at the end:

```
var name1 = "Jon"
var name2 = "Kim"
var name3 = "Kailey"
var name4 = "Kara"

print(name1, name2, name3, name4, separator:", ", terminator:"")
```

There is one other parameter that we can add to our `print()` function. This is the `to:` parameter. This parameter will let us redirect the output of the `print()` function. In the following example, we redirect the output to a variable named `line`:

```
var name1 = "Jon"
var name2 = "Kim"
var name3 = "Kailey"
var name4 = "Kara"

var line = ""

print(name1, name2, name3, name4, separator:", ", terminator:"", to:&line)
```

Previously, the `print()` function was simply a useful tool for basic debugging but now, with the new enhanced `print()` function, we can use it for a lot more.

Summary

We began this chapter with a discussion on the Swift language and gave a brief history about the language. We also mentioned some of the changes that will be present in Swift 4 and noted that ABI stabilization will be pushed out to a future version of Swift. We then showed how to start and use Playgrounds to experiment with Swift programming. We also covered the basic Swift language syntax and discussed proper language styles. The chapter concluded with two Hello World examples.

In the next chapter, we will see how to use variables and constants in Swift. We will also look at the various data types and how to use operators in Swift.

2
Learning about Variables, Constants, Strings, and Operators

The first program I ever wrote was written in the BASIC programming language and was the typical Hello World application. This application was exciting at first, but the excitement of printing static text wore off pretty quickly. For my second application, I used BASIC's input command to prompt the user for a name and then printed out a custom hello message to the user with their name in it. At the age of 12, it was pretty cool to display *Hello Han Solo*. This application led me to create numerous Mad Lib-style applications that prompted the user for various words and then put those words into a story that was displayed after the user had entered all the required words. These applications introduced me to, and taught me, the importance of variables. Every useful application I've created since then has used variables.

In this chapter, we will cover the following topics:

- What are variables and constants?
- What is the difference between explicit and inferred typing?
- What are numeric, string, and Boolean types?
- Defining what Optional types are?
- Explaining how enumerations work in Swift?
- Explaining how Swift's operators work?

Constants and variables

Constants and variables associate an identifier (such as `myName` or `currentTemperature`) with a value of a particular type (such as the `String` or `Int` type), where the identifier can be used to retrieve the value. The difference between a constant and a variable is that a variable can be updated or changed, while a constant cannot be changed once a value is assigned to it.

Constants are good for defining values that you know will never change, like the temperature that water freezes at or the speed of light. Constants are also good for defining a value that we use many times throughout our application, such as a standard font size or the maximum number of characters in a buffer. There will be numerous examples of constants throughout this book, and it is recommended that we use constants rather than variables whenever possible.

Variables tend to be more common in software development than constants. This is mainly because developers tend to prefer variables over constants. In Swift, we receive a warning if we declare a variable that is never changed. We can make useful applications without using constants (although it is a good practice to use them); however, it is almost impossible to create a useful application without variables.

 The use of constants is encouraged in Swift. If we do not expect or want a value to change, we should declare it as a constant. This adds a very important safety constraint to our code that ensures that the value never changes.

You can use almost any character in the naming/identifier of a variable or constant (even Unicode characters); however, there are a few rules that you must follow:

1. An identifier must not contain any whitespace.
2. It must not contain any mathematical symbols or arrows.
3. An identifier must not contain private-use or invalid Unicode characters.
4. It must not contain line- or box-drawing characters.
5. It must not start with a number, but it can contain numbers.
6. If you use a Swift keyword as an identifier, surround it with back ticks; using a Swift keyword as an identifier is strongly discouraged.

Keywords are words that are used by the Swift programming language. Some examples of keywords that you will see in this chapter are `var` and `let`. You should avoid using Swift keywords as identifiers to avoid confusion when reading your code.

Defining constants and variables

Constants and variables must be defined prior to using them. To define a constant, you use the `let` keyword, and to define a variable, you use the `var` keyword. The following code shows how to define both constants and variables:

```
// Constants
let freezingTemperatureOfWaterCelsius = 0
let speedOfLightKmSec = 300000

// Variables
var currentTemperature = 22
var currentSpeed = 55
```

We can declare multiple constants or variables in a single line by separating them with a comma. For example, we could shrink the preceding four lines of code down to two lines, as shown here:

```
// Constants
let freezingTempertureOfWaterCelsius = 0, speedOfLightKmSec = 300000

// Variables
var currentTemperture = 22, currentSpeed = 55
```

We can change the value of a variable to another value of a compatible type; however, as we noted earlier, we cannot change the value of a constant. Let's look at the following Playground. Can you tell what is wrong with the code from the error message that is shown?

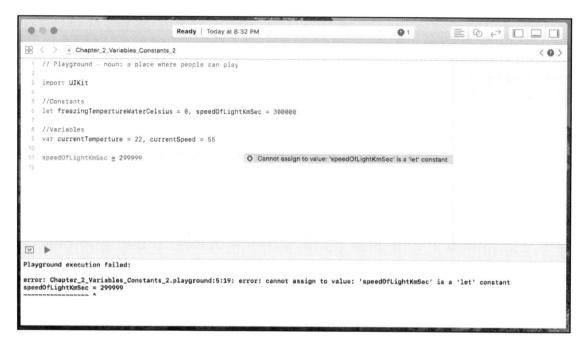

Did you figure out what was wrong with the code? Any physicist can tell you that we cannot change the speed of light, and in our code `speedOfLightKmSec` is a constant, so we cannot change it here either. When we attempted to change the `speedOfLightKmSec` constant, an error was thrown. We are able to change the value of `highTemperature` without an error because it is a variable. We have mentioned the difference between variables and constants a couple of times because it is a very important concept to grasp, especially when we move on to define mutable and immutable collection types in `Chapter 3`, *Using Swift Collections and the Tuple Type*.

 A mutable type/collection is a type or collection that can be changed like a variable. An immutable type/collection is a type or collection that cannot be changed.

Type safety

Swift is a type-safe language, which means we are required to define the types of the values we are going to store in a variable. We will get an error if we attempt to assign a value to a variable that is of the wrong type. The following Playground shows what happens if we attempt to put a string value into a variable that expects integer values.

We will go over the most popular types a little later in the chapter.

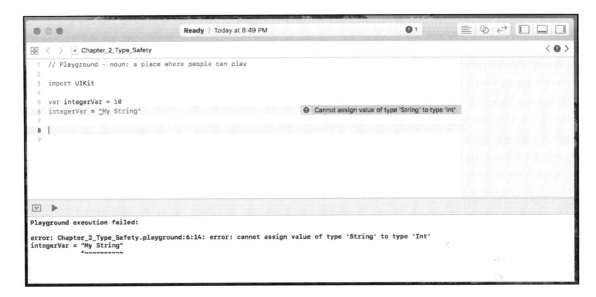

Swift performs a type check when it compiles code, therefore, it will flag any mis-matched types with an error. The error message in this Playground explains quite clearly that we are trying to insert a string value into an integer variable.

How does Swift know that the constant `integerVar` is of the `Int` type? Swift uses type inference to figure out the appropriate type. Let's look at what type inference is.

Type inference

Type inference allows us to omit the variable type when we define it. The compiler will infer the type based on the initial value. For example, in Objective-C we would define an integer like this:

```
int myInt = 1
```

This tells the compiler that the `myInt` variable is of the `int` type, and the initial value is the number 1. In Swift, we would define the same integer like this:

```
var myInt = 1
```

Swift infers that the variable type is an integer because the initial value is an integer. Let's look at a couple more examples:

```
var x = 3.14   // Double type
var y = "Hello"  // String type
var z = true  // Boolean type
```

In the preceding example, the compiler will correctly infer that variable x is a `Double`, variable, y is a `String`, and variable z is a `Boolean`, based on their initial values.

Explicit types

Type inference is a very nice feature in Swift and is one that you will probably get used to very quickly. However, there are times when we would like to explicitly define a variable's type. For example, in the preceding example, the variable x is inferred to be Double, but what if we wanted the variable type to be `Float`? We can explicitly define a variable type like this:

```
var x: Float = 3.14
```

Notice the `Float` declaration (the colon and the word `Float`) after the variable identifier. This tells the compiler to define this variable to be that of the `Float` type and gives it an initial value of 3.14. When we define a variable in this manner, we need to make sure that the initial value is of the same type that we are defining the variable to be. If we try to give a variable an initial value that is of a different type than we are defining it as, we will receive an error. As an example, the following line will throw an error because we are explicitly defining the variable to be that of the `Float` type even though we are trying to put a `String` value in it:

```
var x: Float = "My str"
```

We will need to explicitly define the variable type if we are not setting an initial value. For example, the following line of code is invalid because the compiler does not know what type to set the variable x to:

```
var x
```

If we use this code in our application, we will receive a `Type annotation missing in pattern` error. If we are not setting an initial value for a variable, we are required to define the type like this:

```
var x: Int
```

Now that we have seen how to explicitly define a variable type, let's look at some of the most commonly used types.

Numeric types

Swift contains many of the standard numeric types that are suitable for storing various integer and floating-point values. Let's start off by looking at the integer type.

Integer types

An integer is a whole number and can be either signed (positive, negative, or zero) or unsigned (positive or zero). Swift provides several integer types of different sizes. The following chart shows the value ranges for the different integer types on a 64-bit system:

Type	Minimum	Maximum
Int8	-128	127
Int16	-32,768	32,767
Int32	-2,147,483,648	2,147,483,647
Int64	- 9,223,372,036,854,775,808	9,223,372,036,854,775,807
Int	- 9,223,372,036,854,775,808	9,223,372,036,854,775,807
UInt8	0	255
UInt16	0	65,535
UInt32	0	4,294,967,295

| UInt64 | 0 | 18,446,744,073,709,551,615 |
| UInt | 0 | 18,446,744,073,709,551,615 |

 Unless there is a specific reason to define the size of an integer, I would recommend using the standard `Int` or `UInt` types. This will save you from needing to convert between different types of integers later.

In Swift, the integer type and other numerical types are actually named types, implemented in the Swift standard library using structures. This gives us a consistent mechanism for memory management of all the data types as well as properties that we can access. For the preceding chart, I retrieved the minimum and maximum values of each integer type using the `min` and `max` properties of the integer types. Look at the following Playground to see how I retrieved the values:

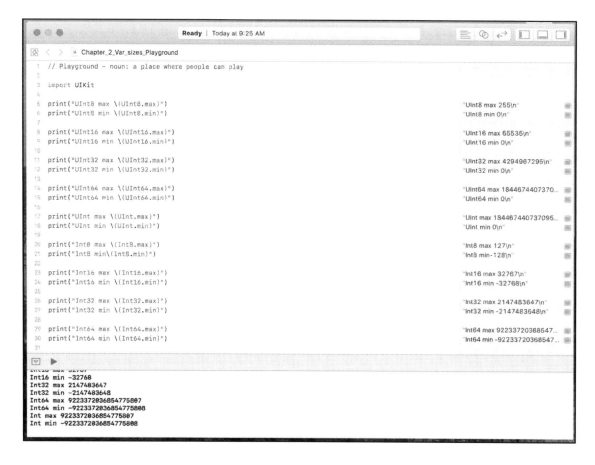

Integers can also be represented as binary, octal, and hexadecimal numbers. We just need to add a prefix to the number to tell the compiler which base the number should be in. The following chart shows the prefix for each numerical base:

Base	Prefix
Decimal	None
Binary	0b
Octal	0o
Hexadecimal	0x

The following Playground shows how the number 95 is represented in each of the numerical bases:

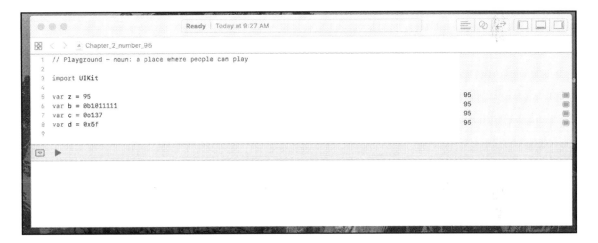

Swift also allows us to insert arbitrary underscores in our numeric literals. This can improve the readability of our code without changing the underlying value. As an example, if we were defining the speed of light, which is constant, we could define it like this:

```
let speedOfLightKmSec = 300_000
```

The Swift compiler will ignore these underscores and interpret this value as if the underscores were not there.

Floating-point and Double values

A floating-point number is a number with a decimal component. There are two standard floating-point types in Swift: Float and Double. The Float type represents a 32-bit floating-point number, while the Double type represents a 64-bit floating-point number. Swift also supports an extended floating-point type: Float80. The Float80 type is an 80-bit floating-point number.

It is recommended that we use the Double type over the Float type unless there is a specific reason to use the latter. The Double type has a precision of at least 15 decimal digits, while the Float type's precision can be as small as six decimal digits. Let's look at an example of how this can affect our application without us knowing it. The following screenshot shows the results if we add two decimal numbers together using both a Float type and a Double type:

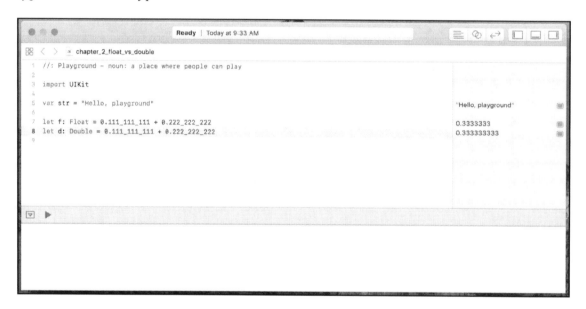

As we can see from the screenshot, the two decimal numbers that we are adding contain nine digits past the decimal point; however, the results in the Float type only contain seven digits, while the results in the Double type contain the full nine digits. The loss of precision can cause issues if we are working with currency or other numbers that need accurate calculations.

The floating-point accuracy problem is not an issue confined to Swift; all the languages that implement the IEEE 754 floating-point standard have similar issues. The best practice is to use the `Double` type for all floating-point numbers unless there is a specific reason not to.

What if we have two variables, where one is an integer and the other is a double? Do you think we can add them as the following code shows?

```
var a: Int = 3
var b: Double = 0.14
var c = a + b
```

If we put the preceding code into a Playground, we would receive the following error:

```
operator '+' cannot be applied to operands of type Int and Double
```

This error lets us know that we are trying to add two different types of numbers, which is not allowed. To add an integer and a double together, we need to convert the integer value into a double value. The following code shows how to do this:

```
var a: Int = 3
var b: Double = 0.14
var c = Double(a) + b
```

Notice how we use the `Double()` function to initialize a `Double` value with the integer value. All numeric types in Swift have an initializer to do these types of conversion. These initializers are called convenience initializers, similar to the `Double()` function shown in the preceding code sample. For example, the following code shows how you can initialize a `Float` or `uint16` value with an integer value:

```
var intVar = 32
var floatVar = Float(intVar)
var uint16Var = UInt16(intVar)
```

The Boolean type

Boolean values are often referred to as logical values because they can be either `true` or `false`. Swift has a built-in `Boolean` type that accepts one of the two built-in `Boolean` constants: true and false.

Boolean constants and variables can be defined like this:

```
let swiftIsCool = true
var itIsRaining = false
```

Boolean values are especially useful when working with conditional statements, such as the if, while, and guard statements. For example, what do you think this code would do?

```
let isSwiftCool = true
let isItRaining = false
if isSwiftCool {
  print("YEA, I cannot wait to learn it")
}
if isItRaining {
  print("Get a rain coat")
}
```

If you answered that this code would print out YEA, I cannot wait to learn it, then you would be correct. This line is printed out because the isSwiftCool Boolean type is set to true. As the is ItRaining variable is set to false, the Get a rain coat message is not printed.

The string type

A string is an ordered collection of characters, such as Hello or Swift. In Swift, the String type represents a string. We have seen several examples of strings in this book, so the following code should look familiar. This code shows how to define two strings:

```
var stringOne = "Hello"
var stringTwo = " World"
```

We can also create a string using a multiline string literal. The following code shows how we can do that:

```
var multiLine = """
This is a multiline string literal. This shows how we can create a string
over multiple lines.
"""
```

Notice that we put three double quotes around the multiline string. We can use quotes in our multiline string to quote specific text. The following code shows how to do this:

```
var multiLine = """
This is a multiline string literal. This shows how we can create a string
over multiple lines. Jon says, "multiline string literals are cool"
"""
```

Since a string is an ordered collection of characters, we can iterate through each character of a string. The following code shows how to do this:

```
var stringOne = "Hello"
for char in stringOne.characters {
  print(char)
}
```

The preceding code will display the results shown in the following screenshot:

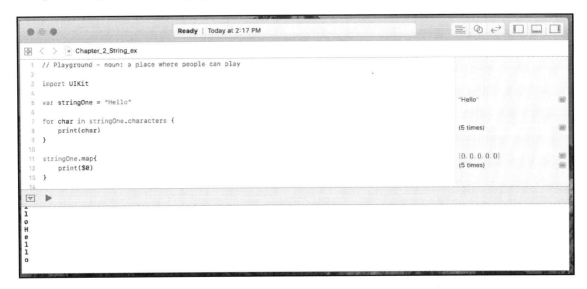

We can also use the map() method of the String type to retrieve each character, as shown in the following code:

```
stringOne.map {
  print($0)
}
```

We will look at the map() method, and how it works, later on in this book.

There are two ways to add one string to another. We can concatenate them or include them in-line. To concatenate two strings, we use the + or += operators. The following code shows us how to concatenate two strings. The first example appends `stringB` to the end of `stringA` and the results are put into the new `stringC` variable. The second example appends `stringB` directly to the end of `stringA` without creating a new string:

```
var stringC = stringA + stringB
stringA += stringB
```

To include a string in-line with another string, we use a special sequence of characters: \(). The following code shows how to include a string in-line with another string:

```
var stringA = "Jon"
var stringB = "Hello \(stringA)"
```

In the previous example, `stringB` will contain the message `Hello Jon`, because Swift will replace the \(stringA) sequence of characters with the value of the `stringA` variable.

In Swift, we define the mutability of variables and collections by using the `var` and `let` keywords. If we define a string as a variable using `var`, the string is mutable, meaning that we can change and edit the value. If we define a string as a constant using let, the string is immutable, meaning that we cannot change or edit the value once it is set. The following code shows the difference between a mutable and an immutable string:

```
var x = "Hello"
let y = "HI"
var z = " World"

//This is valid because x is mutable
x += z

//This is invalid because y is not mutable.
y += z
```

Strings in Swift have two methods that can convert the case of the string. These methods are `lowercased()` and `uppercased()`. The following example demonstrates these methods:

```
var stringOne = "hElLo"
print("Lowercase String:   " + stringOne.lowercased())
print("Uppercase String:   " + stringOne.uppercased())
```

If we run this code, the results will be as follows:

```
Lowercase String:   hello
Uppercase String:   HELLO
```

Swift provides four ways to compare a string; these are string equality, prefix equality, suffix equality, and `isEmpty`. The following example demonstrates these ways:

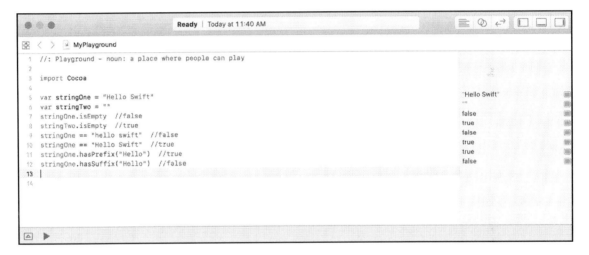

We can replace all the occurrences of a target string with another string. This is done with the `replacingOccurrances(of:)` method. The following code demonstrates this:

```
var stringOne = "one,to,three,four"
print(stringOne.replacingOccurrences(of: "to", with: "two"))
```

The preceding example will print `one, two, three, four` to the screen because we are replacing all the occurrences of `to` with `two` in the `stringOne` variable.

We can also retrieve substrings and individual characters from our strings; however, when we retrieve a substring from a string, the substring is an instance of the `Substring` type and not the `String` type. The `Substring` type contains most of the same methods as the String type, so you can use them in a similar way. Unlike `String` types, however, they are meant to be used only for short periods of time while we are working with a `String` value. If you need to use a `Substring` type for a long period of time, you should convert it to a `String` type. The following example shows we can work with substrings:

```
var path = "/one/two/three/four"

//Create start and end indexes
let startIndex = path.index(path.startIndex, offsetBy: 4)
let endIndex = path.index(path.startIndex, offsetBy: 14)

let sPath = path[startIndex ..< endIndex] //returns the "/two/three"
//convert the substring to a string
let newStr = String(sPath)

path.substring(to: startIndex)   //returns the "/one"
path.substring(from: endIndex)   //returns the "/four"

path.last
path.first
```

In the preceding example, we use the subscript `path` to retrieve the substring between a start and end index. The indices are created with the `index(_: offsetBy:)` function. The first property in the `index(_: offsetBy:)` function gives the index of where we wish to start, and the `offsetBy` property tells us how much to increase the index by.

The `substring(to:)` method creates a substring from the beginning of the string to the index. The `substring(from:)` method creates a substring from the index to the end of the string. We then use the `last` property to get the last character of the string and the `first` property to get the first character.

We can retrieve the number of characters in a string by using the `count` property. The following example shows how you can use this function:

```
var path = "/one/two/three/four"
var length = path.count
```

This completes our whirlwind tour of strings. We went through these properties and functions very quickly, but we will be using strings extensively throughout this book, so we will have a lot of time to get used to them.

Optional variables

All the variables we have looked at so far are considered to be non-optional variables. This means that the variables are required to have a non-nil value; however, there are times when we may want or need our variables to contain no or `nil` values.

In Swift, an optional variable is a variable that we can assign `nil` (no value) to. Optional variables and constants are defined using the `?` (question mark).

The following Playground will show us how to define an optional type and what happens if we assign a `nil` value to a non-optional variable:

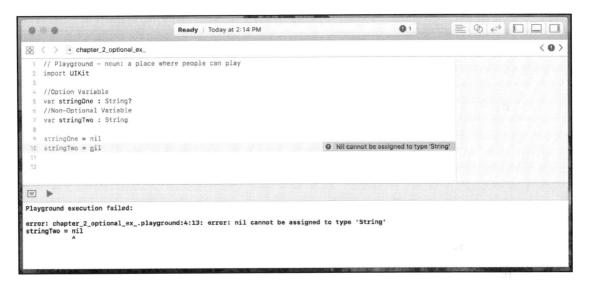

Notice the error we receive when we try to assign a nil value to the non-optional variable.

Optional variables were added to the Swift language as a safety feature. They provide a compile-time check of our variables to verify that they contain valid values. Unless the code specifically defines a variable as optional, we can assume that it contains a valid value, and we do not have to check for nil values. Since we can define a variable prior to initializing it, this could give us a nil value in a non-optional variable; however, the compiler is able to check for this.

The following Playground shows the error that we receive if we attempt to use a non-optional variable prior to initializing it:

To verify that an optional variable or constant contains a valid (non-nil) value, one may attempt to use the != (not equals to) operator to verify that the variable is not equal to nil. While this is valid, there are better ways to do this. Swift provides us with two tools to verify that an optional contains a non-nil value. These tools are optional binding and optional chaining. Before we cover optional binding and optional chaining, let's see how to use the != (not equals to) operator and what force unwrapping is.

When we use the term unwrapping in Swift we are referring to the process of retrieving the value from an optional. To use force unwrapping, we must first make sure that the optional has a non-nil value and then we can use the exclamation point (!) to access that value. The following example shows how we can do this:

```swift
var name: String?
name = "Jon"

if name != nil {
  var newString = "Hello " + name!
}
```

In this example, we create an optional variable named name and we assign it a value of Jon. We then use the != operator to verify that the optional is not equal to nil. If it is not equal to nil, we use the exclamation point to access its value. While this is a perfectly viable option, it is recommended that we use the optional binding method that we will discuss next instead of force unwrapping.

Optional binding

Optional binding is used to check whether an optional variable or constant has a non-nil value, and if so, assign that value to a temporary, non-optional variable. For optional binding, we use the if let or if var keywords together. If we use if let, the temporary value is a constant and cannot be changed. If we use the if var keyword, it puts the temporary value into a variable that can be changed. The following code illustrates how optional binding is used:

```
var myOptional: String?
if let temp = myOptional {
  print(temp)
  print("Can not use temp outside of the if bracket")
} else {
  print("myOptional was nil")
}
```

In the preceding example, we use the if let keywords to check whether the myOptional variable is nil. If it is not nil, we assign the value to the temp variable and execute the code between the brackets. If the myOptional variable is nil, we execute the code in the else bracket, which prints out the message, myOptional was nil. One thing to note is that the temp variable is scoped only for the conditional block and cannot be used outside the conditional block.

It is perfectly acceptable, and preferred with optional binding, to assign the value to a variable of the same name. The following code illustrates this:

```
var myOptional: String?
if let myOptional = myOptional {
  print(myOptional)
  print("Cannot use temp outside of the if bracket")
} else {
  print("myOptional was nil")
}
```

To illustrate the scope of the temporary variable, let's look at the following code:

```
var myOptional: String?
myOptional = "Jon"
if var myOptional = myOptional {
  myOptional = "test"
  print("Inside:  \(myOptional)")
}
print("Outside: \(myOptional)")
```

In this example, the first line that is printed to the console is Inside: test, because we are within the scope of the `if var` statement where we assign the value of `test` to the `myOptional` variable. The second line that is printed to the console is `Outside: Optional(Jon)` because we are outside the scope of the `if var` statement where the `myOptional` variable is set to `Jon`.

We can also test multiple optional variables in one line. We do this by separating each optional check with a comma. The following example shows how to do this:

```
if let myOptional = myOptional, let myOptional2 = myOptional2, let
myOptional3 = myOptional3 {
  // only reach this if all three optionals
  // have non-nil values
}
```

Optional chaining

Optional chaining allows us to call properties, methods, and subscripts on an optional that might be nil. If any of the chained values return nil, the return value will be nil. The following code gives an example of optional chaining using a fictitious `car` object. In this example, if either the `car` or tires optional variables are nil, the variable `tireSize` will be nil, otherwise the `tireSize` variable will be equal to the `tireSize` property:

```
var tireSize = car?.tires?.tireSize
```

The following Playground illustrates the three ways of verifying whether an optional contains a valid value prior to using it:

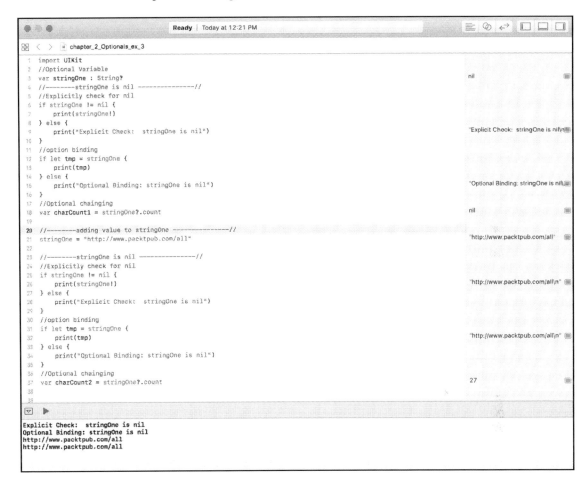

In the preceding Playground, we begin by defining the optional string variable, stringOne. We then explicitly check for nil by using the != (not equal to) operator. If stringOne is not equal to nil, we print the value of stringOne to the console. If stringOne is nil, we print the Explicit Check: stringOne is nil message to the console. As we can see in the results console, Explicit Check: stringOne is nil is printed to the console because we have not assigned a value to stringOne yet.

When an optional value is defined without giving it a value, it is the same as setting its initial value to nil.

We then use optional binding to verify that `stringOne` is not nil. If `stringOne` is not nil, the value of `stringOne` is put into the `tmp` temporary variable, and we print the value of `tmp` to the console. If `stringOne` is nil, we print the `Optional Binding: stringOne is nil` message to the console. As we can see in the results console, `Optional Binding: stringOne is nil` is printed to the console because we have not assigned a value to `stringOne` yet.

We use optional chaining to assign the value of the `count` property of the `stringOne` variable to the `charCount1` variable if `stringOne` is not nil. The `charCount1` variable is nil because we have not yet assigned a value to `stringOne`.

We then assign a value of `http://www.packtpub.com/all` to the `stringOne` variable and rerun all three tests again. This time, `stringOne` has a non-nil value; therefore, the value of `charCount2` is printed to the console.

It would be tempting to say that I need to set this variable to nil and define it as optional, but that would be a mistake. The mindset regarding optionals should be to only use them if there is a specific reason for the variable to have a nil value.

We will be discussing optionals is much greater detail in `Chapter 10`, *Using Optional Types.*

Enumerations

Enumerations (also known as enums) are a special data type that enables us to group related types together and use them in a type-safe manner. Enumerations in Swift are not tied to integer values as they are in other languages, such as C or Java. In Swift, we are able to define an enumeration with a type (string, character, integer, or floating-point) and then define its actual value (known as the raw value). Enumerations also support features that are traditionally only supported by classes, such as computed properties and instance methods. We will discuss these advanced features in depth in `Chapter 5`, *Classes and Structures.* In this section, we will look at the traditional features of enumerations.

We will define an enumeration that contains a list of `Planets`, like this:

```
enum Planets {
  case Mercury
  case Venus
  case Earth
  case Mars
  case Jupiter
  case Saturn
  case Uranus
  case Neptune
}
```

The values defined in an enumeration are considered to be the member values (or simply the members) of the enumeration. In most cases, you will see the member values defined like the preceding example because it is easy to read; however, there is a shorter version. This shorter version lets us define multiple members in a single line, separated by commas, as the following example shows:

```
enum Planets {
  case Mercury, Venus, Earth, Mars, Jupiter
  case Saturn, Uranus, Neptune
}
```

We can then use the Planets enumeration like this:

```
var planetWeLiveOn = Planets.Earth
var furthestPlanet = Planets.Neptune
```

The type for the `planetWeLiveOn` and `furthestPlanet` variables is inferred when we initialize the variable with one of the member values of the `Planets` enumeration. Once the variable type is inferred, we can then assign a new value without the `Planets` prefix, as shown here:

```
planetWeLiveOn = .Mars
```

We can compare an enumeration value using the traditional equals (==) operator or use a switch statement. The following example shows how to use the `equals` operator and the `switch` statement with an enum:

```
// Using the traditional == operator
if planetWeLiveOn == .Earth {
  print("Earth it is")
}

// Using the switch statement
switch planetWeLiveOn {
```

```
    case .Mercury:
      print("We live on Mercury, it is very hot!")
    case .Venus:
      print("We live on Venus, it is very hot!")
    case .Earth:
      print("We live on Earth, just right")
    case .Mars:
      print("We live on Mars, a little cold")
    default:
      print("Where do we live?")
}
```

Enumerations can come prepopulated with raw values, which are required to be of the same type. The following example shows how to define an enumeration with string values:

```
enum Devices: String {
  case MusicPlayer = "iPod"
  case Phone = "iPhone"
  case Tablet = "iPad"
}

print("We are using an \(Devices.Tablet.rawValue)")
```

The preceding example creates an enumeration with three types of device. We then use the rawValue property to retrieve the stored value for the Tablet member of the Devices enumeration. This example will print a message saying, We are using an iPad.

Let's create another Planets enumeration, but this time, assign numbers to the members, as follows:

```
enum Planets: Int {
  case Mercury = 1
  case Venus
  case Earth
  case Mars
  case Jupiter
  case Saturn
  case Uranus
  case Neptune
}
print("Earth is planet number \(Planets.Earth.rawValue)")
```

The big difference between these last two enumerations examples is that in the second example, we only assign a value to the first member (Mercury). If integers are used for the raw values of an enumeration then we do not have to assign a value to each member. If no value is present, the raw values will be auto-incremented.

In Swift, enumerations can also have associated values. Associated values allow us to store additional information along with member values. This additional information can vary each time we use the member. It can also be of any type, and the types can be different for each member. Let's look at how we might use associate types by defining a `Product` enumeration, which contains two types of products:

```swift
enum Product {
  case Book(Double, Int, Int)
  case Puzzle(Double, Int)
}

var masterSwift = Product.Book(49.99, 2017, 310)
var worldPuzzle = Product.Puzzle(9.99, 200)

switch masterSwift {
  case .Book(let price, let year, let pages):
    print("Mastering Swift was published in \(year) for the price of
\(price)
          and has \(pages) pages")
  case .Puzzle(let price, let pieces):
    print("Mastering Swift is a puzzle with \(pieces) and sells for
\(price)")
}

switch worldPuzzle {
  case .Book(let price, let year, let pages):
    print("World Puzzle was published in \(year) for the price of \(price)
and
          has \(pages) pages")
  case .Puzzle(let price, let pieces):
    print("World Puzzle is a puzzle with \(pieces) and sells for \(price)")
}
```

In the preceding example, we begin by defining a `Product` enumeration with two members: `Book` and `Puzzle`. The `Book` member has associated values of the `Double`, `Int`, and `Int` types, while the `Puzzle` member has associated values of the `Double` and `Int` types. Notice that we are using named associated types where we assign a name for each associated type. We then create two products `masterSwift` and `worldPuzzle`. We assign the `masterSwift` variable a value of `Product.Book` with the associated values of 49.99, 2016, and 310. We then assign the `worldPuzzle` variable a value of `Product.Puzzle` with the associated values of 9.99 and 200.

We can then check the `Products` enumeration using a `switch` statement, as we did in an earlier example. We then extract the associated values within the `switch` statement. In this example, we extracted the associated values as constants with the `let` keyword, but you can also extract the associated values as variables with the `var` keyword.

If you put the previous code into a Playground, the following results will be displayed:

```
"Master Swift was published in 2017 for the price of 49.99 and has 310
pages"
"World Puzzle is a puzzle with 200 and sells for 9.99"
```

We have only scratched the surface of what enumerations can do in Swift. In `Chapter 5`, *Classes and Structures*, we will look at some additional features of enumerations with Swift and explore why they are so powerful.

Operators

An operator is a symbol or combination of symbols that we can use to check, change, or combine values. We have used operators in most of the examples so far in this book, but we did not specifically call them operators. In this section, we will show you how to use most of the basic operators that Swift supports.

Swift supports most standard C operators and also improves on some of them to eliminate several common coding errors. For example, the assignment operator does not return a value, which prevents it from being used where we are meant to use the equality operator (==).

Let's look at the operators in Swift.

The assignment operator

The assignment operator initializes or updates a variable. Here is a prototype:

```
var A = var B
```

Here is an example:

```
let x = 1
var y = "Hello"
a = b
```

Comparison operators

The comparison operator returns a Boolean `true` if the statement is `true` or a Boolean `false` if the statement is not `true`.

Here are some prototypes:

```
Equality:
  varA == varB
Not equal:
  varA != varB
Greater than:
  varA > varB
Less than:
  varA < varB
Greater than or equal to:
  varA >= varB
Less than or equal to:
  varA <= varB
```

Here are some examples:

```
2 == 1 //false, 2 does not equal 1
2 != 1 //true, 2 does not equal 1
2 > 1 //true, 2 is greater than 1
2 < 1 //false, 2 is not less than 1
2 >= 1 //true, 2 is greater or equal to 1
2 <= 1 //false, 2 is not less or equal to 1
```

Arithmetic operators

The arithmetic operators perform the four basic mathematical operations.

Here are some prototypes:

```
Addition:
  varA + varB
Subtraction:
  varA - varB
Multiplication:
  varA * varB
Division:
  varA / varB
```

Here are some examples:

```
var x = 4 + 2 //x will equal 6
var x = 4 - 2 //x will equal 2
var x = 4 * 2 //x will equal 8
var x = 4 / 2 //x will equal 2
var x = "Hello " + "world"  //x will equal "Hello World"
```

The remainder operator

The remainder operator calculates the remainder if the first operand is divided by the second operand. In other languages, this is sometimes referred to as the modulo or modulus operator.

Here is a prototype:

```
varA % varB
```

Here is an example:

```
var x = 10 % 3    //x will equal 1
var x = 10 % 2.6  //x will equal 2.2
```

Compound assignment operators

The compound assignment operators combine an arithmetic operator with an assignment operator.

Here are some prototypes:

```
varA += varB
varA -= varB
varA *= varB
varA /= varB
```

Here are some examples:

```
var x = 6
x += 2  //x is equal to 8
x -= 2  //x is equal to 4
x *= 2  //x is equal to 12
x /= 2  //x is equal to 3
```

The ternary conditional operator

The ternary conditional operator assigns a value to a variable based on the evaluation of a comparison operator or `Boolean` value.

Here is a prototype:

```
(boolValue ? valueA : valueB)
```

Here is an example:

```
var x = 2
var y = 3
var z = (y >x ? "Y is greater" : "X is greater")
//z equals "Y is greater"
```

The logical NOT operator

The logical NOT operator inverts a `Boolean` value. Here is a prototype:

```
varA = !varB
```

Here is a example:

```
var x = true
var y = !x  //y equals false
```

The logical AND operator

The logical AND operator returns true if both operands are `true`; otherwise, it returns `false`.

Here is a prototype:

```
varA && varB
```

Here is a example:

```
var x = true
var y = false
var z = x && y  //z equals false
```

The logical OR operator

The logical OR operator returns `true` if either of the operands are true.

Here is a prototype:

```
varA || varB
```

Here is a example:

```
var x = true
var y = false
var z = x || y  //z equals true
```

For those who are familiar with the C language, or similar languages, these operators should look pretty familiar. For those of you who aren't that familiar with the C operators, rest assured that, once you begin to use them frequently, they will become second nature.

Summary

In this chapter, we covered topics ranging from variables and constants to data types and operators. The items in this chapter will act as the foundation for every application that you write; therefore, it is important to understand the concepts discussed here.

In this chapter, we have seen that we should prefer constants to variables when the value is not going to change. Swift will give you a compile time warning if you set but never change a variables value. We also saw that we should prefer type inference over declaring a type.

Numeric and string types, implemented as primitives in other languages, are named types implemented with structures in Swift. In future chapters, you will see why this is important. One of the most important things to remember from this chapter is that, if a variable contains a nil value, you must declare it as an optional.

In the next chapter, we will look at how we can use Swift collection types to store related data. These collection types are the dictionary and array types. We will also look at how we can use the Cocoa and Foundation data types in Swift.

3
Using Swift Collections and the Tuple Type

Once I got past the basic `Hello, World!` beginner applications, I quickly began to realize the shortcomings of variables, especially with the Mad Libs-style applications that I was starting to write. These applications requested that the user enter numerous strings, which resulted in the creation of separate variables for each input field that the user entered. Having all these separate variables quickly became very cumbersome. I remember talking to a friend about this, and he asked me why I was not using arrays. At that time, I was not familiar with arrays, so I asked him to show me what they were. Even though he had a TI-99/4A and I had a Commodore Vic-20, the concept of arrays was the same. Even today, the arrays found in modern development languages have the same basic concepts as the arrays I used on my Commodore Vic-20. While it is definitely possible to create a useful application without using collections, such as arrays, when used properly collections do make application development significantly easier.

In this chapter, we will cover the following topics:

- What an array is in Swift and how to use it?
- What a dictionary is in Swift and how to use it?
- What a set is in Swift and how to use it?
- What a tuple is in Swift and how to use it?

Swift collection types

A collection groups multiple items into a single unit. Swift provides three native collection types. These collection types are arrays, sets, and dictionaries. *Arrays* store data in an ordered collection, sets are unordered collections of unique values, and *dictionaries* are unordered collections of key-value pairs. In an array, we access the data by the location or index in the array, whereas in a set we iterate through the collection while dictionaries are accessed using a unique key.

The data stored in a Swift collection is required to be of the same type. This means, as an example, that we are unable to store a string value in an array of integers. Since Swift does not allow us to mismatch data types in a collection, we can be certain of the data type when we retrieve elements from a collection. This is another feature that, on the surface, might seem like a shortcoming, but actually helps eliminate common programming mistakes.

 Having a collection that contains arbitrary data types usually leads to problems, and should be considered a design problem. Later in this chapter, we will see how to use the `Any` and `AnyObject` aliases, but we should avoid this wherever possible.

Mutability

For those who are familiar with Objective-C, you will know that there are different classes for mutable and immutable collections. For example, to define a mutable array, we use the `NSMutableArray` class, and to define an immutable array, we use the `NSArray` class. Swift is a little different, because it does not contain separate classes for mutable and immutable collections. Instead, we define whether a collection is constant (immutable) or variable (mutable) by using the `let` and `var` keywords. This should seem familiar by now since we define constants with the `let` keyword and variables with the `var` keyword.

 It is good practice to create immutable collections unless there is a specific need to change the objects within the collection. This allows the compiler to optimize performance.

Let's begin our tour of collections by looking at the most common collection type: the array type.

Arrays

Arrays are a very common component of modern programming languages, and can be found in virtually all modern programming languages. In Swift, an array is an ordered list of objects of the same type.

When an array is created, we must declare the type of data that can be stored in it by explicit type declaration or through type inference. Typically, we only explicitly declare the data type of an array when we are creating an empty array. If we initialize an array with data, the compiler uses type inference to infer the data type for the array.

Each object in an array is called an **element**. Each of these elements is stored in a set order and can be accessed by searching for its location (index) in the array.

Creating and initializing arrays

We can initialize an array with an array literal. An array literal is a set of values that prepopulate the array. The following example shows how to define an immutable array of integers using the `let` keyword:

```
let arrayOne = [1,2,3]
```

As mentioned, if we need to create a mutable array, we will use the `var` keyword to define the array. The following example shows how to define a mutable array:

```
var arrayTwo = [4,5,6]
```

In the preceding two examples, the compiler inferred the type of values stored in the array by looking at the type of values stored in the array literal. If we want to create an empty array, we will need to explicitly declare the type of values to store in the array. There are two ways to declare null arrays in Swift. The following examples show how to declare an empty mutable array that can be used to store integers:

```
var arrayThree = [Int]()
var arrayThree: [Int] = []
```

In the preceding examples, we created arrays with integer values, and the majority of the array examples in this chapter will also use integer values; however, we can create arrays in Swift with any type. The only rule is that, once an array is defined as containing a particular type, all the elements in the array must be of that type. The following example shows how we can create arrays of various data types:

```
var arrayOne = [String]()
var arrayTwo = [Double]()
var arrayThree = [MyObject]()
```

Swift provides special type aliases for working with nonspecific types. These aliases are AnyObject and Any. We can use these aliases to define arrays whose elements are of different types like this:

```
var myArray: [Any] = [1,"Two"]
```

The AnyObject aliases can represent an instance of any class type, while the Any aliases can represent an instance of the Any type. We should use the Any and AnyObject aliases only when there is an explicit need for this behavior. It is always better to be specific about the types of data our collections contain.

We can also initialize an array of a certain size with all the elements of the array set to a predefined value. This can be very useful if we want to create an array and prepopulate it with default values. The following example defines an array with seven elements, with each element containing the number 3:

```
var arrayFour = [Int](repeating: 3, count: 7)
```

While the most common array is a one-dimensional array, multidimensional arrays can also be created. A multidimensional array is really nothing more than an array of arrays. For example, a two-dimensional array is an array of arrays, while a three-dimensional array is an array of arrays of arrays. The following examples show the two ways to create a two-dimensional array in Swift:

```
var multiArrayOne = [[1,2],[3,4],[5,6]]
var multiArrayTwo = [[Int]]()
```

Accessing the array elements

The subscript syntax is used to retrieve values from an array. Subscript syntax, for an array, is where a number appears between two square brackets, and that number specifies the location (index) within the array of the element we wish to retrieve. The following example shows how to retrieve elements from an array using the subscript syntax:

```
let arrayOne = [1,2,3,4,5,6]
print(arrayOne[0])   //Displays '1'
print(arrayOne[3])   //Displays '4'
```

In the preceding code, we begin by creating an array of integers that contains six numbers. We then print out the value at indexes 0 and 3.

 One important fact to note is that indices in Swift arrays start with the number zero. This means that the first item in an array has an index of 0. The second item in an array has an index of 1.

If we want to retrieve an individual value within a multidimensional array, we need to provide a subscript for each dimension of the array. If we do not provide a subscript for each dimension, we will retrieve an array rather than an individual value within the array. The following example shows how we can define a two-dimensional array and retrieve an individual value within the two dimensions:

```
let multiArray = [[1,2],[3,4],[5,6]]
let arr = multiArray[0] //arr contains the array [1,2]
let value = multiArray[0][1] //value contains 2
```

In the preceding code, we begin by defining a two-dimensional array. When we retrieve the value at index 0 of the first dimension (multiArray[0]), we retrieve the array [1,2]. When we retrieve the value at index 0 of the first dimension and index 1 of the second dimension (multiArray[0][1]), we retrieve the integer 2.

We can retrieve the first and last elements of an array using the first and last properties. The first and last properties return an optional value, since the values may be nil if the array is empty. The following example shows how to use these properties to retrieve the first and last elements of both a one-dimensional and a multidimensional array:

```
let arrayOne = [1,2,3,4,5,6]
let first = arrayOne.first  //first contains 1
let last = arrayOne.last  //last contains 6

let multiArray = [[1,2],[3,4],[5,6]]
let arrFirst1 = multiArray[0].first //arrFirst1 contains 1
```

```
let arrFirst2 = multiArray.first //arrFirst2 contains[1,2]
let arrLast1 = multiArray[0].last //arrLast1 contains 2
let arrLast2 = multiArray.last  //arrLast2 contains [5,6]
```

Counting the elements of an array

At times, it is essential to know the number of elements in an array. The array type in Swift contains a read-only `count` property. The following example shows how to use this property to retrieve the number of elements in both single-dimensional and multidimensional arrays:

```
let arrayOne = [1,2,3]
let multiArrayOne = [[3,4],[5,6],[7,8]]
print(arrayOne.count)  //Displays 3
print(multiArrayOne.count)  //Displays 3 for the three arrays
print(multiArrayOne[0].count)  //Displays 2 for the two elements
```

The value that is returned by the `count` property is the number of elements in the array and not the largest valid index of the array. For nonempty arrays, the largest valid index is the number of elements in the array minus 1. This is because the first element of the array has an index number of 0. As an example, if an array has two elements, the valid indexes are 0 and 1, while the `count` property would return 2. This is illustrated with the following code:

```
let arrayOne = [0,1]
print(arrayOne[0])  //Displays 0
print(arrayOne[1])  //Displays 1
print(arrayOne.count) //Displays 2
```

If we attempt to retrieve an element from an array that is outside the range of the array, the application will throw an `array index out of range` error. Therefore, if we are unsure of the size of an array, it is good practice to verify that the index is not outside the range of the array. The following examples illustrate this concept:

```
//This example will throw an array index out of range error
let arrayOne = [1,2,3,4]
print(arrayOne[6])

//This example will not throw an array index out of range error
let arrayTwo = [1,2,3,4]
if (arrayTwo.count > 6) {
  print(arrayTwo[6])
}
```

In the preceding code, the first block would throw an `array index out of range error` because we are attempting to access the value from the `arrayOne` array at index 6; however, there are only four elements in the array. The second example would not throw the error because we are checking whether the `arrayTwo` array contains more than six elements before trying to access the element at the sixth index.

Is the array empty?

To check whether an array is empty (does not contain any elements), we use the `isEmpty` property. This property will return `true` if the array is empty and `false` if it is not. The following example shows how to check whether an array is empty or not:

```
var arrayOne = [1,2]
var arrayTwo = [Int]()
arrayOne.isEmpty  //Returns false because the array is not empty
arrayTwo.isEmpty  //Returns true because the array is empty
```

Appending to an array

A static array is somewhat useful, but having the ability to add elements dynamically is what makes arrays really useful. To add an item to the end of an array, we can use the `append` method. The following example shows how to append an item to the end of an array:

```
var arrayOne = [1,2]
arrayOne.append(3)  //arrayOne will now contain 1, 2 and 3
```

Swift also allows us to use the addition assignment operator (+=) to append an array to another array. The following example shows how to use the addition assignment operator to append an array to the end of another array:

```
var arrayOne = [1,2]
arrayOne += [3,4]  //arrayOne will now contain 1, 2, 3 and 4
```

The way you append an element to the end of an array is really up to you. Personally, I prefer the assignment operator because, to me, it is a bit easier to read, but we will be using both in this book.

Inserting a value into an array

We can insert a value into an array by using the `insert` method. The `insert` method will move all the items up one spot, starting at the specified index, to make room for the new element, and then insert the value into the specified index. The following example shows how to use this method to insert a new value into an array:

```
var arrayOne = [1,2,3,4,5]
arrayOne.insert(10, at: 3) //arrayOne now contains 1, 2,3, 10, 4 and 5
```

You cannot insert a value that is outside the current range of the array. Attempting to do so will throw an `Index out of range exception`. For example, in the preceding code, if we attempt to insert a new integer at index 10, we will receive an `Index out of range exception error` because `arrayOne` contains only five elements. The exception to this is that we can insert an item directly after the last element, and therefore we can insert an item at index 6. However, it is recommended that we use the `append` function to append an item to avoid errors.

Replacing elements in an array

We use the subscript syntax to replace elements in an array. Using the subscript, we pick the element of the array we wish to update and then use the assignment operator to assign a new value. The following example shows how we will replace a value in an array:

```
var arrayOne = [1,2,3]
arrayOne[1] = 10  //arrayOne now contains 1,10,3
```

You cannot update a value that is outside the current range of the array. Attempting to do so will throw the same `Index out of range exception` that was thrown when we tried to insert a value outside the range of the array.

Removing elements from an array

There are three methods that we can use to remove one or all of the elements in an array. These methods are `removeLast()`, `remove(at:)`, and `removeAll()`. The following example shows how to use the three methods to remove elements from the array:

```
var arrayOne = [1,2,3,4,5]
arrayOne.removeLast()  //arrayOne now contains 1, 2, 3 and 4
```

```
arrayOne.remove(at:2)   //arrayOne now contains 1, 2 and 4
arrayOne.removeAll()    //arrayOne is now empty
```

The `removeLast()` and `remove(at:)` methods will also return the value of the element being removed. Therefore, if we want to know the value of the item that was removed, we can rewrite the `remove(at:)` and `removeLast()` lines to capture the value, as shown in the following example:

```
var arrayOne = [1,2,3,4,5]
var removed1 = arrayOne.removeLast() //removed1 contains the value 5
var removed = arrayOne.remove(at: 2)//removed contains the value 3
```

Merging two arrays

To create a new array by adding two arrays together, we use the addition (+) operator. The following example shows how to use the addition (+) operator to create a new array that contains all the elements of two other arrays:

```
let arrayOne = [1,2]
let arrayTwo = [3,4]
var combined = arrayOne + arrayTwo //combine contains 1, 2, 3 and 4
```

In the preceding code, `arrayOne` and `arrayTwo` are left unchanged, while the `combined` array contains the elements from `arrayOne`, followed by the elements from `arrayTwo`.

Retrieving a subarray from an array

We can retrieve a subarray from an existing array by using the subscript syntax with a range operator. The following example shows how to retrieve a range of elements from an existing array:

```
let arrayOne = [1,2,3,4,5]
var subArray = arrayOne[2...4] //subArray contains 3, 4 and 5
```

The operator (three periods) is known as a **two-sided range** operator. The range operator, in the preceding code, says that I want all the elements from 2 to 4 inclusively (elements 2 and 4 as well as what is between them). There is another two-sided range operator-..<, known as the half-open range operator. The half-open range operator functions the same as the previous range operator, but excludes the last element. The following example shows how to use the ..< operator:

```
let arrayOne = [1,2,3,4,5]
var subArray = arrayOne[2..<4] //subArray contains 3 and 4
```

In the preceding example, the subarray will contain two elements, 3 and 4. A two-sided range operator has numbers on either side of the operator. In Swift, we are not limited to two-sided range operators; we can also use one-sided range operators. The following examples show how we can use one-sided range operators:

```
let arrayOne = [1,2,3,4,5]
var a = arrayOne[..<3]   //subArray contains 1, 2 and 3
var b = arrayOne[...3]   //subArray contains 1, 2, 3 and 4
var c = arrayOne[2...]   //subArray contains 3, 4 and 5
```

The one-sided range operators were added to Swift 4.

Making bulk changes to an array

We can use the subscript syntax with a range operator to change the values of multiple elements. The following example shows how to do this:

```
var arrayOne = [1,2,3,4,5]
arrayOne[1...2] = [12,13]//arrayOne contains 1,12,13,4 and 5
```

In the preceding code, the elements at indices 1 and 2 will be changed to numbers 12 and 13; therefore, arrayOne will contain 1, 12, 13, 4, and 5.

The number of elements that you are changing in the range operator does not need to match the number of values that you are passing in. Swift makes bulk changes by first removing the elements defined by the range operator and then inserting the new values. The following example demonstrates this concept:

```
var arrayOne = [1,2,3,4,5]
arrayOne[1...3] = [12,13] //arrayOne now contains 1, 12, 13 and 5
```

In the preceding code, the `arrayOne` array starts with five elements. We then replace the range of elements 1 to 3 inclusively. This causes elements 1 through 3 (three elements) to be removed from the array first. After those three elements are removed, then the two new elements (12 and 13) are added to the array, starting at index 1. After this is complete, `arrayOne` will contain these four elements: 1, 12, 13, and 5. Using the same logic we can also add more elements then we remove. The following example illustrates this:

```
var arrayOne = [1,2,3,4,5]
arrayOne[1...3] = [12,13,14,15]
//arrayOne now contains 1, 12, 13, 14, 15 and 5 (six elements)
```

In the preceding code, `arrayOne` starts with five elements. We then say that we want to replace the range of elements 1 through 3 inclusively. As in the previous example, this causes elements 1 to 3 (three elements) to be removed from the array. We then add four elements (12, 13, 14, and 15) to the array, starting at index 1. After this is complete, `arrayOne` will contain these six elements: 1, 12, 13, 14, 15, and 5.

Algorithms for arrays

Swift arrays have several methods that take a closure as the argument. These methods transform the array in a way defined by the code in the closure. Closures are self-contained blocks of code that can be passed around, and are similar to blocks in Objective-C and lambdas in other languages. We will discuss closures in depth in `Chapter 12`, *Working with Closures*. For now, the goal is to become familiar with how the algorithms work in Swift.

Sort

The sort algorithm sorts an array in place. This means that, when the `sort()` method is used, the original array is replaced with the sorted one. The closure takes two arguments (represented by `$0` and `$1`), and it should return a Boolean value that indicates whether the first element should be placed before the second element. The following code shows how to use the sort algorithm:

```
var arrayOne = [9,3,6,2,8,5]
arrayOne.sort(){ $0 < $1 }
//arrayOne contains 2,3,5,6,8 and 9
```

The preceding code will sort the array in ascending order. We can tell this because the rule will return true if the first number ($0) is less than the second number ($1). Therefore, when the sort algorithm begins, it compares the first two numbers (9 and 3) and returns true if the first number (9) is less than the second number (3). In our case, the rule returns false, so the numbers are reversed. The algorithm continues sorting in this manner until all of the numbers are sorted in the correct order.

The preceding example sorted the array in numerically increasing order; if we wanted to reverse the order, we would reverse the arguments in the closure. The following code shows how to reverse the sort order:

```
var arrayOne = [9,3,6,2,8,5]
arrayOne.sort(){ $1 < $0 }
//arrayOne contains 9,8,6,5,3 and 2
```

When we run this code, arrayOne will contain the elements 9, 8, 6, 5, 3, and 2.

Sorted

While the sort algorithm sorts the array in place (replaces the original array), the sorted algorithm does not change the original array; it instead creates a new array with the sorted elements from the original array. The following example shows how to use the sorted algorithm:

```
var arrayOne = [9,3,6,2,8,5]
let sorted = arrayOne.sorted(){ $0 < $1 }
//sorted contains 2,3,5,6,8 and 9
//arrayOne contains 9,3,6,2,8 and 5
```

After we run this code, arrayOne will contain the original unsorted array (9, 3, 6, 2, 8, and 5) and the sorted array will contain the new sorted array (2, 3, 5, 6, 8, and 9).

Filter

The filter algorithm will return a new array by filtering the original array. This is one of the most powerful array algorithms and may end up as the one you use the most. If you need to retrieve a subset of an array based on a set of rules, I recommend using this algorithm rather than trying to write your own method to filter the array.

The closure takes one argument, and it should return a Boolean `true` if the element should be included in the new array, as shown in the following code:

```
var arrayOne = [1,2,3,4,5,6,7,8,9]
let filtered = arrayOne.filter{$0 > 3 && $0 < 7}
//filtered contains 4,5 and 6
```

In the preceding code, the rule that we are passing to the algorithm returns true if the number is greater than 3 and less than 7; therefore, any number that is greater than 3 and less than 7 is included in the new `filtered` array.

This next example shows how we can retrieve a subset of cities that contain the letter o in their name:

```
var city = ["Boston", "London", "Chicago", "Atlanta"]
let filtered = city.filter{$0.range(of:"o") != nil}
//filtered contains "Boston", "London" and "Chicago"
```

In the preceding code, we use the `range(of:)` method to return `true` if the string contains the letter o. If the method returns `true`, the string is included in the `filteredarray`.

Map

While the filter algorithm is used to select only certain elements of an array, map is used to apply logic to all elements in the array. The following example shows how to use the map algorithm to divide each number by 10:

```
var arrayOne = [10, 20, 30, 40]
let applied = arrayOne.map{ $0 / 10}
//applied contains 1,2,3 and 4
```

In the preceding code, the new array contains the numbers 1, 2, 3, and 4, which is the result of dividing each element of the original array by 10.

The new array created by the map algorithm is not required to contain the same element types as the original array; however, all the elements in the new array must be of the same type. In the following example, the original array contains integer values, but the new array created by the map algorithm contains string elements:

```
var arrayOne = [1, 2, 3, 4]
let applied = arrayOne.map{ "num:\($0)"}
//applied contains "num:1", "num:2", "num:3" and "num:4"
```

In the preceding code, we created an array of strings that appends the numbers from the original array to the num: string.

forEach

We can use the `forEach` algorithm to iterate over a sequence. The following example shows how we would do this:

```
var arrayOne = [10, 20, 30, 40]
arrayOne.forEach{ print($0) }
```

This example will print the following results to the console:

```
10
20
30
40
```

While using the `forEach` algorithm is very easy, it does have some limitations. The recommended way to iterate over an array is to use the `for-in` loop, which we will see in the next section.

Iterating over an array

We can iterate over all elements of an array, in order, with a `for-in` loop. The `for-in` loop will execute one or more statements for each element of the array. We will discuss the `for-in` loop in greater detail in Chapter 4, *Control Flow and Functions*. The following example shows how we would iterate over the elements of an array:

```
var arrayOne = ["one", "two", "three"]
for item in arrayOne {
  print(item)
}
```

In the preceding example, the `for-in` loop iterates over the array and executes the `print(item)` line for each element in the array. If we run this code, it will display the following results in the console:

```
one
two
three
```

There are times when we would like to iterate over an array, as we did in the preceding example, but we would also like to know the index, as well as the value of the element. To do this, we can use the `enumerated` method of an array, which returns a tuple (see the *Tuples* section later in this chapter) for each item in the array that contains both the index and value of the element. The following example shows how to use this function:

```
var arrayOne = ["one", "two", "three"]
for (index,value) in arrayOne.enumerated() {
  print("\(index) \(value)")
}
```

The preceding code will display the following results in the console:

```
0 one
1 two
2 three
```

Now that we have introduced arrays in Swift, let's move on to dictionaries.

Dictionaries

While dictionaries are not as commonly used as arrays, they have additional functionality that makes them incredibly powerful. A dictionary is a container that stores multiple key-value pairs, where all the keys are of the same type and all the values are of the same type. The key is used as a unique identifier for the value. A dictionary does not guarantee the order in which the key-value pairs are stored since we look up the values by the key rather than by the index of the value.

Dictionaries are good for storing items that map to unique identifiers, where the unique identifier should be used to retrieve the item. Countries with their abbreviations are a good example of items that can be stored in a dictionary. In the following chart, we show countries with their abbreviations as key-value pairs:

Key	Value
US	United States
IN	India
UK	United Kingdom

Creating and initializing dictionaries

We can initialize a dictionary using a dictionary literal, similarly to how we initialized an array with the array literal. The following example shows how to create a dictionary using the key-value pairs in the preceding chart:

```
let countries = ["US":"UnitedStates","IN":"India","UK":"UnitedKingdom"]
```

The preceding code creates an immutable dictionary that contains each of the key-value pairs in the chart we saw before. Just like the array, to create a mutable dictionary we will need to use the var keyword in place of let. The following example shows how to create a mutable dictionary containing the countries:

```
var countries = ["US":"UnitedStates","IN":"India","UK":"UnitedKingdom"]
```

In the preceding two examples, we created a dictionary where the key and value were both strings. The compiler inferred that the key and value were strings because that was the type of the keys and values used to initiate the dictionary. If we wanted to create an empty dictionary, we would need to tell the compiler what the key and value types are. The following examples create various dictionaries with different key-value types:

```
var dic1 = [String:String]()
var dic2 = [Int:String]()
var dic3 = [String:MyObject]()
var dic4: [String:String] = [:]
var dic5: [Int:String] = [:]
```

 If we want to use a custom object as the key in a dictionary, we will need to make the custom object conform to the **Hashable** protocol from Swift's standard library. We will discuss protocols and classes in Chapter 5, *Classes and Structures,* but for now just understand that it is possible to use custom objects as a key in a dictionary.

Accessing dictionary values

We use the subscript syntax to retrieve the value for a particular key. If the dictionary does not contain the key we are looking for, the dictionary will return nil; therefore, the variable returned from this lookup is an optional variable. The following example shows how to retrieve a value from a dictionary using its key in the subscript syntax:

```
let countries = ["US":"United States", "IN":"India","UK":"UnitedKingdom"]
var name = countries["US"]
```

In the preceding code, the variable name will contain this string: United States.

Counting the key or values in a dictionary

We use the `count` property of the dictionary to get the number of key-value pairs in the dictionary. The following example shows how to use this property:

```
let countries = ["US":"United States", "IN":"India","UK":"United Kingdom"];
var cnt = countries.count  //cnt contains 3
```

In the preceding code, the `cnt` variable will contain the number 3 since there are three key-value pairs in the `countries` dictionary.

Is the dictionary empty?

To test whether the dictionary contains any key-value pairs at all, we can use the `isEmpty` property. This property will return `false` if the dictionary contains one or more key-value pairs and `true` if it is empty. The following example shows how to use this property to determine whether our dictionary contains any key-value pairs:

```
let countries = ["US":"United States", "IN":"India","UK":"United Kingdom"]
var empty = countries.isEmpty
```

In the preceding code, the `isEmpty` property returned `false` as there are three key-value pairs in the `countries` dictionary.

Updating the value of a key

To update the value of a key in a dictionary, we can use either the subscript syntax or the `updateValue(_: ,forKey:)` method. The `updateValue(_:, forKey:)` method has an additional feature that the subscript syntax doesn't: it returns the original value associated with the key prior to changing the value. The following example shows how to use both the subscript syntax and the `updateValue(_:, forKey:)` method to update the value of a key:

```
var countries = ["US":"United States", "IN":"India","UK":"United Kingdom"]

countries["UK"] = "Great Britain"
//The value of UK is now set to "Great Britain"

var orig = countries.updateValue("Britain", forKey: "UK")
//The value of UK is now set to "Britain"
//The orig variable equals "Great Britain"
```

In the preceding code, we use the subscript syntax to change the value associated with the key UK from United Kingdom to Great Britain. The original value of United Kingdom was not saved prior to replacing it. We then used the updateValue(_:, forKey:) method to change the value associated with the key UK from Great Britain to Britain. With the updateValue(_:, forKey:) method, the original value of Great Britain is assigned to the orig variable, prior to changing the value in the dictionary.

Adding a key-value pair

To add a new key-value pair to a dictionary, we can use the subscript syntax or the same updateValue(_:, forKey:) method that we used to update the value of a key. If we use the updateValue(_:, forKey:) method and the key is not currently present in the dictionary, this method will add a new key-value pair and return nil. The following example shows how to use both the subscript syntax and the updateValue(_:, forKey:) method to add a new key-value pair to a dictionary:

```
var countries = ["US":"United States", "IN":"India","UK":"United Kingdom"]
countries["FR"] = "France" //The value of "FR" is set to"France"
var orig = countries.updateValue("Germany", forKey: "DE")
//The value of "DE" is set to "Germany" and orig is nil
```

In the preceding code, the countries dictionary starts with three key-value pairs and we then add a fourth key-value pair (FR/France) to the dictionary using the subscript syntax. We use the updateValue(_:,forKey:) method to add a fifth key-value pair (DE/Germany) to the dictionary. The orig variable is set to nil because the countries dictionary did not contain a value associated with the DE key.

Removing a key-value pair

There may be times when we need to remove values from a dictionary. There are three ways to achieve this: using the subscript syntax, the removeValue(forKey:) method, and the removeAll() method. The removeValue(forKey:) method returns the value of the key prior to removing it. The removeAll() method removes all the elements from the dictionary. The following example shows how to use all three methods to remove key-value pairs from a dictionary:

```
var countries = ["US":"UnitedStates","IN":"India","UK":"United Kingdom"];
countries["IN"] = nil //The "IN" key/value pair is removed
var orig = countries.removeValue(forKey:"UK")
//The "UK" key value pair is removed and orig contains "United Kingdom"
```

```
countries.removeAll()
//Removes all key/value pairs from the countries dictionary
```

In the preceding code, the `countries` dictionary starts off with three key-value pairs. We then set the value associated with the key `IN` to nil, which removes the key-value pair from the dictionary. We use the `removeValue(forKey:)` method to remove the key associated with the `UK` key. Prior to removing the value associated with the `UK` key, the `removeValue(forKey:)` method saves the value in the `orig` variable. Finally, we use the `removeAll()` method to remove all the remaining key-value pairs in the countries dictionary.

Now let's look at the set type.

Set

The set type is a generic collection that is similar to the array type. While the array type is an ordered collection that may contain duplicate items, the set type is an unordered collection where each item must be unique.

Like the key in a dictionary, the type stored in an array must conform to the **Hashable** protocol. This means that the type must provide a way to compute a hash value for itself. All of Swift's basic types, such as `String`, `Double`, `Int`, and `Bool`, conform to this protocol and can be used in a set by default.

Let's look at how we would use the set type.

Initializing a set

There are a couple of ways in which we can initialize a set. Just like the array and dictionary types, Swift needs to know what type of data is going to be stored in it. This means that we must either tell Swift the type of data to store in the set or initialize it with some data so that it can infer the data type.

Just like the array and dictionary types, we use the `var` and `let` keywords to declare if the set is mutable or not:

```
//Initializes an empty set of the String type
var mySet = Set<String>()

//Initializes a mutable set of the String type with initial values
var mySet = Set(["one", "two", "three"])
```

```
//Creates a immutable set of the String type.
let mySet = Set(["one", "two", "three"])
```

Inserting items into a set

We use the `insert` method to insert an item into a set. If we attempt to insert an item that is already in the set, the item will be ignored. Here are some examples of inserting items into a set:

```
var mySet = Set<String>()
mySet.insert("One")
mySet.insert("Two")
mySet.insert("Three")
```

The `insert` method returns a tuple that we can use to verify that the value was successfully added to the set. We will look at tuples later in this chapter, but the following example shows how to check the returned value to see if it was added successfully:

```
var mySet = Set<String>()
mySet.insert("One")
mySet.insert("Two")
var results = mySet.insert("One")
if results.inserted {
  print("Success")
} else {
  print("Failed")
}
```

In this example, `Failed` would be printed to the console since we are attempting to add the value `One` to the set when it is already in the set.

Determining the number of items in a set

We can use the `count` property to determine the number of items in a set. Here is an example of how to use this method:

```
var mySet = Set<String>()
mySet.insert("One")
mySet.insert("Two")
mySet.insert("Three")
print("\(mySet.count) items")
```

When executed, this code will print the message `3 items` to the console because the set contains three items.

Checking whether a set contains an item

We can verify whether a set contains an item by using the `contains()` method, as shown here:

```
var mySet = Set<String>()
mySet.insert("One")
mySet.insert("Two")
mySet.insert("Three")
var contain = mySet.contains("Two")
```

In the preceding example, the `contain` variable is set to true because the set contains the string `Two`.

Iterating over a set

We can use the `for-in` statement to iterate over the items in a set. The following example shows how we would iterate through the items in a set:

```
for item in mySet {
 print(item)
}
```

The preceding example will print out each item in the set to the console.

Removing items in a set

We can remove a single item or all the items in a set. To remove a single item, we would use the `remove(_:)` method and, to remove all the items, we would use the `removeAll()` method. The following example shows how to remove items from a set:

```
//The remove method will return and remove an item from a set
var item = mySet.remove("Two")

//The removeAll method will remove all items from a set
mySet.removeAll()
```

Set operations

Apple has provided four methods that we can use to construct a set from two other sets. These operations can be performed in place, on one of the sets, or used to create a new set. These operations are as follows:

- **union and formUnion**: These create a set with all the unique values from both sets
- **subtracting and subtract**: These create a set with values from the first set that are not in the second set
- **intersection and fromIntersection**: These create a set with values that are common to both sets
- **symmetricDifference and fromSymmetricDifference**: These create a new set with values that are in either set, but not in both sets

Let's look at some examples and see the results that can be obtained from each of these operations. For all the examples of set operations, we will be using the following two sets:

```
var mySet1 = Set(["One", "Two", "Three", "abc"])
var mySet2 = Set(["abc","def","ghi", "One"])
```

The first example will use the `union` method. This method will take the unique values from both sets to make another set:

```
var newSetUnion = mySet1.union(mySet2)
```

The `newSetUnion` variable will contain the following values: `One`, `Two`, `Three`, `abc`, `def`, and `ghi`. We can use the `formUnion` method to perform the `union` function in place without creating a new set:

```
mySet1.formUnion(mySet2)
```

In this example, the `mySet1set` set will contain all the unique values from the `mySet1` and `mySet2` sets.

Now let's look at the `subtract` and `subtracting` methods. These methods will create a set with the values from the first set that are not in the second set:

```
var newSetSubtract = mySet1.subtracting(mySet2)
```

In this example, the `newSetSubtract` variable will contain the values `Two` and `Three` because those are the only two values that are not also in the second set.

We use the subtract method to perform the subtraction function in place without creating a new set:

```
mySet1.subtract(mySet2)
```

In this example, the `mySet1` set will contain the values `Two` and `Three` because those are the only two values that are not in the `mySet2` set.

Now let's look at the `intersection` methods. This method creates a new set from the values that are common between the two sets:

```
var newSetIntersect = mySet1.intersection(mySet2)
```

In this example, the `newSetIntersect` variable will contain the values `One` and `abc` since they are the values that are common between the two sets.

We can use the `formIntersection()` method to perform the intersection function in place without creating a new set:

```
mySet1.formIntersection(mySet2)
```

In this example, the `mySet1` set will contain the values `One` and `abc` since they are the values that are common between the two sets.

Finally, let's look at the `symmetricDifference` methods. These methods will create a new set with values that are in either set, but not in both:

```
var newSetExclusiveOr = mySet1.symmetricDifference(mySet2)
```

In this example, the `newSetExclusiveOr` variable will contain the values `Two`, `Three`, `def`, and `ghi`.

To perform this method in place we use the `fromSymmetricDifference()` method:

```
mySet1.formSymmetricDifference(mySet2)
```

These four operations (union, subtraction, intersection, and symmetric difference methods) add functionality that is not present with arrays. Combined with faster lookup speeds, as compared to an array, the set type can be a very useful alternative when the order of the collection is not important and the instances in the collection must be unique.

Tuples

Tuples group multiple values into a single compound value. Unlike arrays and dictionaries, the values in a tuple do not have to be of the same type. While tuples are included in this chapter about collections, they actually behave more like a custom type than a collection.

The following example shows how to define a tuple:

```
var team = ("Boston", "Red Sox", 97, 65, 59.9)
```

In the preceding example, an unnamed tuple was created that contains two strings, two integers, and one double. The values of the tuple can be decomposed into a set of variables, as shown in the following example:

```
var team = ("Boston", "Red Sox", 97, 65, 59.9)
var (city, name, wins, loses, percent) = team
```

In the preceding code, the `city` variable will contain `Boston`, the `name` variable will contain `Red Sox`, the `wins` variable will contain 97, the `loses` variable will contain 65, and finally the `percent` variable will contain 0.599.

The values of the tuple can be retrieved by specifying the location of the value. The following example shows how we can retrieve values by their location:

```
var team = ("Boston", "Red Sox", 97, 65, 59.9)
var city = team.0
var name = team.1
var wins = team.2
var loses = team.3
var percent = team.4
```

Naming tuples, known as named tuples, allows us to avoid the decomposition step. A named tuple associates a name (key) with each element of the tuple. The following example shows how to create a named tuple:

```
var team = (city:"Boston", name:"Red Sox", wins:97, loses:65, percent:59.9)
```

Values from a named tuple can be accessed using the dot syntax. In the preceding code, we will access the `city` element of the tuple like this: `team.city`. In the preceding code, the `team.city` element will contain `Boston`.

Tuples are incredibly useful, and can be used for all sorts of purposes. I have found that they are very useful for replacing classes and structures that are designed to simply store data and do not contain any methods. We will learn more about classes and structures in `Chapter 5`, *Classes and Structures*.

Summary

In this chapter, we covered Swift collections and the tuple type. Having a good understanding of the native collection types of Swift is essential to architecting and developing applications in Swift since all but the most basic applications use them.

The three Swift collection types are arrays, sets, and dictionaries. Arrays store data as an ordered collection. Sets store data as an unordered collection of unique values. Dictionaries store data in an unordered collections of key-value pairs.

We also looked at the tuple, which allows us to group multiple values into a single compound value. Unlike standard collection types in Swift, the values in a tuple do not have to be of the same type or indeed any type.

In the next chapter, we will begin to move away from the foundations of the Swift language and learn the building blocks of application development by looking at control flow and functions.

4

Control Flow and Functions

Every month, while I was learning BASIC programming on my Vic-20, I would read several of the early computer magazines, such as *Byte Magazine*. I remember one particular review that I read for a game called *Zork*. While Zork was not a game that was available for my Vic-20, the concept of the game fascinated me because I was really into sci-fi and fantasy. I remember thinking how cool it would be to write a game like that, so I decided to figure out how to do it. One of the biggest concepts that I had to grasp at that time was how to control the flow of the application depending on the user's actions.

In this chapter, we will cover the following topics:

- What conditional statements are and how to use them?
- What loops are and how to use them?
- What control transfer statements are and how to use them?
- How to create and use functions in Swift?

What have we learned so far?

Up to this point, we have been laying the foundation for writing applications with Swift. While it is possible to write a very basic application with what we have learned so far, it would be really difficult to write a useful application using only what we've covered in the first three chapters.

Starting with this chapter, we will begin to move away from the foundations of the Swift language, and begin to learn the building blocks of application development with Swift. In this chapter, we will go over control flow and functions. To become a master of the Swift programming language, it is important that you fully understand and comprehend the concepts discussed in this chapter and in `Chapter 5`, *Classes and Structure*.

Before we cover control flow and functions, let's look at how curly brackets and parentheses are used in Swift.

Curly brackets

In Swift, unlike other C-like languages, curly brackets are required for conditional statements and loops. In other C-like languages, if there is only one statement to execute for a conditional statement or a loop, curly brackets around that line are optional. This has led to numerous errors and bugs, such as Apple's `goto fail` bug. When Apple was designing Swift, they decided to introduce the use of curly brackets, even when there is only one line of code to execute. Let's look at some code that illustrates this requirement. This first example is not valid in Swift because it is missing the curly brackets; however, it will be valid in most other languages:

```
if (x > y)
x=0
```

In Swift, you are required to have the curly brackets, as illustrated in the following example:

```
if (x > y) {
   x=0
}
```

Parentheses

Unlike other C-like languages, the parentheses around conditional expressions in Swift are optional. In the preceding example, we put parentheses around the conditional expression, but they are not required. The following example would be valid in Swift, but not valid in most C-like languages:

```
if x > y {
   x=0
}
```

Control flow

Control flow, also known as flow of control, refers to the order in which statements, instructions, or functions are executed within an application. Swift supports most of the familiar control flow statements that are used in C-like languages. These include loops (including `while`), conditional statements (including `if`, `switch`, and `guard`), and the transfer of control statements (including `break` and `continue`). It is worth noting that Swift does not include the traditional C `for` loop and, rather than the traditional `do-while` loop, Swift has the `repeat-while` loop.

In addition to the standard C control flow statements, Swift has also included statements such as the `for-in` loop and enhanced some of the existing statements, such as the `switch` statement.

Let's begin by looking at conditional statements in Swift.

Conditional statements

A conditional statement will check a condition and execute a block of code only if the condition is true. Swift provides both the `if` and `if...else` conditional statements. Let's look at how to use these conditional statements to execute blocks of code if a specified condition is `true`.

The if statement

The `if` statement will check a conditional statement and, if it is `true`, it will execute the block of code. This statement takes the following format:

```
if condition {
  block of code
}
```

Now, let's look at how to use the `if` statement:

```
let teamOneScore = 7
let teamTwoScore = 6
if teamOneScore>teamTwoScore {
  print("Team One Won")
}
```

In the preceding example, we begin by setting the `teamOneScore` and `teamTwoScore` constants. We then use the `if` statement to check whether the value of `teamOneScore` is greater than the value of `teamTwoScore`. If the value is greater, we print Team One Won to the console. If we run this code, we will indeed see that Team One Won is printed to the console, but if the value of `teamTwoScore` is greater than the value of `teamOneScore`, nothing will be printed. That would not be the best way to write an application, as we want the user to know which team actually won. The `if...else` statement can help us with this problem.

Conditional code execution with the if...else statement

The `if...else` statement will check a conditional statement and, if it is `true`, it will execute a block of code. If the conditional statement is not `true`, it will execute a separate block of code. This statement follows this format:

```
if condition {
  block of code if true
} else {
  block of code if not true
}
```

Let's modify the preceding example to use the `if...else` statement to tell the user which team won:

```
let teamOneScore = 7
let teamTwoScore = 6
if teamOneScore>teamTwoScore{
  print("Team One Won")
} else {
  print("Team Two Won")
}
```

This new version will print out Team One Won if the value of `teamOneScore` is greater than the value of `teamTwoScore`; otherwise, it will print out the message, Team Two Won. This fixed one problem with our code, but what do you think the code will do if the value of `teamOneScore` is equal to the value of `teamTwoScore`? In the real world, we would see a tie, but in the preceding code, we would print out Team Two Won, which would not be fair to team one. In cases like this, we can use multiple `else if` statements and an `else` statement at the end to act as the default path if no conditional statements are met.

The following code sample illustrates this:

```
let teamOneScore = 7
let teamTwoScore = 6
if teamOneScore>teamTwoScore {
  print("Team One Won")
} else if teamTwoScore>teamOneScore {
  print("Team Two Won")
} else {
  print("We have a tie")
}
```

In the preceding code, if the value of `teamOneScore` is greater than the value of `teamTwoScore`, we print `Team One Won` to the console. We then have an `else if` statement, which means the conditional statement is checked only if the first `if` statement returns `false`. Finally, if both of the `if` statements return `false`, the code in the `else` block is called and `We have a tie` is printed to the console.

This is a good time to point out that it is not good practice to have numerous `else if` statements stacked up, as we showed you in the previous example. It is better to use the `switch` statement, which we will look at later in this chapter.

The guard statement

In Swift, and most modern languages, our conditional statements tend to focus on testing if a condition is `true`. As an example, the following code tests to see whether the variable x is greater than 10 and; if so, we will perform some function. If the condition is `false`, we handle the following error condition:

```
var x = 9
if x > 10 {
  // Functional code here
} else {
  // Do error condition
}
```

This type of code embeds our functional code within our checks and tucks the error conditions away at the end of our functions, but what if that is not what we really want? Sometimes, it might be nice to take care of our error conditions at the beginning of the function. In our simple example, we could easily check if x is less than or equal to 10 and; if so, it will perform the error condition. Not all conditional statements are that easy to rewrite, especially items such as optional binding.

In Swift, we have the `guard` statement. This statement focuses on performing a function if a condition is false; this allows us to trap errors and perform the error conditions early in our functions. We could rewrite our previous example using the `guard` statement like this:

```
var x = 9
guard x > 10 else {
  // Do error condition
  return
}
//Functional code here
```

In this new example, we check to see whether the variable `x` is greater than 10, and if not, we perform the error condition. If the variable is greater than 10, the code continues. You will notice that we have a `return` statement embedded within the guard condition. The code within the `guard` statement must contain a transfer of control statement; this is what prevents the rest of the code from executing. If we forget the transfer of control statement, Swift will show a compile time error.

Let's look at some more examples of the `guard` statement. The following example shows how we would use the `guard` statement to verify that an optional contains a valid value:

```
func guardFunction(str: String?) {
  guard let goodStr = str else {
    print("Input was nil")
    return
  }
  print("Input was \(goodStr)")
}
```

In this example, we create a function named `guardFunction()` that accepts an optional that contains a string or nil value. We then use the `guard` statement with optional binding to verify that the string optional is not `nil`. If it does contain nil, then the code within the `guard` statement is executed and the `return` statement is used to exit the function. The really nice thing about using the `guard` statement with optional binding is that the new variable is in the scope of the rest of the function, rather than just within the scope of the optional binding statement.

A conditional statement checks the condition once and; if the condition is met, it executes the block of code. What if we wanted to continuously execute the block of code until a condition is met? For this, we would use one of the looping statements in Swift.

The for-in loop

The `for` loop variants are probably the most widely-used looping statements. While Swift does not offer the standard C-based `for` loop, it does have the `for-in` loop. The standard C-based `for` loop was removed from the Swift language in Swift 3 because it was rarely used. You can read the full proposal to remove this loop on the Swift evolution site at https://github.com/apple/swift-evolution/blob/master/proposals/7-remove-c-style-for-loops.md. The `for...in` statement is used to execute a block of code for each item in a range, collection, or sequence.

Using the for...in loop

The `for-in` loop iterates over a collection of items or a range of numbers and executes a block of code for each item in the collection or range. The format for the `for-in` statement looks like this:

```
for variable in collection/range {
  block of code
}
```

As we can see in the preceding code, the `for-in` loop has two sections:

- **Variable**: This variable will change each time the loop executes and will hold the current item from the collection or range
- **Collection/range**: This is the collection or range to iterate through

Let's look at how to use the `for-in` loop to iterate through a range of numbers:

```
for index in 1...5 {
  print(index)
}
```

In the preceding example, we iterated over a range of numbers from 1 to 5 and printed each of the numbers to the console. This loop used the closed range operator (. . .) to give the loop a range to iterate through. Swift also provides the half-open range operator (. .<) and the one-sided range operators that we saw in the previous chapter.

Now, let's look at how to iterate over an array with the `for-in` loop:

```
var countries = ["USA","UK", "IN"]
for item in countries {
  print(item)
}
```

In the preceding example, we iterated through the `countries` array and printed each element of the array to the console. As we can see, iterating through an array with the `for-in` loop is safer, cleaner, and a lot easier than using the standard C-based `for` loop. Using the `for-in` loop prevents us from making common mistakes, such as using the <= (less than or equal to) operator rather than the < (less than) operator in our conditional statement.

Let's look at how to iterate over a dictionary with the `for-in` loop:

```
var dic = ["USA": "United States", "UK": "United Kingdom","IN":"India"]

for (abbr, name) in dic {
  print("\(abbr) --\(name)")
}
```

In the preceding example, we used the `for-in` loop to iterate through each key-value pair of the dictionary. In this example, each item in the dictionary is returned as a (key,value) tuple. We can decompose (key,value) tuple members as named constants within the body of the loop. One thing to note is that, since a dictionary does not guarantee the order that items are stored in, the order that they are iterated through may not be the same as the order in which they were inserted.

Now, let's look at another type of loop, the `while` loop.

The while loop

The `while` loop executes a block of code until a condition is met. Swift provides two forms of the `while` loop; these are the `while` and `repeat-while` loops. In Swift 2.0, Apple replaced the `do-while` loop with the `repeat-while` loop. The `repeat-while` loop functions in the same way as the `do-while` loop did. Swift uses the `do` statement for error handling.

We use `while` loops when the number of iterations to perform is not known and usually dependent on some business logic. A `while` loop is used when you want to run a loop zero or more times, while a `repeat-while` loop is used when you want to run the loop one or more times.

Using the while loop

The `while` loop starts by evaluating a conditional statement and then repeatedly executes a block of code while the conditional statement is `true`. The format for the `while` statement is as follows:

```
while condition {
  block of code
}
```

Let's look at how to use a `while` loop. In the following example, the `while` loop will continue to execute the block of code while the randomly-generated number is less than 7. In this example, we are using the `arc4random_uniform()` function to generate a random number between 0 and 9:

```
var ran = 0
while ran < 7 {
  ran = Int(arc4random_uniform(10))
}
```

In the preceding example, we began by initializing the `ran` variable to 0. The `while` loop then checks that variable and; if the value is less than 7, a new random number between 0 and 9 is generated. The `while` loop will continue to loop while the randomly-generated number is less than 7. Once the randomly-generated number is equal to or greater than 7, the loop will exit.

In the preceding example, the `while` loop checked the conditional statement prior to generating a new random number. What if we did not want to check the conditional statement prior to generating a random number? We could generate a random number when we first initialize the variable, but that would mean we would need to duplicate the code that generates the random numbers, and duplicating code is never an ideal solution. It would be preferable to use the `repeat-while` loop.

Using the repeat-while loop

The difference between the `while` and `repeat-while` loops is that the `while` loops check the conditional statement prior to executing the block of code for the first time; therefore, all the variables in the conditional statements need to be initialized prior to executing the `while` loop.

The `repeat-while` loop will run through the loop block prior to checking the conditional statement for the first time. This means that we can initialize the variables in the conditional block of code. Use of the `repeat-while` loop is preferred when the conditional statement is dependent on the code in the loop block. The `repeat-while` loop takes the following format:

```
repeat {
  block of code
} while condition
```

Let's look at this specific example by creating a `repeat-while` loop where we initialize the variable we are checking within the loop block:

```
var ran: Int
repeat {
  ran = Int(arc4random_uniform(10))
} while ran < 4
```

In the preceding example, we defined the `ran` variable as an integer; however, we did not initialize it until we entered the loop block and generated a random number. If this is attempted with the `while` loop (leaving the `ran` variable uninitialized), we will receive a using variable before being initialized as an exception.

Earlier we mentioned that the `switch` statement is preferred over using multiple `else if` blocks. Let's see how we can use the `switch` statement.

The switch statement

The `switch` statement takes a value, compares it to several possible matches, and executes the appropriate block of code based on the first successful match. The `switch` statement is an alternative to using multiple `else if` statements when there could be several possible matches. The `switch` statement takes the following format:

```
switch value {
  case match1:
    block of code
  case match2:
    block of code
  //as many cases as needed
  default:
    block of code
}
```

Unlike the switch statement in most other languages, in Swift it does not fall through to the next case statement; therefore, we do not need to use a break statement to prevent this fall through. This is another safety feature that has been built into Swift, as one of the most common programming mistakes regarding the switch statement made by beginner programmers is to forget the break statement at the end of the case statement. Let's look at how to use the switch statement:

```
var speed = 300000000
switch speed {
  case 300000000:
    print("Speed of light")
  case 340:
    print("Speed of sound")
  default:
    print("Unknown speed")
}
```

In the preceding example, the switch statement took the value of the speed variable and compared it to the two case statements. If the value of speed matches either case, it will print out the speed. If it does not find a match, it will print out the Unknown speed message.

Every switch statement must have a match for all the possible values. This means that, unless we are matching against an enumeration that has a defined number of values, each switch statement must have a default case. Let's look at a case where we do not have a default case:

```
var num = 5
switch num {
  case 1 :
    print("number is one")
  case 2 :
    print("Number is two")
  case 3 :
    print("Number is three")
}
```

If we put the preceding code into a Playground and attempt to compile the code, we will receive a switch must be exhaustive, consider adding a default clause error. This is a compile time error, and therefore we will not be notified until we attempt to compile the code.

It is possible to include multiple items in a single case. To do this, we need to separate the items with a comma. Let's look at how we use the switch statement to tell us if a character is a vowel or a consonant:

```
var char : Character = "e"
switch char {
  case "a", "e", "i", "o", "u":
    print("letter is a vowel")
  case "b", "c", "d", "f", "g", "h", "j", "k", "l", "m","n", "p", "q", "r",
      "s", "t", "v", "w","x", "y", "z":
    print("letter is a consonant")
  default:
    print("unknown letter")
}
```

We can see in the preceding example that each case has multiple items. Commas separate these items and the switch statement attempts to match the char variable to each item listed in the case statements.

It is also possible to check the value of a switch statement to see whether it is included in a range. To do this, we use one of the range operators in the case statement, as shown in the following example:

```
var grade = 93
switch grade {
  case 90...100:
    print("Grade is an A")
  case 80...89:
    print("Grade is a B")
  case 70...79:
    print("Grade is an C")
  case 60...69:
    print("Grade is a D")
  case 0...59:
    print("Grade is a F")
  default:
    print("Unknown Grade")
}
```

In the preceding example, the switch statement took the grade variable, compared it with the ranges in each case statement, and printed out the appropriate grade.

In Swift, any `case` statement can contain an optional `where` clause, which provides an additional condition that needs validating. The guard condition is defined with the `where` keyword. Let's say that, in our preceding example, we have students who are receiving special assistance in class and we wanted to define a grade of `D` for them as a range of 55 to 69. The following example shows how we would do this:

```
var studentId = 4
var grade = 57
switch grade {
  case 90...100:
    print("Grade is an A")
  case 80...89:
    print("Grade is a B")
  case 70...79:
    print("Grade is an C")
  case 55...69 where studentId == 4:
    print("Grade is a D for student 4")
  case 60...69:
    print("Grade is a D")
  case 0...59:
    print("Grade is a F")
  default:
    print("Unknown Grade")
}
```

One thing to keep in mind with the `where` expression is that Swift will attempt to match the value starting with the first case statement and working its way down, checking each case statement in order. This means that, if we put the `case` statement with the `where` expression after the grade F case statement, then the `case` statement with the `where` expression will never be reached. The following example illustrates this:

```
var studentId = 4
var grade = 57
switch grade {
  case 90...100:
    print("Grade is an A")
  case 80...89:
    print("Grade is a B")
  case 70...79:
    print("Grade is an C")
  case 60...69:
    print("Grade is a D")
  case 0...59:
    print("Grade is a F")
  //The following case statement would never be reached because the
    grades would always match one of the previous two
  case 55...69 where studentId == 4:
```

```
    print("Grade is a D for student 4")
  default:
    print("Unknown Grade")
}
```

 A good rule of thumb is that, if you are using the where clause, always put the `case` statements with the where clause before any similar `case` statements without the where clause.

Switch statements are also extremely useful for evaluating enumerations. Since an enumeration has a finite number of values, if we provide a `case` statement for all the values in the enumeration, we do not need to provide a default case. The following example shows how we can use a `switch` statement to evaluate an enumeration:

```
enum Product {
  case Book(String, Double, Int)
  case Puzzle(String, Double)
}
var order = Product.Book("Mastering Swift 4", 49.99, 2017)
switch order {
  case .Book(let name, let price, let year):
    print("You ordered the book \(name): \(year) for \(price)")
  case .Puzzle(let name, let price):
    print("You ordered the Puzzle \(name) for \(price)")
}
```

In this example, we began by defining an enumeration named `Product` with two values, each with the associated values. We then created an `order` variable of the product type and used the `switch` statement to evaluate it. Notice that we did not put a default case at the end of the `switch` statement. If we were to add additional values to the `product` enumeration later, we would need to either put a default case at the end of the `switch` statement or add additional `case` statements to handle the additional values.

Using case and where statements with conditional statements

As we saw in the last section, the `case` and `where` statements within a `switch` statement can be very powerful. Using `case` and `where` statements within our conditional statements can also make our code much smaller and easier to read. Conditional statements, such as `if`, `for`, and `while`, can also make use of the `where` and `case` keywords. Let's look at some examples, starting off with using the `where` statement to filter the results in a `for-in` loop.

Filtering with the where statement

In this example, we will take an array of integers and print out only the even numbers. However, before we look at how to filter the results with the `where` statement, let's look at how to do this without the `where` statement:

```
for number in 1...30 {
  if number % 2 == 0 {
    print(number)
  }
}
```

In this example, we use a `for-in` loop to cycle through the numbers 1 to 30. Within the `for-in` loop, we use an `if` conditional statement to filter out the odd numbers. In this simple example, the code is fairly easy to read, but let's see how we can use the `where` statement to use fewer lines of code and make them easier to read:

```
for number in 1...30 where number % 2 == 0 {
  print(number)
}
```

We still have the same `for-in` loop as in the previous example. However, we have now put the `where` statement at the end; therefore, we only loop through the even numbers. Using the `where` statement shortens our example by two lines and makes it easier to read because the `where` clause is on the same line as the `for-in` loop, rather than being embedded in the loop itself.

Now let's look at how we could filter with the `for-case` statement.

Filtering with the for-case statement

In this next example, we will use the `for-case` statement to filter through an array of tuples and print out only the results that match our criteria. The `for-case` example is very similar to using the `where` statement where it is designed to eliminate the need for an `if` statement within a loop to filter the results. In this example, we will use the `for-case` statement to filter through a list of World Series winners and print out the year(s) a particular team won the World Series:

```
var worldSeriesWinners = [
  ("Red Sox", 2004),
  ("White Sox", 2005),
  ("Cardinals", 2006),
  ("Red Sox", 2007),
  ("Phillies", 2008),
```

```
        ("Yankees", 2009),
        ("Giants", 2010),
        ("Cardinals", 2011),
        ("Giants", 2012),
        ("Red Sox", 2013),
        ("Giants", 2014),
        ("Royals", 2015)
]

for case let ("Red Sox", year) in worldSeriesWinners {
    print(year)
}
```

In this example, we created an array of tuples named `worldSeriesWinners`, where each tuple in the array contained the name of the team and the year that they won the World Series. We then use the `for-case` statement to filter through the array and only print out the years that the Red Sox won the World Series. The filtering is done within the `case` statement, where `("Red Sox", year)` states that we want all the results that have the string `Red Sox` in the first item of the tuple, and the value of the second item in the `year` constant. The `for-in` loop then loops through the results of the `case` statement, printing out the value of the `year` constant.

The `for-case-in` statement also makes it very easy to filter out the `nil` values in an array of optionals. Let's look at an example of this:

```
let myNumbers: [Int?] = [1, 2, nil, 4, 5, nil, 6]

for case let .some(num) in myNumbers {
    print(num)
}
```

In this example, we created an array of optionals named `myNumbers` that could contain either an integer value or `nil`. As we will see in `Chapter 10`, *Using Optional Types*, an optional is internally defined as an enumeration, as shown in the following code:

```
enum Optional<Wrapped> {
    case none,
    case some(Wrapped)
}
```

If an optional is set to nil, it will have a value of `none`, but if it is not nil it will have a value of `some`, with an associated type of the actual value. In our example, when we filter for `.some(num)`, we are looking for any optional that has a non-nil value. As shorthand for `.some()`, we could use the `?` (question mark) symbol, as we will see in the following example. This example also combines the `for-case-in` statement with a `where` statement to perform additional filtering.

```
let myNumbers: [Int?] = [1, 2, nil, 4, 5, nil, 6]

for case let num? in myNumbers where num > 3 {
  print(num)
}
```

This example is the same as the previous example, except that we have inputted the additional filtering with the `where` statement. In the previous example, we looped through all of the non-nil values, but in this example, we have looped through the non-nil values that are greater than 3. Let's see how we do this same filtering without the `case` or `where` statements:

```
let myNumbers: [Int?] = [1, 2, nil, 4, 5, nil, 6]

for num in myNumbers {
  if let num = num {
    if num > 3 {
      print(num)
    }
  }
}
```

Using the `for-case-in` and `where` statements can greatly reduce the number of lines needed. It also makes our code much easier to read because all the filtering statements are on the same line.

Let's look at one more filtering example. This time, we will look at the `if-case` statement.

Using the if-case statement

Using the `if-case` statement is very similar to using the `switch` statement. Most of the time the `switch` statement is preferred when we have over two cases we are trying to match, but there are instances where the `if-case` statement is needed. One of those times is when we are only looking for one or two possible matches, and we do not want to handle all the possible matches. Let's look at an example of this:

```
enum Identifier {
  case Name(String)
  case Number(Int)
  case NoIdentifier
}
var playerIdentifier = Identifier.Number(2)
if case let .Number(num) = playerIdentifier {
  print("Player's number is \(num)")
}
```

In this example, we created an enumeration named `Identifier` that contains three possible values: `Name`, `Number`, and `NoIdentifier`. We then created an instance of the `Identifier` enumeration named `playerIdentifier`, with a value of `Number` and an associated value of 2. We then used the `if-case` statement to see if the `playerIdentifier` had a value for `Number` and; if so, we printed a message to the console.

Just like the `for-case` statement, we can perform additional filtering with the `where` statement. The following example uses the same `Identifier` enumeration as we used in the previous example:

```
var playerIdentifier = Identifier.Number(2)

if case let .Number(num) = playerIdentifier, num == 2 {
  print("Player is either XanderBogarts or Derek Jeter")
}
```

In this example, we have used the `if-case` statement to see if the `playerIdentifier` had a value of `Number`, but we also added the `where` statement to see if the associated value was equal to 2. If so, we identified the player as either `XanderBogarts` or `Derek Jeter`.

As we saw in our examples, using the `case` and `where` statements with our conditional statements can reduce the number of lines needed to perform certain types of filtering. It can also make our code easier to read. Now let's look at control transfer statements.

Control transfer statements

Control transfer statements are used to transfer control to another part of the code. Swift offers six control transfer statements; these are continue, break, fallthrough, guard, throws, and return. We will look at the return statement in the *Functions* section later on in this chapter and will discuss the throws statement in Chapter 8, *Writing Safer Code with Availability and Error Handling*. The remaining control transfer statements will be discussed in this section.

The continue statement

The continue statement tells a loop to stop executing the code block and to go to the next iteration of the loop. The following example shows how we can use this statement to print out only the odd numbers in a range:

```
for i in 1...10 {
  if i % 2 == 0 {
    continue
  }
  print("\(i) is odd")
}
```

In the preceding example, we looped through a range of 1 through 10. For each iteration of the for-in loop, we used the remainder (%) operator to see whether the number was odd or even. If the number is even, the continue statement tells the loop to immediately go to the next iteration of the loop. If the number is odd, we print out that the number is odd and then move on. The output of the preceding code is as follows:

```
1 is odd
3 is odd
5 is odd
7 is odd
9 is odd
```

Now let's look at the break statement.

The break statement

The `break` statement immediately ends the execution of a code block within the control flow. The following example shows how to break out of a `for-in` loop when we encounter the first even number:

```
for i in 1...10 {
  if i % 2 == 0 {
    break
  }
  print("\(i) is odd")
}
```

In the preceding example, we loop through the range of 1 through 10. For each iteration of the `for-in` loop, we use the remainder (`%`) operator to see whether the number is odd or even. If the number is even, we use the `break` statement to immediately exit the loop. If the number is odd, we print out that the number is odd, and then go to the next iteration of the loop. The preceding code has the following output:

```
1 is odd
```

The fallthrough statement

In Swift, the `switch` statement does not fall through like other languages; however, we can use the `fallthrough` statement to force them to fall through. The `fallthrough` statement can be very dangerous because, once a match is found, the next case defaults to true and that code block is executed. The following example illustrates this:

```
var name = "Jon"
var sport = "Baseball"
switch sport {
  case "Baseball":
    print("\(name) plays Baseball")
    fallthrough
  case "Basketball":
    print("\(name) plays Basketball")
    fallthrough
  default:
    print("Unknown sport")
}
```

In the preceding example, the baseball case was matched, however, there was a `fallthrough` keyword in both the baseball and basketball case; therefore, all three cases are matched. The output will look like this:

```
Jon plays Baseball
Jon plays Basketball
Unknown sport
```

Now that we have seen how control flow statements work in Swift, let's introduce functions.

Functions

In Swift, a function is a self-contained block of code that performs a specific task. Functions are generally used to logically break our code into reusable named blocks. The function's name is used to call the function.

When we define a function, we can also optionally define one or more parameters (also known as arguments). Parameters are named values that are passed into the function by the code that calls it. These parameters are generally used within the function to perform the task of the function. We can also define default values for the parameters to simplify how the function is called.

Every Swift function has a type associated with it. This type is referred to as the return type and it defines the type of data returned from the function to the code that called it. If a value is not returned from a function, the return type is `Void`.

Let's look at how to define functions in Swift.

Using a single parameter function

The syntax used to define a function in Swift is very flexible. This flexibility makes it easy for us to define simple C-style functions, or more complex functions, with local and external parameter names. Let's look at some examples of how to define functions. The following example accepts one parameter and does not return any value back to the code that called it:

```swift
func sayHello(name: String) -> Void {
  let retString = "Hello " + name
  print(retString)
}
```

In the preceding example, we defined a function named `sayHello()` that accepted one parameter named `name`. Inside the function, we printed out a greeting to the name of the person. Once the code within the function is executed, the function exits and control is returned back to the code that called it. Rather than printing out the greeting, we could return it to the code that called it by adding a return type, as follows:

```
func sayHello2(name: String) ->String {
    let retString = "Hello " + name
    return retString
}
```

The `->` `string` defines that the return type associated with the function is a string. This means that the function must return an instance of the String type to the code that calls it. Inside the function, we build a string constant named `retString` with the greeting message and then return it using the return statement.

Calling a Swift function is a similar process to calling functions or methods in other languages, such as C or Java. The following example shows how to call the `sayHello(name:)` function that prints the greeting message to the screen:

```
sayHello(name:"Jon")
```

Now, let's look at how to call the `sayHello2(name:)` function that returns a value back to the code that called it:

```
var message = sayHello2(name:"Jon")
print(message)
```

In the preceding example, we called the `sayHello2(name:)` function and inputted the value returned in the `message` variable. If a function defines a return type as the `sayHello2(name:)` function does, it must return a value of that type to the code that called it. Therefore, every possible conditional path within the function must end by returning a value of the specified type. This does not mean that the code that called the function is required to retrieve the returned value. As an example, both lines in the following snippet are valid:

```
sayHello2(name:"Jon")
var message = sayHello2(name:"Jon")
```

If you do not specify a variable for the return value to go into, the value is dropped. When the code is compiled you will receive a warning if a function returns a value and you do not put it into a variable or a constant. You can avoid this warning by using the underscore, as shown in the following example:

```
_ = sayHello2(name:"Jon")
```

The underscore tells the compiler that you are aware of the return value but you do not want to use it. Using the `@discardableResult` attribute when declaring a function will also silence the warning. This attribute is used as follows:

```
@discardableResult func sayHello2(name: String) ->String {
    let retString = "Hello " + name
    return retString
}
```

Let's look at how we would define multiple parameters for our functions.

Using a multi-parameter function

We are not limited to just one parameter with our functions, we can also define multiple parameters. To create a multi-parameter function, we list the parameters in the parentheses and separate the parameter definitions with commas. Let's look at how to define multiple parameters in a function:

```
func sayHello(name: String, greeting: String) {
    print("\(greeting) \(name)")
}
```

In the preceding example, the function accepts two arguments: name and greeting. We then print a greeting to the console using both parameters.

Calling a multi-parameter function is a little different from calling a single-parameter function. When calling a multi-parameter function, we separate the parameters with commas. We also need to include the parameter name for all the parameters. The following example shows how to call a multi-parameter function:

```
sayHello(name:"Jon", greeting:"Bonjour")
```

We do not need to supply an argument for each parameter of the function if we define default values. Let's look at how to configure default values for our parameters.

Defining a parameter's default values

We can define default values for any parameter by using the equals to operator (=) within the function definition when we declare the parameters. The following example shows how to declare a function with a parameter's default values:

```
func sayHello(name: String, greeting: String = "Bonjour") {
  print("\(greeting) \(name)")
}
```

In the function declaration, we have defined one parameter without a default value (name:String) and one parameter with a default value (greeting: String = "Bonjour"). When a parameter has a default value declared, we are able to call the function with or without setting a value for that parameter. The following example shows how to call the sayHello() function without setting the greeting parameter, and also how to call it when you do set the greeting parameter:

```
sayHello(name:"Jon")
sayHello(name:"Jon", greeting: "Hello")
```

In the sayHello(name:"Jon") line, the function will print out the message Bonjour Jon since it uses the default value for the greeting parameter. In the sayHello(name:"Jon", greeting: "Hello") line, the function will print out the message Hello Jon since we have overridden the default value for the greeting parameter.

We can declare multiple parameters with default values and override only the ones we want by using the parameter names. The following example shows how we would do this by overriding one of the default values when we call it:

```
func sayHello(name: String = "Test", name2: String = "Kim", greeting:
String = "Bonjour") {
  print("\(greeting) \(name) and \(name2)")
}

sayHello(name:"Jon",greeting: "Hello")
```

In the preceding example, we declared a function with three parameters, each with a default value. We then called the function leaving the name2 parameter with its default value, while overriding the default values for the remaining two parameters.

The preceding example will print out the message Hello Jon and Kim.

Returning multiple values from a function

There are a couple of ways to return multiple values from a Swift function. One of the most common ways is to put the values into a collection type (an array or dictionary) and then return the collection. The following example shows how to return a collection type from a Swift function:

```
func getNames() -> [String] {
  var retArray = ["Jon", "Kim", "Kailey", "Kara"]
  return retArray
}

var names = getNames()
```

In the preceding example, we declared the getNames() function with no parameters and a return type of [String]. The return type of [String] specifies the return type to be an array of string types.

In the preceding example, our array could only return string types. If we needed to return numbers with our strings, we could return an array of the Any type and then use typecasting to specify the object type. However, this would not be a good design for our application, as it would be prone to errors. A better way to return values of different types would be to use a tuple type.

When we return a tuple from a function, it is recommended that we use a named tuple to allow us to use the dot syntax to access the returned values. The following example shows how to return a named tuple from a function and access the values from the named tuple that is returned:

```
func getTeam() -> (team:String, wins:Int, percent:Double) {
  let retTuple = ("Red Sox", 99, 0.611)
  return retTuple
}

var t = getTeam()
print("\(t.team) had \(t.wins) wins")
```

In the preceding example, we defined the `getTeam()` function that returned a named tuple containing three values: `String`, `Int`, and `Double`. Within the function, we created the tuple that we were going to return. Notice that we did not need to define the tuple that we were going to return as a named tuple, as the value types within the tuple matched the value types in the function definition. We can now call the function, as we would any other function, and use the dot syntax to access the values of the tuple that is returned. In the preceding example, the code would print out the following line:

```
Red Sox had 99 wins
```

Returning optional values

In the previous sections, we returned non-nil values from our function; however, that is not always what we need our code to do. What happens if we need to return a `nil` value from a function? The following code would not be valid and would cause a `nil is incompatible with return type 'String'` exception:

```
func getName() ->String {
  return nil
}
```

The reason this code throws an exception is because we have defined the return type as a `String` value, but we are attempting to return a `nil` value. If there is a reason to return nil, we need to define the return type as an optional type to let the code calling it know that the value may be `nil`. To define the return type as an optional type, we use the question mark (?) in the same way as we did when we defined a variable as an optional type. The following example shows how to define an optional return type:

```
func getName() ->String? {
  return nil
}
```

The preceding code would not cause an exception.

We can also set a tuple as an optional type, or any value within a tuple as an optional type. The following example shows how we would return a tuple as an optional type:

```
func getTeam2(id: Int) -> (team:String, wins:Int, percent:Double)? {
  if id == 1 {
    return ("Red Sox", 99, 0.611)
  }
  return nil
}
```

In the following example, we could return a tuple as defined within our function definition or `nil`; either option is valid. If we needed an individual value within our tuple to be nil, we would need to add an optional type within our tuple. The following example shows how to return a value of nil within the tuple:

```
func getTeam() -> (team:String, wins:Int, percent:Double?) {
  let retTuple: (String, Int, Double?) = ("Red Sox", 99, nil)
  return retTuple
}
```

In the preceding example, we set the `percent` value to either `Double` or `nil`.

Adding external parameter names

In the preceding examples in this section, we defined the parameters' names and value types in the same way we would define parameters in C code. In Swift, we are not limited to this syntax as we can also use external parameter names.

External parameter names are used to indicate the purpose of each parameter when we call a function. An external parameter name for each parameter needs to be defined in conjunction with its local parameter name. The external parameter name is added before the local parameter name in the function definition. The external and local parameter names are separated by a space.

Let's look at how to use external parameter names. But before we do, let's review how we have previously defined functions. In the following two examples, we will define a function without external parameter names, and then redefine it with external parameter names:

```
func winPercentage(team: String, wins: Int, loses: Int) -> Double{
  return Double(wins) / Double(wins + loses)
}
```

In the preceding example, the `winPercentage()` function accepted three parameters. These parameters were `team`, `wins`, and `loses`. The `team` parameter should be of type `String` and the `wins` and `loses` parameters should be of type `int`. The following line of code shows how to call the `winPercentage()` function:

```
var per = winPercentage(team: "Red Sox", wins: 99, loses: 63)
```

Now, let's define the same function with external parameter names:

```
func winPercentage(baseballTeam team: String, withWins wins: Int, andLoses
losses: Int) -> Double {
   return Double(wins) / Double(wins + losses)
}
```

In the preceding example, we redefined the `winPercentage()` function with external parameter names. In this redefinition, we have the same three parameters: `team`, `wins`, and `losses`. The difference is how we define the parameters. When using external parameters, we define each parameter with both an external parameter name and a local parameter name separated by a space. In the preceding example, the first parameter had an external parameter name of `baseballTeam` and an internal parameter name of `team`.

When we call a function with external parameter names, we need to include the external parameter names in the function call. The following code shows how to call this function:

```
var per = winPercentage(baseballTeam:"Red Sox", withWins:99,
                        andLoses:63)
```

While using external parameter names requires more typing, it does make your code easier to read. In the preceding example, it is easy to see that the function is looking for the name of a baseball team, the second parameter is the number of wins, and the last parameter is the number of losses.

Using variadic parameters

A **variadic** parameter is one that accepts zero or more values of a specified type. Within the function's definition, we define a variadic parameter by appending three periods (. . .) to the parameter's type name. The values of a variadic parameter are made available to the function as an array of the specified type. The following example shows how we would use a variadic parameter with a function:

```
func sayHello(greeting: String, names: String...) {
   for name in names {
     print("\(greeting) \(name)")
   }
}
```

In the preceding example, the `sayHello()` function takes two parameters. The first parameter is of the `String` type, which is the greeting to use. The second parameter is a variadic parameter of the `String` type, which are the names to send the greeting to. Within the function, a variadic parameter is an array that contains the type specified; therefore, in our example, the `names` parameter is an array of `String` values. In this example, we used a `for-in` loop to access the values within the `names` parameter.

The following line of code shows how to call the `sayHello()` function with a variadic parameter:

```
sayHello(greeting:"Hello", names: "Jon", "Kim")
```

The preceding line of code will print a greeting to each of the names.

Inout parameters

If we want to change the value of a parameter and we want those changes to persist once the function ends, we need to define the parameter as an `inout` parameter. Any changes made to an `inout` parameter are passed back to the variable that was used in the function call.

Two things to keep in mind when we use `inout` parameters are that these parameters cannot have default values and that they cannot be variadic parameters.

Let's look at how to use the `inout` parameters to swap the values of two variables:

```
func reverse(first: inout String, second: inout String) {
  let tmp = first
  first = second
  second = tmp
}
```

This function will accept two parameters and swap the values of the variables that are used in the function call. When we make the function call, we put an ampersand (`&`) in front of the variable name, indicating that the function can modify its value. The following example shows how to call the `reverse` function:

```
var one = "One"
var two = "Two"
reverse(first: &one, second: &two)
print("one: \(one) two: \(two)")
```

In the preceding example, we set variable one to a value of One and variable two to a value of Two. We then called the reverse() function with the one and two variables. Once the reverse() function has returned, the variable named one will contain the value Two, while the variable named two will contain the value One.

Putting it all together

To reinforce what we have learned in this chapter, let's look at one more example. For this example, we will create a function that will test to see if a string value contains a valid IPv4 address. An IPv4 address is the address assigned to a computer that uses the **Internet Protocol (IP)** to communicate. An IP address consists of four numeric values ranging from 0-255, separated by a dot (period). An example of a valid IP address is 10.0.1.250:

```
func isValidIP(ipAddr: String?) ->Bool {

  guard let ipAddr = ipAddr else {
    return false
  }
  let octets = ipAddr.characters.split { $0 == "."}.map{String($0)}
  guard octets.count == 4 else {
    return false
  }
  for octet in octets {
    guard validOctet(octet: octet) else {
      return false
    }
  }
  return true
}
```

Since the sole parameter in the isValidIp() function is an optional type, the first thing we do is verify that the ipAddr parameter is not nil. To do this, we use a guard statement with optional binding and; if the optional binding fails, we return a Boolean false value because nil is not a valid IP address.

If the ipAddr parameter contains a non-nil value, we then split the string into an array of strings, using the dots as delimiters. Since an IP address is supposed to contain four numbers separated by a dot, we use the guard statement again to check whether the array contains four elements. If it does not, we return false because we know that the ipAddr parameter did not contain a valid IP address.

Then, we loop through the values in the array that we created by splitting the original `ipAddr` parameter at the dots and passing the values to the `validOctet()` function. If all four values are verified by the `validOctet()` function, we have a valid IP address and we return a Boolean `true` value; however, if any of the values fail the `validOctet()` function, we return a Boolean `false` value. Now, let's look at the code for the `validOctet()` function:

```
func validOctet(octet: String) ->Bool {
  guard let num = Int(String(octet)),num>= 0 &&num<256 else {
    return false
  }
}
```

The `validOctet()` function has one `String` parameter named `octet`. This function will verify that the `octet` parameter contains a numeric value between 0 and 255; and if it does, will return a Boolean `true` value. Otherwise, it will return a Boolean `false` value.

Summary

In this chapter, we covered control flow and functions in Swift. It is essential to understand the concepts in this chapter before moving ahead. Every application that we write, beyond the simple Hello World applications, will rely very heavily on control flow statements and functions.

Control flow statements are used to make decisions within our application, and functions are used to group our code into sections that are reusable and organized.

In the next chapter, we will learn how to group our code into classes and structures.

5
Classes and Structures

The first programming language that I learned was BASIC. It was a good language to begin programming with, but once I traded in my Commodore Vic-20 for a PCjr (yes, I had a PCjr and I really enjoyed it), I realized that there were other, more advanced languages out there, and I spent a lot of time learning Pascal and C. It wasn't until I started college that I heard the term 'object-oriented programming language'. At that time, object-oriented programming languages were so new that there were no real courses on them, but I was able to experiment a little with C++. After I graduated, I left object-oriented programming behind, and it really wasn't until several years later, when I started to experiment with C++ again, that I really discovered the power and flexibility of object-oriented programming.

In this chapter, we will cover the following topics:

- What are classes and structures?
- How to add properties and property observers to classes and structures?
- How to add methods to classes and structures?
- How to add initializers to classes and structures?
- How and when to use access controls?
- How to create a class hierarchy?
- How to extend a class?
- How Swift manages memory?

What are classes and structures?

In Swift, classes and structures are very similar. If we really want to master Swift, it is very important to not only understand what makes classes and structures so similar, but to also understand what sets them apart, because they are the building blocks of our applications. Apple describes classes and structures as follows:

"Classes and structures are general-purpose, flexible constructs that become the building blocks of your program's code. You define properties and methods to add functionality to your classes and structures by using the already familiar syntax of constants, variables, and functions."

Let's begin by taking a quick look at some of the similarities between classes and structures.

Similarities between classes and structures

In Swift, classes and structures are more similar than they are in other languages, such as Objective-C. The following is a list of some of the features that classes and structures share:

- **Properties**: These are used to store information in our classes and structures
- **Methods**: These provide functionality for our classes and structures
- **Initializers**: These are used when initializing instances of our classes and structures
- **Subscripts**: These provide access to values using the subscript syntax
- **Extensions**: These help extend both classes and structures

Now let's take a quick look at some of the differences between classes and structures.

Differences between classes and structures

While classes and structures are very similar, there are also several very important differences. The following is a list of some of the differences between classes and structures in Swift:

- **Type**: A structure is a value type, while a class is a reference type
- **Inheritance**: A structure cannot inherit from other types, while a class can
- **Deinitializers**: Structures cannot have custom deinitializers, while a class can

Throughout this chapter, we will be emphasizing the differences between classes and structures to help us understand when to use each. Before we really dive into classes and structures, let's look at the difference between value types (structures) and reference types (classes). To fully understand when to use classes and structures and how to properly use them, it is important to understand the difference between value and reference types.

Value versus reference types

Structures are value types. When we pass instances of a structure within our application, we pass a copy of the structure and not the original structure. Classes are reference types, therefore when we pass an instance of a class, within our application, a reference to the original instance is passed. It is very important to understand this difference. We will give a very high-level view here, and will provide additional details in the *Memory management* section at the end of this chapter.

When we pass structures within our application, we are passing copies of the structures and not the original structures. Since the function gets its own copy of the structure, it can change it as needed without affecting the original instance of the structure.

When we pass an instance of a class within our application, we are passing a reference to the original instance of the class. Since we're passing the instance of the class to the function, the function is getting a reference to the original instance; therefore, any changes made within the function will remain once the function exits.

To illustrate the difference between value and reference types, let's look at a real-world object: a book. If we have a friend who wants to read *Mastering Swift*, we could either buy them their own copy or share ours.

If we bought our friend their own copy of the book, then any notes they made within the book would remain in their copy of the book and would not be reflected in our copy. This is how passing by value works with structures and variables. Any changes that are made to the structure or variable within the function are not reflected in the original instance of the structure or variable.

If we share our copy of the book, then any notes they made within the book would stay in the book when they return it to us. This is how passing by reference works. Any changes that are made to the instance of the class remains when the function exits.

To read more about value versus reference types, see the *Memory management* section at the end of this chapter.

Creating a class or structure

We use the same syntax to define classes and structures. The only difference is that we define a class using the `class` keyword and a structure using the `struct` keyword. Let's look at the syntax used to create both classes and structures:

```
class MyClass {
  // MyClass definition
}

struct MyStruct {
  // MyStruct definition
}
```

In the preceding code, we define a new class named `MyClass` and a new structure named `MyStruct`. This effectively creates two new Swift types named `MyClass` and `MyStruct`. When we name a new type, we want to use the standard naming convention set by Swift, where the name is in camel case with the first letter being uppercase. This is also known as PascalCase. Any method or property defined within the class or structure should also be named using camel case with the first letter being uppercase.

Empty classes and structures are not that useful, so let's look at how we can add properties to our classes and structures.

Properties

Properties associate values with a class or a structure. There are two types of properties:

- **Stored properties**: Stored properties will store variable or constant values as part of an instance of a class or structure. Stored properties can also have property observers that can monitor the property for changes and respond with custom actions when the value of the property changes.
- **Computed properties**: These do not store a value themselves, but retrieve and possibly set other properties. The value returned by a computed property can also be calculated when it is requested.

Stored properties

A stored property is a variable or constant that is stored as part of an instance of a class or structure. These are defined with the var and let keywords just like normal variables and constants. In the following code, we will create a structure named MyStruct and a class named MyClass. The structure and the class both contain two stored properties, c and v. The stored property c is a constant because it is defined with the let keyword, and v is a variable because it is defined with the var keyword. Let's look at the following code:

```
struct MyStruct {
   let c = 5
   var v = ""
}

class MyClass {
   let c = 5
   var v = ""
}
```

As we can see from the example, the syntax to define a stored property is the same for both classes and structures. Let's look at how we would create an instance of both the structure and class. The following code creates an instance of the MyStruct structure named myStruct and an instance of the MyClass class named myClass:

```
var myStruct = MyStruct()
var myClass = MyClass()
```

One of the differences between structures and classes is that, by default, a structure creates an initializer that lets us populate the stored properties when we create an instance of the structure. Therefore, we could also create an instance of MyStruct like this:

```
var myStruct = MyStruct(v: "Hello")
```

In the preceding example, the initializer is used to set the variable v, and the c constant will still contain the number 5 that is defined in the structures. If we did not give the constant an initial value, as shown in the following example, the default initializer would be used to set the constant as well:

```
struct MyStruct {
   let c: Int
   var v = ""
}
```

The following example shows how the initializer for this new structure would work:

```
var myStruct = MyStruct(c: 10, v: "Hello")
```

This allows us to define a constant where we set the value when we initialize the class or structure at runtime, rather than hardcoding the value of the constant within the type.

The order in which the parameters appear in the initializer is the order that we defined them. In the previous example, we defined the c constant first, therefore, it is the first parameter in the initializer. We defined the v parameter next, therefore, it is the second parameter in the initializer.

To set or read a stored property, we use the standard dot syntax. Let's look at how we would set and read stored properties in Swift:

```
var x = myClass.c
myClass.v = "Howdy"
```

In the first line of code, we read the c property and store it into a variable named x. In the second line of code we set the property v to the string Howdy.

Before we move on to computed properties, let's create both a structure and class that will represent an employee. We will be using and expanding these throughout this chapter to show how classes and structures are similar, and how they differ:

```
struct EmployeeStruct {
  var firstName = ""
  var lastName = ""
  var salaryYear = 0.0
}

public class EmployeeClass {
  var firstName = ""
  var lastName = ""
  var salaryYear = 0.0
}
```

The employee structure is named EmployeeStruct and the employee class is named EmployeeClass. Both the class and structure have three stored properties: firstName, lastName, and salaryYear.

Within the structure and class, we can access these properties by using the name of the property and the `self` keyword. Every instance of a structure or class has a property named `self`. This property refers to the instance itself, therefore, we can use it to access the properties within the instance. The following examples show how we can access the properties with the `self` keyword within the instance of the structure or class:

```
self.firstName = "Jon"
self.lastName = "Hoffman"
```

Computed properties

Computed properties are properties that do not have backend variables that are used to store the values associated with the property. The values of a computed property are usually computed when code requests it. You can think of a computed property as a function disguised as a property. Let's look at how we would define a read-only computed property:

```
var salaryWeek: Double {
  get{
    return self.salaryYear/52
  }
}
```

To create a read-only computed property, we begin by defining it as if it were a normal variable with the `var` keyword, followed by the variable name, colon, and the variable type. What comes next is different; we add a curly bracket at the end of the declaration and then define a getter method that is called when the value of our computed property is requested. In this example, the getter method divides the current value of the `salaryYear` property by 52 to get the employee's weekly salary.

We can simplify the definition of the read-only computed property by removing the `get` keyword, as shown in the following example:

```
var salaryWeek: Double {
  return self.salaryYear/52
}
```

Computed properties are not limited to being read-only, we can also write to them. To enable the salaryWeek property to be writeable, we will add a setter method. The following example shows how we add a setter method that will set the salaryYear property, based on the value being passed into the salaryWeek property:

```
var salaryWeek: Double {
  get {
    return self.salaryYear/52
  }
  set (newSalaryWeek){
    self.salaryYear = newSalaryWeek*52
  }
}
```

We can simplify the setter definition by not defining a name for the new value. In this case, the value will be assigned to a default variable named newValue, as shown in the following example.

```
var salaryWeek: Double {
  get{
    return self.salaryYear/52
  }
  set{
    self.salaryYear = newValue*52
  }
}
```

The salaryWeek computed property, as written in the preceding examples, could be added to either the EmployeeClass class or the EmployeeStruct structure without any modifications. Let's see how we can do this by adding the salaryWeek property to our EmployeeClass class:

```
public class EmployeeClass {
  var firstName = ""
  var lastName = ""
  var salaryYear = 0.0

  var salaryWeek: Double {
    get{
      return self.salaryYear/52
    }
    set (newSalaryWeek){
      self.salaryYear = newSalaryWeek*52
    }
  }
}
```

Now, let's look at how we can add the `salaryWeek` computed property to the `EmployeeStruct` structure:

```
struct EmployeeStruct {
  var firstName = ""
  var lastName = ""
  var salaryYear = 0.0

  var salaryWeek: Double {
    get{
      return self.salaryYear/52
    }
    set (newSalaryWeek){
      self.salaryYear = newSalaryWeek*52
    }
  }
}
```

As we can see, the class and structure definitions are the same so far, except for the initial `class` or `struct` keywords that are used to define them.

We read and write to a computed property exactly as we would to a stored property. Code that is external to the class or structure should not be aware that the property is a computed property. Let's see this in action by creating an instance of the `EmployeeStruct` structure:

```
var f = EmployeeStruct(firstName: "Jon", lastName: "Hoffman", salaryYear:
39_000)
print(f.salaryWeek) //prints 750.00 to the console
f.salaryWeek = 1000
print(f.salaryWeek) //prints 1000.00 to the console
print(f.salaryYear) //prints 52000.00 to the console
```

The preceding example starts off by creating an instance of the `EmployStruct` structure with the `salaryYear` value being set to 39,000. Next, we print the value of the `salaryWeek` property to the console. This value is currently 750.00. We then set the `salaryWeek` property to 1,000.00 and print out both the `salaryWeek` and `salaryYear` properties to the console. The values of the `salaryWeek` and `salaryYear` properties are now 1,000.00 and 52,000 respectively. As we can see, in this example, setting either the `salaryWeek` or `salaryYear` property changes the values returned by both.

Computed properties can be very useful for offering different views of the same data. For example, if we had a value that represented the length of something, we could store the length in centimeters and then use computed properties that calculate the values for meters, millimeters, and kilometers.

Now, let's look at property observers.

Property observers

Property observers are called every time the value of the property is set. We can add property observers to any non-lazy stored property. We can also add property observers to any inherited stored or computed property by overriding the property in the subclass. We will look at the *Overriding properties* section a little later in this chapter.

There are two property observers that we can set in Swift: `willSet` and `didSet`. The `willSet` observer is called right before the property is set, and the `didSet` observer is called right after the property is set.

One thing to note about property observers is that they are not called when the value is set during initialization. Let's look at how we can add a property observer to the salary property of our `EmployeeClass` class and `EmployeeStruct` structure:

```
var salaryYear: Double = 0.0 {
  willSet(newSalary) {
    print("About to set salaryYear to \(newSalary)")
  }
  didSet {
    if salaryWeek>oldValue {
      print("\(firstName) got a raise.")
    }else {
      print("\(firstName) did not get a raise.")
    }
  }
}
```

When we add a property observer to a stored property, we need to include the type of the value being stored within the definition of the property. In the preceding example, we did not need to define our `salaryYear` property as a `Double` type, however, when we add property observers, the definition is required.

After the property definition, we define the `willSet` observer that simply prints out the new value that the `salaryYear` property will be set to. We also define a `didSet` observer that will check whether the new value is greater than the old value, and if so, it will print out that the employee got a raise; otherwise, it will print out that the employee did not get a raise.

As with the getter method with computed properties, we do not need to define the name for the new value of the `willSet` observer. If we do not define a name, the new value is put in a constant named `newValue`. The following example shows how we can rewrite the previous `willSet` observer without defining a name for the new value:

```
willSet {
  print("About to set salaryYear to \(newValue)")
}
```

As we have seen, properties are mainly used to store information associated with a class or structure. Methods are mainly used to add the business logic to a class or structure. Let's look at how we add methods to a class or structure.

Methods

Methods are functions that are associated with an instance of a class or structure. A method, like a function, will encapsulate the code for a specific task or functionality that is associated with the class or structure. Let's look at how we can define methods for classes and structures. The following code will return the full name of the employee by using the `firstName` and `lastName` properties:

```
func getFullName() -> String {
  return firstName + " " + lastName
}
```

We define this method exactly as we would define any function. A method is simply a function that is associated with a specific class or structure, and everything that we learned about functions in the previous chapters applies to methods. The `getFullName()` function can be added directly to the `EmployeeClass` class or `EmployeeStruct` structure without any modification.

To access a method, we use the same dot syntax we used to access properties. The following code shows how we access the `getFullName()` method of a class and a structure:

```
var e = EmployeeClass()
var f = EmployeeStruct(firstName: "Jon", lastName: "Hoffman", salaryYear:
50000)

e.firstName = "Jon"
e.lastName = "Hoffman"
e.salaryYear = 50000.00

print(e.getFullName()) //Jon Hoffman is printed to the console
print(f.getFullName()) //Jon Hoffman is printed to the console
```

In the preceding example, we initialize an instance of both the `EmployeeClass` class and `EmployeeStruct` structure. We populate the structure and class with the same information and then use the `getFullName()` method to print the full name of the employee to the console. In both cases, `Jon Hoffman` is printed to the console.

There is a difference in how we define methods for classes and structures that need to update property values. Let's look at how we define a method that gives an employee a raise within the `EmployeeClass` class:

```
func giveRaise(amount: Double) {
  self.salaryYear += amount
}
```

If we add the preceding code to our `EmployeeClass`, it works as expected and when we call the method with an amount, the employee gets a raise. However, if we try to add this method as it is written to the `EmployeeStruct` structure, we receive a `mark` method `mutating to make self mutable` error. By default, we are not allowed to update property values within a method of a structure. If we want to modify a property, we can opt into mutating behavior for that method by adding the `mutating` keyword before the `func` keyword of the method declaration. Therefore, the following code would be the correct way to define the `giveRaise(amount:)` method for the `EmployeeStruct` structure:

```
mutating func giveRase(amount: Double) {
  self.salaryYear += amount
}
```

In the preceding examples, we use the `self` property to refer to the current instance of the type within the instance itself, so when we write `self.salaryYear`, we ask for the value of the `salaryYear` property for the current instance of the type.

 The `self` property should only be used when necessary. We are using it in these past few examples to illustrate what it is and how to use it.

The `self` property is mainly used to distinguish between local and instance variables that have the same name. Let's look at an example that illustrates this. We can add this function to either the `EmployeeClass` or `EmployeeStruct` type:

```
func isEqualFirstName(firstName: String) -> Bool {
  return self.firstName == firstName
}
```

In the preceding example, the method accepts an argument named `firstName`. There is also a property within the type that has the same name. We use the `self` property to specify that we want the instance property with the name `firstName`, and not the local variable with this name.

Other than the `mutating` keyword being required for methods that change the value of the structure's properties, methods can be defined and used exactly as functions are defined and used. Therefore, everything we learned about functions in the previous chapter can be applied to methods.

There are times when we want to initialize properties or perform some business logic when a class or structure is first initialized. For this, we will use an initializer.

Custom initializers

Initializers are called when we initialize a new instance of a type (class or structure). Initialization is the process of preparing an instance for use. The initialization process can include setting initial values for stored properties, verifying that external resources are available, or setting up the UI properly. Initializers are generally used to ensure that the instance of the class or structure is properly initialized prior to first use.

Initializers are special methods that are used to create a new instance of a type. We define an initializer similar to defining other methods, but we must use the `init` keyword as the name of the initializer to tell the compiler that this method is an initializer. In its simplest form, the initializer does not accept any arguments. Let's look at the syntax used to write a simple initializer:

```
init() {
  //Perform initialization here
}
```

This format works for both classes and structures. By default, all classes and structures have an empty default initializer that can be overriden. We used these default initializers when we initialized the `EmployeeClass` class and `EmployeeStruct` structure in the previous section. Structures also have an additional default initializer, which we saw with the `EmployeeStruct` structure that accepts a value for each stored property and initializes them with those values. Let's look at how we add custom initializers to the `EmployeeClass` class and `EmployeeStruct` structure.

In the following code, we create three custom initializers that will work for both the `EmployeeClass` class and `EmployeeStruct` structure:

```
init() {
  self.firstName = ""
  self.lastName = ""
  self.salaryYear = 0.0
}
init(firstName: String, lastName: String) {
  self.firstName = firstName
  self.lastName = lastName
  self.salaryYear = 0.0
}
init(firstName: String, lastName: String, salaryYear: Double) {
  self.firstName = firstName
  self.lastName = lastName
  self.salaryYear = salaryYear
}
```

The first initializer, `init()`, when used, will set all of the stored properties to their default values. The second initializer, `init(firstName: String, lastName: String)`, when used, will populate the `firstName` and `lastName` properties with the values of the arguments. The third initializer, `init(firstName: String, lastName: String, salaryYear: Double)`, will populate all the properties with the values of the arguments.

In the previous example, we can see that in Swift, an initializer does not have an explicit return value but it does return an instance of the type. This means that we do not define a return type for the initializer or have a return statement within the initializer. Let's look at how we could use these initializers:

```
var g = EmployeeClass()
var h = EmployeeStruct(firstName: "Me", lastName: "Moe")
var i = EmployeeClass(firstName: "Me", lastName: "Moe", salaryYear: 45_000)
```

The variable `g` uses the `init()` initializer to create an instance of the `EmployeeClass` class; therefore, all the properties of this instance contain their default values.

The `h` variable uses the `init(firstName: String, lastName: String)` initializer to create an instance of the `EmployeeStruct` structure, therefore, the `firstName` property is set to `Me` and the `lastName` property is set to `Moe`, which are the two arguments passed into the initializer. The `salaryYear` property is still set to the default value of 0.0.

The i variable uses the `init(firstName: String, lastName: String, salaryYear: Double)` initializer to create an instance of the `EmployeeClass` class; therefore, the `firstName` property is set to `Me`, the `lastName` property is set to `Moe`, and the `salaryYear` property is set to `45_000`.

Since all the initializers are identified with the `init` keyword, the parameters and parameter types are used to identify which initializer to use.

A class, unlike a structure, can have a deinitializer. A deinitializer is called just before an instance of the class is destroyed and removed from memory. In the *Memory management* section of this chapter, we will show examples of the deinitializer and see when it is called.

Let's look at internal and external parameter names with initializers.

Internal and external parameter names

Just like functions, the parameters associated with an initializer can have separate internal and external names. If we do not supply external parameter names for our parameters, Swift will automatically generate them for us. In the previous examples, we did not include external parameter names in the definition of the initializers, so Swift created them for us using the internal parameter name as the external parameter name.

If we wanted to supply our own parameter names, we would do so by putting the external parameter name before the internal parameter name, exactly as we do with any normal function. Let's look at how we can define our own external parameter names by redefining one of the initializers within our `EmployeeClass` class:

```
init(employeeWithFirstName firstName: String, lastName lastName: String,
andSalary salaryYear: Double) {
  self.firstName = firstName
  self.lastName = lastName
  self.salaryYear = salaryYear
}
```

In the preceding example, we created the `init(employeeWithFirstName firstName: String, lastName lastName: String, andSalary salaryYear: Double)` initializer. This initializer will create an instance of the `EmployeeClass` class and populate the instance properties with the value of the arguments. In this example, each of the parameters has both external and internal property names. Let's look at how we would use this initializer, with the external property names:

```
var i = EmployeeClass(employeeWithFirstName: "Me", lastName: "Moe",
andSalary: 45000)
```

Notice that we are now using the external parameter names as defined in the initializer. Using external parameter names can help make our code more readable and help differentiate between different initializers.

So, what will happen if our initializer fails? For example, what if our class relies on a specific resource, such as a web service that is not currently available? This is where failable initializers come in.

Failable initializers

A failable initializer is an initializer that may fail to initialize the resources needed for a class or a structure, thereby rendering the instance unusable. When using a failable initializer, the result of the initializer is an optional type, containing either a valid instance of the type or nil.

An initializer can be made failable by adding a question mark (?) after the init keyword. Let's look at how we can create a failable initializer that will not allow a new employee to be initialized with a salary of less than $20,000 a year:

```
init?(firstName: String, lastName: String, salaryYear: Double) {
  self.firstName = firstName
  self.lastName = lastName
  self.salaryYear = salaryYear
  if self.salaryYear < 20_000 {
    return nil
  }
}
```

In the previous examples, we did not include a return statement within the initializer because Swift does not need to return the initialized instance, however, in a failable initializer, if the initialization fails, it will return nil. If the initializer successfully initializes the instance, we do not need to return anything. Therefore, in our example, if the yearly salary that is passed in is less than $20,000 a year, we return nil, indicating that the initialization failed, otherwise nothing will be returned. Let's look at how we would use a failable initializer to create an instance of a class or structure:

```
if let f = EmployeeClass(firstName: "Jon", lastName: "Hoffman", salaryYear:
29_000) {
  print(f.getFullName())
} else {
  print("Failed to initialize")
}
```

In the previous example, we initialize the instance of the `EmployeeClass` class with a yearly salary of greater than $20,000, therefore, the instance gets initialized correctly and the full name of `Jon Hoffman` is printed to the console. Now, let's try to initialize an instance of the `EmployeeClass` class with a yearly salary of less than $20,000, to see how it fails:

```
if let f = EmployeeClass(firstName: "Jon", lastName: "Hoffman", salaryYear:
19_000) {
  print(f.getFullName())
} else {
  print("Failed to initialize")
}
```

In the example, the yearly salary that we are attempting to initialize for our employee is less than $20,000, therefore, the initialization fails and a `Failed to initialize` message is printed to the console.

There are times when we want to restrict access to certain parts of our code. For this we use access controls.

Access controls

Access controls enable us to hide implementation details and only expose the interfaces we want to expose. This feature is handled with access controls. We can assign specific access levels to both classes and structures. We can also assign specific access levels to properties, methods, and initializers that belong to our classes and structures.

In Swift, there are five access levels:

- **Open**: This is the most visible access control level. It allows us to use the property, method, class, and so on anywhere we want to import the module. Basically, anything can use an item that has an access control level of open. Anything that is marked open can be subclassed or overridden by any item within the module they are defined in and any module that imports the module it is defined in. This level is primarily used by frameworks to expose the framework's public API. The open access control is only available to classes and members of a class.
- **Public**: This access level allows us to use the property, method, class, and so on anywhere we want to import the module. Basically, anything can use an item that has an access control level of public. Anything that is marked public can be subclassed or overridden only by any item within the module they are defined in. This level is primarily used by frameworks to expose the framework's public API.

- **Internal**: This is the default access level. This access level allows us to use the property, method, class, and so on in the module the item is defined in. If this level is used in a framework, it lets other parts of the framework use the item but code outside the framework will be unable to access it.
- **Fileprivate**: This access control allows access to the properties and methods from any code within the same source file that the item is defined in.
- **Private**: This is the least visible access control level. It only allows us to use the property, method, class, and so on, within extensions of that declaration defined in the source file that defines it.

When we are developing frameworks, the access controls really become useful. We will need to mark the public facing interfaces as public or open, so other modules such as applications that import the framework can use them. We will then use the internal and private access control levels to mark the interfaces that we want to use internally to the framework and the source file, respectively.

To define access levels, we place the name of the level before the definition of the entity. The following code shows examples of how we add access levels to several entities:

```
private struct EmployeeStruct {}
public class EmployeeClass {}
internal class EmployeeClass2 {}
public var firstName = "Jon"
internal var lastName = "Hoffman"
private var salaryYear = 0.0
public func getFullName() -> String {}
private func giveRaise(amount: Double) {}
```

There are some limitations with access controls, but these limitations are there to ensure that access levels in Swift follow a simple guiding principle--no entity can be defined in terms of another entity that has a lower (more restrictive) access level. What this means is we cannot assign a higher (less restrictive) access level to an entity when it relies on another entity that has a lower (more restrictive) access level.

The following examples demonstrate this principle:

- We cannot mark a method as being public when one of the arguments or the return type has an access level of private, because external code would not have access to the private type
- We cannot set the access level of a method or property to public when the class or structure has an access level of private, because external code would not be able to access the constructor when the class is private

Inheritance

The concept of inheritance is a basic object-oriented development concept. Inheritance allows a class to be defined as having a certain set of characteristics and then other classes can be derived from that class. The derived class inherits all of the features of the class it is inheriting from (unless the derived class overrides those characteristics) and then usually adds additional characteristics of its own.

With inheritance, we can create what is known as a class hierarchy. In a class hierarchy, the class at the top of the hierarchy is known as the base class and the derived classes are known as subclasses. We are not limited to only creating subclasses from a base class, we can also create subclasses from other subclasses. The class that a subclass is derived from is known as the parent or superclass. In Swift, a class can have only one parent class. This is known as single inheritance.

 Inheritance is one of the fundamental differences that separate classes from structures. Classes can be derived from a parent or superclass, but a structure cannot.

Subclasses can call and access the properties, methods, and subscripts of their superclass. They can also override the properties, methods, and subscripts of their superclass. Subclasses can add property observers to properties that they inherit from a superclass, so they can be notified when the values of the properties change. Let's look at an example that illustrates how inheritance works in Swift.

We will start off by defining a base class named `Plant`. The `Plant` class will have two properties, `height` and `age`. It will also have one method, `growHeight()`. The `height` property will represent the height of the plant, the `age` property will represent the age of the plant, and the `growHeight()` method will be used to increase the height of the plant. Here is how we would define the `Plant` class:

```
class Plant {
  var height = 0.0
  var age = 0
  func growHeight(inches: Double) {
    height += inches;
  }
}
```

Now that we have our `Plant` base class, let's see how we would define a subclass of it. We will name this subclass `Tree`. The `Tree` class will inherit the `age` and `height` properties of the `Plant` class and add one more property named `limbs`. It will also inherit the `growHeight()` method of the `Plant` class and add two more methods: `limbGrow()`, where new limbs are grown, and `limbFall()`, where limbs fall off the tree. Let's have a look at the following code:

```
class Tree: Plant {
  var limbs = 0
  func limbGrow() {
    self.limbs += 1
  }
  func limbFall() {
    self.limbs -= 1
  }
}
```

We indicate that a class has a superclass by adding a colon and the name of the superclass to the end of the class definition. In this example, we indicated that the `Tree` class has a superclass named `Plant`.

Now, let's look at how we could use the `Tree` class that inherited the `age` and `height` properties from the `Plant` class:

```
var tree = Tree()
tree.age = 5
tree.height = 4
tree.limbGrow()
tree.limbGrow()
```

The preceding example begins by creating an instance of the `Tree` class. We then set the `age` and `height` properties to 5 and 4, respectively, and add two limbs to the tree by calling the `limbGrow()` method twice.

We now have a base class named `Plant` that has a subclass named `Tree`. This means that the super (or parent) class of `Tree` is the `Plant` class. This also means that one of the subclasses (or child classes) of `Plant` is named `Tree`. There are, however, lots of different kinds of trees in the world. Let's create two subclasses from the `Tree` class. These subclasses will be the `PineTree` class and the `OakTree` class:

```
class PineTree: Tree {
  var needles = 0
}
```

```
class OakTree: Tree {
  var leaves = 0
}
```

The class hierarchy now looks like this:

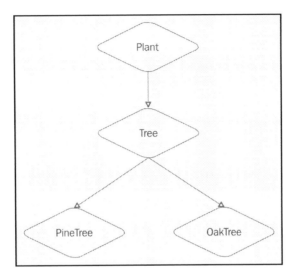

It is important to keep in mind that in Swift, a class can have multiple subclasses; however, a class can have only one superclass. There are times when a subclass needs to provide its own implementation of a method or property that it inherited from its superclass. This is known as **overriding**.

Overriding methods and properties

To override a method, property, or subscript, we need to prefix the definition with the override keyword. This tells the compiler that we intend to override something in the superclass and that we did not make a duplicate definition by mistake. The override keyword prompts the Swift compiler to verify that the superclass (or one of its parents) has a matching declaration that can be overridden. If it cannot find a matching declaration in one of the superclasses, an error will be thrown.

Overriding methods

Let's look at how we can override a method. We will start by adding a `getDetails()` method to the `Plant` class that we will then override in the child classes. The following code shows the code for the new `Plant` class:

```
class Plant {
  var height = 0.0
  var age = 0
  func growHeight(inches: Double) {
    self.height += inches;
  }
  func getDetails() -> String {
    return "Plant Details"
  }
}
```

Now, let's see how we can override the `getDetails()` method in the `Tree` class:

```
class Tree: Plant {
  private var limbs = 0
  func limbGrow() {
    self.limbs += 1
  }
  func limbFall() {
    self.limbs -= 1
  }
  override func getDetails() -> String {
    return "Tree Details"
  }
}
```

The thing to note here is that we do not use the `override` keyword in the `Plant` class because it is the first class to implement this method, however, we do include it in the `Tree` class since we are overriding the `getDetails()` method from the `Plant` class. Now, let's see what happens if we call the `getDetails()` method from an instance of the `Plant` and `Tree` classes:

```
var plant = Plant()
var tree = Tree()
print("Plant: \(plant.getDetails())")
print("Tree: \(tree.getDetails())")
```

The previous example will print the following two lines to the console:

```
Plant: Plant Details
Tree: Tree Details
```

As we can see, the `getDetails()` method in the `Tree` subclass overrides the `getDetails()` of its parent `Plant` class.

Inside the `Tree` class, we can still call the `getDetails()` method (or any overridden method, property, or subscript) of its superclass by using the `super` prefix. We will begin by replacing the `getDetails()` method in the `Plant` class with the following method that will generate a string containing the values of the `height` and `age` properties:

```
func getDetails() -> String {
  return "Height:\(height) age:\(age)"
}
```

Now we will replace the `getDetails()` method for the `Tree` class with the following method that will call the `getDetails()` method of the superclass:

```
override func getDetails() -> String {
  let details = super.getDetails()
  return "\(details) limbs:\(limbs)"
}
```

In the preceding example, we begin by calling the `getDetails()` method of the superclass (the `Plant` class in this case) to get a string containing the tree's height and age. We then build a new string object that combines the results of the `getDetails()` method and a new string that contains the number of limbs from the `Tree` class. This new string is then returned. Let's look at what happens if we call this new method:

```
var tree = Tree()
tree.age = 5
tree.height = 4
tree.limbGrow()
tree.limbGrow()
print(tree.getDetails())
```

If we run the preceding code, the following line will be printed to the console:

```
Height: 4.0  age: 5  limbs: 2
```

As we can see, the string that is returned contains the `height` and `age` information from the `Plant` class and the `limbs` information from the `Tree` class.

Overriding properties

We can provide custom getters and setters to override any inherited property. When we override a property, we must provide the name and the type of property we are overriding, so the compiler can verify one of the classes in the class hierarchy has a matching property to override.

Let's see how we can override a property by adding the following property to our `Plant` class:

```
var description: String {
  return "Base class is Plant."
}
```

The `description` property is a basic read-only property. This property returns the string, `Base class is Plant`. Now let's override this property by adding the following property to the `Tree` class:

```
override var description: String {
  return "\(super.description) I am a Tree class."
}
```

The same `override` keyword is used when overriding both properties and methods. This keyword tells the compiler that we want to override a property, so the compiler can verify that another class in the class hierarchy contains a matching property to override. We then implement the property as we would any other property. Calling the `description` property for an instance of the `Tree` class will result in the `Base class is Plant. I am a Tree class` string being returned.

There are times when we want to prevent a subclass from overriding the properties and methods. There are also times when we want to prevent an entire class from being subclassed. Let's see how to do this.

Preventing overrides

To prevent overrides or subclassing, we can use the `final` keyword. To use the `final` keyword, we add it before the item's definition. Examples are `final func`, `final var`, and `final class`.

Any attempt to override an item marked with this keyword will result in a compile-time error.

Protocols

There are times when we would like to describe the implementations (methods, properties, and other requirements) of a type without actually providing any implementation. For this, we can use protocols.

Protocols define a blueprint of methods, properties, and other requirements for a class or a structure. A class or a structure can then provide an implementation that conforms to those requirements. The class or structure that provides the implementation is said to conform to the protocol.

Protocols are very important to the Swift language. The entire Swift standard library is based on them and we will be looking at protocols in-depth and how to use them in Chapter 6, *Using Protocols and Protocol Extensions* and Chapter 7, *Protocol-Oriented Design*.

Protocol syntax

The syntax to define a protocol is very similar to how we define a class or a structure. The following example shows the syntax used to define a protocol:

```
protocol MyProtocol {
   //protocol definition here
}
```

We state that a class or structure conforms to a protocol by placing the name of the protocol after the type's name, separated by a colon. Here is an example of how we would state that a structure conforms to the MyProtocol protocol:

```
struct MyStruct: MyProtocol {
   //class implementation here
}
```

A type can conform to multiple protocols. We list the protocols that the type conforms to by separating them with commas. The following example shows how we would state that our structure conforms to multiple protocols:

```
Struct MyStruct: MyProtocol, AnotherProtocol, ThirdProtocol {
   // class implementation here
}
```

If we need a class to both inherit from a superclass and implement a protocol, we would list the superclass first, followed by the protocols. The following example illustrates this:

```
Class MyClass: MySuperClass, MyProtocol, MyProtocol2 {
  // Class implementation here
}
```

Property requirements

A protocol can require that the conforming type provides certain properties with a specified name and type. The protocol does not say if the property should be a stored or computed property because the implementation details are left up to the conforming type.

When defining a property within a protocol, we must specify whether the property is a read-only or a read-write property by using the `get` and `set` keywords. Let's look at how we would define properties within a protocol by creating a protocol named `FullName`:

```
protocol FullName {
  var firstName: String { get set }
  var lastName: String { get set }
}
```

The `FullName` protocol defines two properties, which any type that conforms to the protocol must implement. These are the `firstName` and `lastName` properties and both are read-write properties. If we wanted to specify that the property is read-only, we would define it with only the `get` keyword, like this:

```
var readOnly: String { get }
```

Let's see how we can create a `Scientist` class that conforms to this protocol:

```
class Scientist: FullName {
  var firstName = ""
  var lastName = ""
}
```

If we had forgotten to include either the required properties, we would have received an error message letting us know the property we forgot. We also need to make sure that the type of the property is the same. For example, if we change the definition of the `lastName` property in the `Scientist` class to `var lastName = 42`, we will also receive an error message because the protocol specifies that we must have a `lastName` property of the string type.

Method requirements

A protocol can require that the conforming class or structure provides certain methods. We define a method within a protocol exactly as we do within a class or structure, except without the curly braces or method body. Let's add a `getFullName()` method to our `FullName` protocol and `Scientist` class.

```
protocol FullName {
  var firstName: String { get set }
  var lastName: String { get set }
  func getFullName() -> String
}
```

Now, we will need to add a `getFullName()` method to our `Scientist` class so that it will conform to the protocol:

```
class Scientist: FullName {
  var firstName = ""
  var lastName = ""
  var field = ""

  func getFullName() -> String {
    return "\(firstName) \(lastName) studies \(field)"
  }
}
```

Structures can conform to Swift protocols exactly as classes do. In fact, the majority of the Swift standard library are structures that implement the various protocols that make up the standard library. The following example shows how we can create a `FootballPlayer` structure that also conforms to the `FullName` protocol:

```
struct FootballPlayer: FullName {
  var firstName = ""
  var lastName = ""
  var number = 0

  func getFullName() -> String {
    return "\(firstName) \(lastName) has the number \(number)"
  }
}
```

When a class or structure conforms to a Swift protocol, we can be sure that it has implemented the required properties and methods. This can be very useful when we want to ensure that certain properties or methods are implemented over various classes, as our preceding examples show.

Protocols are also very useful when we want to decouple our code from requiring specific types. The following code shows how we would decouple our code using the `FullName` protocol, the `Scientist` class, and the `FootballPlayer` structure that we have already built:

```
var scientist = Scientist()
scientist.firstName = "Kara"
scientist.lastName = "Hoffman"
scientist.field = "Physics"

var player = FootballPlayer();

player.firstName = "Dan"
player.lastName = "Marino"
player.number = 13

var person: FullName
person = scientist
print(person.getFullName())
person = player
print(person.getFullName())
```

In the preceding code, we begin by creating an instance of the `Scientist` class and the `FootballPlayer` structure. We then create a `person` variable that is of the `FullName` (protocol) type and set it to the `scientist` instance that we just created. We then call the `getFullName()` method to retrieve our description. This will print out the `Kara Hoffman studies Physics` message to the console.

We then set the `person` variable equal to the `player` instance and call the `getFullName()` method again. This will print out the `Dan Marino has the number 13` message to the console.

As we can see, the `person` variable does not care what the actual implementation type is. Since we defined the `person` variable to be of the `FullName` type, we can set the variable to an instance of any type that conforms to the `FullName` protocol. This is called polymorphism. We will cover polymorphism and protocols more in Chapter 6, *Using Protocols and Protocol Extensions* and Chapter 7, *Protocol-Oriented Design*.

Extensions

With extensions, we can add new properties, methods, initializers, and subscripts, or make an existing type conform to a protocol without modifying the source code for the type. One thing to note is that extensions cannot override the existing functionality.

To define an extension, we use the `extension` keyword, followed by the type that we are extending. The following example shows how we would create an extension that extends the string class:

```
extension String {
  //add new functionality here
}
```

Let's see how extensions work by adding a `reverse()` method and a `firstLetter` property to Swift's standard string class:

```
extension String {
  var firstLetter: Character? {
    get {
      return self.characters.first
    }
  }

  func reverse() -> String {
    var reverse = ""
    for letter in self.characters {
      reverse = "\(letter)" + reverse
    }
    return reverse
  }
}
```

When we extend an existing type, we define properties, methods, initializers, subscripts, and protocols in exactly the same way as we would normally define them in a standard class or structure. In the string extension example, we see that we define the `reverse()` method and the `firstLetter` property exactly as we would define them in a normal type. We can then use these methods exactly as we would use any other method, as the following example shows:

```
var myString = "Learning Swift is fun"
print(myString.reverse())
print(myString.firstLetter!)
```

Swift 4 did add the reversed() method to the string type which should be preferred over the one we created here. This example just illustrates how to use extensions.

Extensions are very useful for adding extra functionality to an existing type from external frameworks, even for Apple's frameworks, as demonstrated in this example. It is preferred to use extensions to add extra functionality to types from external frameworks rather than subclassing because it allows us to continue to use the type throughout our code rather than changing the type to the subclass.

Memory management

As I mentioned at the start of this chapter, structures are value types and classes are reference types. What this means is that when we pass an instance of a structure within our application, such as a parameter of a method, we create a new instance of the structure in the memory. This new instance of the structure is only valid while the application is in the scope where the structure was created. Once the structure goes out of scope, the new instance of the structure is destroyed and the memory is released. This makes memory management of structures pretty easy and somewhat painless.

Classes, on the other hand, are reference types. This means that we allocate memory for the instance of the class only once, when it is initially created. When we pass an instance of the class within our application, either as a function argument or by assigning it to a variable, we really pass a reference to where the instance is stored in memory. Since the instance of a class may be referenced in multiple scopes (unlike a structure), it cannot be automatically destroyed, and memory is not released when it goes out of scope if it is referenced in another scope. Therefore, Swift needs some form of memory management to track and release the memory used by instances of classes when the class is no longer needed. Swift uses **Automatic Reference Counting (ARC)** to track and manage memory usage.

With ARC, for the most part, memory management in Swift simply works. ARC will automatically track the references to instances of classes, and when an instance is no longer needed (no references pointing to it), ARC will automatically destroy the instance and release the memory. There are a few instances where ARC requires additional information about relationships to properly manage the memory. Before we look at the instances where ARC needs help, let's look at how ARC works.

How ARC works

Whenever we create a new instance of a class, ARC allocates the memory needed to store that class. This ensures that there is enough memory to store the information associated with that instance of the class, and also locks the memory so that nothing overwrites it. When the instance of the class is no longer needed, ARC will release the memory allocated for the class so that it can be used for other purposes. This ensures that we are not tying up memory that is no longer needed.

If ARC were to release the memory for an instance of a class that is still needed, it would not be possible to retrieve the class information from memory. If we did try to access the instance of the class after the memory was released, there is a possibility that the application would crash. To ensure memory is not released for an instance of a class that is still needed, ARC counts how many times the instance is referenced, that is, how many active properties, variables, or constants are pointing to the instance of the class. Once the reference count for an instance of a class equals zero (nothing is referencing the instance), the memory is marked for release.

All the previous examples run properly in a Playground, however, the following examples will not. When we run sample code in a Playground, ARC does not release objects that we create; this is by design so that we can see how the application runs and also the state of the objects at each step. Therefore, we will need to run these samples as an iOS or macOS project. Let's look at an example of how ARC works.

We begin by creating a `MyClass` class with the following code:

```
class MyClass {
   var name = ""
   init(name: String) {
     self.name = name
     print("Initializing class with name \(self.name)")
   }
   deinit {
     print("Releasing class with name \(self.name)")
   }
}
```

This class is very similar to our previous `MyClass` class, except that we add a deinitializer that is called just before an instance of the class is destroyed and removed from memory. This deinitializer prints out a message to the console that lets us know that the instance of the class is about to be removed.

Now, let's look at the code that shows how ARC creates and destroys instances of a class:

```
var class1ref1: MyClass? = MyClass(name: "One")
var class2ref1: MyClass? = MyClass(name: "Two")
var class2ref2: MyClass? = class2ref1

print("Setting class1ref1 to nil")
class1ref1 = nil

print("Setting class2ref1 to nil")
class2ref1 = nil
```

```
print("Setting class2ref2 to nil")
class2ref2 = nil
```

In the example, we begin by creating two instances of the `MyClass` class named `class1ref1` (which stands for class 1 reference 1) and `class2ref1` (which stands for class 2 reference 1). We then create a second reference to `class2ref1` named `class2ref2`. Now, in order to see how ARC works, we need to begin setting the references to `nil`. We start out by setting `class1ref1` to `nil`. Since there is only one reference to `class1ref1`, the deinitializer will be called. Once the deinitializer completes its task, in our case it prints a message to the console letting us know that the instance of the class has been destroyed and the memory has been released.

We then set `class2ref1` to `nil`, but there is a second reference to this class (`class2ref2`) that prevents ARC from destroying the instance so that the deinitializer is not called. Finally, we set `class2ref2` to `nil`, which allows ARC to destroy this instance of the `MyClass` class.

If we run this code, we will see the following output, which illustrates how ARC works:

```
Initializing class with name One
Initializing class with name Two
Setting class1ref1 to nil
Releaseing class with name One
Setting class2ref1 to nil
Setting class2ref2 to nil
Releaseing class with name Two
```

From the example, it seems that ARC handles memory management very well. However, it is possible to write code that will prevent ARC from working properly.

Strong reference cycles

A strong reference cycle is where the instances of two classes holds a strong reference to each other, preventing ARC from releasing either instance. Once again, we are not able to use a Playground for this example, so we need to create an Xcode project. In this project, we start off by creating two classes named `MyClass1_Strong` and `MyClass2_Strong` with the following code:

```
class MyClass1_Strong {
  var name = ""
  var class2: MyClass2_Strong?
  init(name: String) {
    self.name = name
    print("Initializing class1_Strong with name \(self.name)")
```

```
    }
  deinit {
    print("Releasing class1_Strong with name \(self.name)")
  }
}
```

As we can see from the code, `MyClass1_Strong` contains an instance of `MyClass2_Strong`, therefore, the instance of `MyClass2_Strong` cannot be released until `MyClass1_Strong` is destroyed. We can also see from the code that `MyClass2_Strong` contains an instance of `MyClass1_Strong`, therefore, the instance of `MyClass1_Strong` cannot be released until `MyClass2_Strong` is destroyed. This creates a cycle of dependency in which neither instance can be destroyed until the other one is destroyed. Let's see how this works by running the following code:

```
var class1: MyClass1_Strong? = MyClass1_Strong(name: "Class1_Strong")
var class2: MyClass2_Strong? = MyClass2_Strong(name: "Class2_Strong")

class1?.class2 = class2
class2?.class1 = class1

print("Setting classes to nil")
class2 = nil
class1 = nil
```

In this example we create instances of both the `MyClass1_Strong` and `MyClass2_Strong` classes. We then set the `class2` property of the `class1` instance to the `MyClass2_Strong` instance. We also set the `class1` property of the `class2` instance to the `MyClass1_Strong` instance. This means that the `MyClass1_Strong` instance cannot be destroyed until the `MyClass2_Strong` instance is destroyed. This means that the reference counters for each instance will never reach zero, therefore, ARC cannot destroy the instances, which creates a memory leak. A memory leak is where an application continues to use memory and does not properly release it. This can cause an application to eventually crash.

To resolve a strong reference cycle, we need to prevent one of the classes from keeping a strong hold on the instance of the other class, thereby allowing ARC to destroy them both. Swift provides two ways of doing this by letting us define the properties as either a weak or unowned reference.

The difference between a weak reference and an unowned reference is that the instance which a weak reference refers to can be `nil`, whereas the instance that an unowned reference is referring to cannot be `nil`. This means that when we use a weak reference, the property must be an optional property, since it can be `nil`. Let's see how we would use unowned and weak references to resolve a strong reference cycle. Let's start by looking at the unowned reference.

We begin by creating two more classes, MyClass1_Unowned and MyClass2_Unowned:

```
class MyClass1_Unowned {
  var name = ""
  unowned let class2: MyClass2_Unowned
  init(name: String, class2: MyClass2_Unowned) {
    self.name = name
    self.class2 = class2
    print("Initializing class1_Unowned with name \(self.name)")
  }
  deinit {
    print("Releasing class1_Unowned with name \(self.name)")
  }

}

class MyClass2_Unowned {
  var name = ""
  var class1: MyClass1_Unowned?
  init(name: String) {
    self.name = name
    print("Initializing class2_Unowned with name \(self.name)")
  }
  deinit {
    print("Releasing class2_Unowned with name \(self.name)")
  }
}
```

The MyClass1_Unowned class looks pretty similar to classes in the preceding example. The difference here is the MyClass1_Unowned class--we set the class2 property to unowned, which means it cannot be nil and it does not keep a strong reference to the instance that it is referring to. Since the class2 property cannot be nil, we also need to set it when the class is initialized.

Let's see how we can initialize and deinitialize the instances of these classes with the following code:

```
let class2 = MyClass2_Unowned(name: "Class2_Unowned")
let class1: MyClass1_Unowned? = MyClass1_Unowned(name: "class1_Unowned",
                                 class2: class2)

class2.class1 = class1

print("Classes going out of scope")
```

In the preceding code, we create an instance of the MyClass_Unowned class and then use that instance to create an instance of the MyClass1_Unowned class. We then set the class1 property of the MyClass2 instance to the MyClass1_Unowned instance we just created. This creates a reference cycle of dependency between the two classes again, but this time, the MyClass1_Unowned instance is not keeping a strong hold on the MyClass2_Unowned instance, allowing ARC to release both instances when they are no longer needed.

If we run this code, we see the following output, showing that both the MyClass3 and MyClass4 instances are released and the memory is freed:

```
Initializing class2_Unowned with name Class2_Unowned
Initializing class1_Unowned with name class1_Unowned
Classes going out of scope
Releasing class2_Unowned with name Class2_Unowned
Releasing class1_Unowned with name class1_Unowned
```

As we can see, both instances are properly released. Now let's look at how we would use a weak reference to prevent a strong reference cycle. Once again we begin by creating two new classes:

```swift
class MyClass1_Weak {
  var name = ""
  var class2: MyClass2_Weak?
  init(name: String) {
    self.name = name
    print("Initializing class1_Weak with name \(self.name)")
  }
  deinit {
    print("Releasing class1_Weak with name \(self.name)")
  }
}

class MyClass2_Weak {
  var name = ""
  weak var class1: MyClass1_Weak?
  init(name: String) {
    self.name = name
    print("Initializing class2_Weak with name \(self.name)")
  }
  deinit {
    print("Releasing class2_Weak with name \(self.name)")
  }
}
```

The `MyClass1_Weak` and `MyClass2_Weak` classes look very similar to the previous classes we created that showed how a strong reference cycle works. The difference is that we define the `class1` property in the `MyClass2_Weak` class as a weak reference.

Now, let's see how we can initialize and deinitialize instances of these classes with the following code:

```
let class1: MyClass1_Weak? = MyClass1_Weak(name: "Class1_Weak")
let class2: MyClass2_Weak? = MyClass2_Weak(name: "Class2_Weak")

class1?.class2 = class2
class2?.class1 = class1

print("Classes going out of scope")
```

In the preceding code, we create instances of the `MyClass1_Weak` and `MyClass2_Weak` classes and then set the properties of those classes to point to the instance of the other class. Once again, this creates a cycle of dependency, but since we set the `class1` property of the `MyClass2_Weak` class to weak, it does not create a strong reference, allowing both instances to be released.

If we run the code, we will see the following output, showing that both the `MyClass5` and `MyClass6` instances are released and the memory is freed:

```
Initializing class1_Weak with name Class1_Weak
Initializing class2_Weak with name Class2_Weak
Classes going out of scope
Releasing class1_Weak with name Class1_Weak
Releasing class2_Weak with name Class2_Weak
```

It is recommended that you avoid creating circular dependencies, as shown in this section, but there are times when you may need them. For those times, remember that ARC needs some help to release them.

Summary

In this chapter, we took an in depth look at classes and structures. We saw what made them so similar and also what makes them so different. In the coming chapters, it will be important to remember that classes are reference types while structures are value types. We also looked at protocols and extensions.

At the end of this chapter, we looked at memory management with ARC and how to avoid strong reference cycles. While Swift, for the most part, takes care of memory management for us, it is important to understand how memory management works so we can avoid common mistakes such as the strong reference cycles.

As this chapter ends, we end the introduction to the Swift programming language. At this point, we have enough knowledge of the Swift language to begin writing our own applications; however, there is still much to learn.

In the following chapters, we will look in more depth at some of the concepts that we already discussed, such as optionals and subscripts. We will also show how to perform common tasks with Swift, such as parsing common file formats and handling concurrency. Finally, we will have some chapters that will help us write better code, such as a sample Swift style guide, and a chapter on design patterns.

6
Using Protocols and Protocol Extensions

While watching the presentations from WWDC 2015 about protocol extensions and **protocol-oriented programming (POP)**, I will admit that I was very skeptical. I have worked with **object-oriented programming (OOP)** for so long that I was unsure whether this new programming paradigm would solve all of the problems that Apple was claiming it would. Since I am not one who lets my skepticism get in the way of trying something new, I set up a new project that mirrored the one I was currently working on, but wrote the code using Apple's recommendations for POP. I also used protocol extensions extensively in the code. I can honestly say that I was amazed at how much cleaner the new project was compared to the original one. I believe that protocol extensions are going to be one of those defining features that set one programming language apart from the rest. I also believe that many major languages will soon have similar features.

In this chapter, you will learn about the following topics:

- How are protocols used as a type?
- How do we implement polymorphism in Swift using protocols?
- How do we use protocol extensions?
- Why we would want to use protocol extensions?

While protocol extensions are basically syntactic sugar, they are, in my opinion, one of the most important additions to the Swift programming language. With protocol extensions, we are able to provide method and property implementations to any type that conforms to a protocol. To really understand how useful protocols and protocol extensions are, let's get a better understanding of protocols.

While classes, structures, and enumerations can all conform to protocols in Swift, for this chapter, we will be focusing on classes and structures. Enumerations are used when we need to represent a finite number of cases, and while there are valid use cases where we would have an enumeration conform to a protocol, they are very rare in my experience. Just remember that anywhere we refer to a class or structure, we can also use an enumeration.

Let's begin exploring protocols by seeing how they are full-fledged types in Swift.

Protocols as types

Even though no functionality is implemented in a protocol, they are still considered a full-fledged type in the Swift programming language and can be used like any other type. What this means is that we can use protocols as a parameter type or as a return type in a function. We can also use them as the type for variables, constants, and collections. Let's take a look at some examples. For these few examples, we will use the following `PersonProtocol` protocol:

```
protocol PersonProtocol {
  var firstName: String { get set }
  var lastName: String { get set }
  var birthDate: Date { get set }
  var profession: String { get }
  init(firstName: String,lastName: String, birthDate: Date)
}
```

In this first example, a protocol is used as a parameter type and a return type for a function:

```
func updatePerson(person: PersonProtocol) -> PersonProtocol {
  // Code to update person goes here return person
}
```

In this example, the `updatePerson()` function accepts one parameter of the `PersonProtocol` protocol type and also returns a value of the `PersonProtocol` protocol type. This next example shows how to use a protocol as a type for constants, variables, or properties:

```
var myPerson: PersonProtocol
```

In this example, we create a variable of the `PersonProtocol` protocol type that is named `myPerson`. Protocols can also be used as the item type to store for a collection such as arrays, dictionaries, or sets:

```
var people: [PersonProtocol] = []
```

In this final example, we created an array of `PersonProtocol` protocol type. Even though the `PersonProtocol` protocol does not implement any functionality, we can still use protocols when we need to specify a type. However, a protocol cannot be instantiated in the same way as a class or a structure. This is because no functionality is implemented in a protocol. As an example, when trying to create an instance of the `PersonProtocol` protocol, as shown in the following example, we would receive a compile-time error:

```
var test = PersonProtocol(firstName: "Jon", lastName: "Hoffman",
birthDate:bDateProgrammer)
```

We can use the instance of any type that conforms to our protocol wherever the protocol type is required. As an example, if we've defined a variable to be of the `PersonProtocol` protocol type, we can then populate that variable with any class or structure that conforms to this protocol. For this example, let's assume that we have two types named, `SwiftProgrammer` and `FootballPlayer`, which conform to the `PersonProtocol` protocol:

```
var myPerson: PersonProtocol

myPerson = SwiftProgrammer(firstName: "Jon", lastName: "Hoffman",
                           birthDate: bDateProgrammer)
print("\(myPerson.firstName) \(myPerson.lastName)")

myPerson = FootballPlayer(firstName: "Dan", lastName: "Marino",
                          birthDate:bDatePlayer)
print("\(myPerson.firstName) \(myPerson.lastName)")
```

In this example, we start off by creating the `myPerson` variable of the `PersonProtocol` protocol type. We then set the variable with an instance of the `SwiftProgrammer` type and print out the first and last names. Next, we set the `myPerson` variable to an instance of the `FootballPlayer` type and print out the first and last names again. One thing to note is that Swift does not care whether the instance is a class or structure. The only thing that matters is that the type conforms to the `PersonProtocol` protocol type.

As we saw earlier, we can use the `PersonProtocol` protocol as the type for an array. This means that we can populate the array with instances of any type that conforms to the protocol. Once again, it does not matter whether the type is a class or a structure as long as it conforms to the `PersonProtocol` protocol.

Polymorphism with protocols

What we were seeing in the previous examples is a form of polymorphism. The word polymorphism comes from the Greek roots *poly*, meaning many, and *morphe*, meaning form. In programming languages, polymorphism is a single interface to multiple types (many forms). In the previous example, the single interface was the `PersonProtocol` protocol and the multiple types were any type that conforms to that protocol.

Polymorphism gives us the ability to interact with multiple types in a uniform manner. To illustrate this, we can extend the previous example where we created an array of the `PersonProtocol` types and looped through the array. We can then access each item in the array using the properties and methods defined in the `PersonProtocol` protocol, regardless of the actual type. Let's see an example of this:

```
for person in people {
  print("\(person.firstName) \(person.lastName):\(person.profession)")
}
```

We have mentioned a few times in this chapter that, when we define the type of a variable, constant, collection type, and so on to be a protocol type, we can then use the instance of any type that conforms to that protocol. This is a very important concept to understand and is one of the many things that make protocols and protocol extensions so powerful.

When we use a protocol to access instances, as shown in the previous example, we are limited to using only properties and methods that are defined in the protocol itself. If we want to use properties or methods that are specific to the individual types, we need to cast the instance to that type.

Type casting with protocols

Type casting is a way to check the type of the instance and/or to treat the instance as a specified type. In Swift, we use the `is` keyword to check whether an instance is a specific type and the `as` keyword to treat the instance as a specific type.

To start with, let's see how we would check the instance type using the `is` keyword. The following example shows how this is done:

```
for person in people {
  if person is SwiftProgrammer {
    print("\(person.firstName) is a Swift Programmer")
  }
}
```

In this example, we use the if conditional statement to check whether each element in the people array is an instance of the `SwiftProgrammer` type and, if so, we print that the person is a Swift programmer to the console. While this is a good method to check whether we have an instance of a specific class or structure, it is not very efficient if we want to check for multiple types. It would be more efficient to use a `switch` statement, as shown in the next example:

```
for person in people {
  switch person {
    case is SwiftProgrammer:
      print("\(person.firstName) is a Swift Programmer")
    case is FootballPlayer:
      print("\(person.firstName) is a Football Player")
    default:
      print("\(person.firstName) is an unknown type")
  }
}
```

In the previous example, we showed how to use the `switch` statement to check the instance type for each element of the array. To do this check, we use the `is` keyword in each of the `case` statements in an attempt to match the instance type.

In `Chapter 4`, *Control Flow and Functions*, we saw how to filter conditional statements with the `where` statement. We can also use the `where` statement with the `is` keyword to filter the array, as shown in the following example:

```
for person in people where person is SwiftProgrammer {
  print("\(person.firstName) is a Swift Programmer")
}
```

Now let's look at how we can cast an instance of a class or structure to a specific type. To do this, we would use the `as` keyword. Since the cast can fail if the instance is not of the specified type, the `as` keyword comes in two forms: `as?` and `as!`. With the `as?` form, if the casting fails, it returns a nil, and with the `as!` form, if the casting fails, we get a runtime error; therefore it is recommended to use the `as?` form unless we are absolutely sure of the instance type or we perform a check of the instance type prior to doing the cast.

While we do show examples of typecasting with as! in this book, so you are aware that it is there, we highly recommend that you do not use it in your projects because it can cause a runtime error.

Let's look at how we would use the `as?` keyword to cast an instance of a class or structure to a specified type:

```
for person in people {
  if let p = person as? SwiftProgrammer {
    print("\(person.firstName) is a Swift Programmer")
  }
}
```

Since the `as?` keyword returns an optional, we use optional binding to perform the cast, as shown in this example.

Now that we have covered the basics of protocols, let's dive into one of the most exciting features of Swift: protocol extensions.

Protocol extensions

Protocol extensions allow us to extend a protocol to provide method and property implementations to conforming types. They also allow us to provide common implementations to all the conforming types, eliminating the need to provide an implementation in each individual type or the need to create a class hierarchy. While protocol extensions may not seem too exciting, once you see how powerful they really are, they will transform the way you think about and write code.

Let's begin by looking at how we would use protocol extensions within a very simplistic example. We will start off by defining a protocol named `DogProtocol` as follows:

```
protocol DogProtocol {
  var name: String { get set }
  var color: String { get set }
}
```

With this protocol, we state that any type that conforms to the `DogProtocol` protocol must have the two properties of the `String` type named `name` and `color`. Next, let's define the three types that conform to this protocol. We will name these types `JackRussel`, `WhiteLab`, and `Mutt`. The following code shows how we would define these types:

```
struct JackRussel: DogProtocol {
  var name: String
  var color: String
}

class WhiteLab: DogProtocol {
  var name: String
```

```
    var color: String
    init(name: String, color: String) {
      self.name = name
      self.color = color
    }
  }

  struct Mutt: DogProtocol {
    var name: String
    var color: String
  }
```

We purposely created the `JackRussel` and `Mutt` types as structures and the `WhiteLab` type as a class to show the differences between how the two types are set up and to illustrate how they are treated the same when it comes to protocols and protocol extensions.

The biggest difference we can see in this example is that structure types provide a default initiator, but in the class we must provide the initiator to populate the properties.

Now let's say that we want to provide a method named `speak` to each type that conforms to the `DogProtocol` protocol. Prior to protocol extensions, we would have started off by adding the method definition to the protocol, as shown in the following code:

```
protocol DogProtocol {
  var name: String { get set }
  var color: String { get set }
  func speak() -> String
}
```

Once the method is defined in the protocol, we would then need to provide an implementation of the method in every type that conforms to the protocol. Depending on the number of types that conformed to this protocol, this could take a bit of time to implement and affect a lot of code. The following code sample shows how we might implement this method:

```
struct JackRussel: DogProtocol {
  var name: String
  var color: String
  func speak() -> String {
    return "Woof Woof"
  }
}

class WhiteLab: DogProtocol {
  var name: String
  var color: String
  init(name: String, color: String) {self.name = nameself.color = color}
```

```
   func speak() -> String {
   return "Woof Woof"
   }

}
struct Mutt: DogProtocol {
  var name: String
  var color: String
  func speak() -> String {
    return "Woof Woof"
  }

}
```

While this method works, it is not very efficient because anytime we update the protocol, we will need to update all the types that conform to it, and therefore duplicate a lot of code, as shown in this example. If we need to change the default behavior of the speak() method, we would have to go into each implementation and change the method. This is where protocol extensions come in.

With protocol extensions, we could take the speak() method definition out of the protocol itself and define it with the default behavior in the protocol extension.

 If we are implementing a method in a protocol extension, we are not required to define it in the protocol.

The following code shows how we would define the protocol and the protocol extension:

```
protocol DogProtocol {
  var name: String { get set }
  var color: String { get set }
}

extension DogProtocol {
  func speak() -> String {
    return "Woof Woof"
  }
}
```

We begin by defining the DogProtocol with the original two properties. We then create a protocol extension that extends it and contains the default implementation of the speak() method. With this code, there is no need to provide an implementation of the speak() method in all of the types that conform to the DogProtocol because they automatically receive the implementation as part of the protocol.

Let's see how this works by setting the three types that conform to the DogProtocol back to their original implementations and then they should receive the speak() method from the protocol extension:

```
struct JackRussel: DogProtocol {
  var name: String
  var color: String
}
class WhiteLab: DogProtocol {
  var name: String
  var color: String
  init(name: String, color: String) {
    self.name = name
    self.color = color
  }
}

struct Mutt: DogProtocol {
  var name: String
  var color: String
}
```

We can now use each of the types, as shown in the following code:

```
let dash = JackRussel(name: "Dash", color: "Brown and White")
let lily = WhiteLab(name: "Lily", color: "White")
let maple = Mutt(name: "Buddy", color: "Brown")
let dSpeak = dash.speak()   // returns "woof woof"
let lSpeak = lily.speak()   // returns "woof woof"
let bSpeak = maple.speak()   // returns "woof woof"
```

As we can see in this example, by adding the speak() method to the DogProtocol protocol extension, we are automatically adding that method to all the types that conform to the protocol. The speak() method in the protocol extension can be considered a default implementation of the method because we are able to override it in the type implementations. As an example, we could override the speak() method in the Mutt structure, as shown in the following code:

```
struct Mutt: DogProtocol {
  var name: String
  var color: String
  func speak() -> String {
    return "I am hungry"
  }
}
```

When we call the `speak()` method for an instance of the `Mutt` type, it will return the string, `I am hungry`.

In this chapter, we named our protocols with the `protocol` suffix. This was done to make it very clear that this was a protocol. This is not how we would normally name our types. The following example gives a better example of how we would properly name protocols. You can read additional information about Swift's naming conventions in the Swift API design guidelines: `https://swift.org/documentation/api-design-guidelines/#general-conventions`.

Now that we have seen how we would use protocols and protocol extensions, let's look at a more real-world example. In numerous apps across multiple platforms (iOS, Android, and Windows), I have had the requirement to validate user input as it is entered. This validation can be done very easily with regular expressions; however, we do not want various regular expressions littered throughout our code. It is very easy to solve this problem by creating different classes or structures that contain the validation code; however, we would have to organize these types to make them easy to use and maintain. Prior to protocol extensions in Swift, I would use a protocol to define the validation requirements and then created structures that would conform to the protocol for each validation that I needed. Let's look at this pre-protocol extension method.

A regular expression is a sequence of characters that defines a particular pattern. This pattern can then be used to search a string to see whether the string matches the pattern or contains a match of the pattern. Most major programming languages contain a regular expression parser, and if you are not familiar with regular expressions, it may be worthwhile to learn more about them.

The following code shows the `TextValidating` protocol that defines the requirements for any type that we want to use for text validation:

```
protocol TextValidating {
    var regExMatchingString: String { get }
    var regExFindMatchString: String { get }
    var validationMessage: String { get }
    func validateString(str: String) -> Bool
    func getMatchingString(str: String) -> String?
}
```

The Swift API design guidelines
(`https://swift.org/documentation/api-design-guidelines/`) state that protocols that describe what something is should be named as a noun while protocols that describe a capability should be named with a suffix of -able, -ible, or -ing. With this in mind, we named the text validation protocol `TextValidating`.

In this protocol, we define three properties and two methods that any type that conforms to a protocol must implement. The three properties are as follows:

- `regExMatchingString`: This is a regular expression string used to verify that the input string contains only valid characters.
- `regExFindMatchString`: This is a regular expression string used to retrieve a new string from the input string that contains only valid characters. This regular expression is generally used when we need to validate the input in real time as the user enters information because it will find the longest matching prefix of the input string.
- `validationMessage`: This is the error message to display if the input string contains non-valid characters.

The two methods for this protocol are as follows:

- `validateString`: This method will return `true` if the input string contains only valid characters. The `regExMatchingString` property will be used in this method to perform the match.
- `getMatchingString`: This method will return a new string that contains only valid characters. This method is generally used when we need to validate the input in real time as the user enters information because it will find the longest matching prefix of the input string. We will use the `regExFindMatchString` property in this method to retrieve the new string.

Now let's see how we can create a structure that conforms to this protocol. The following structure would be used to verify that the input string contains only alpha characters:

```
struct AlphaValidation1: TextValidating {
  static let sharedInstance = AlphaValidation1()
  private init(){}
  let regExFindMatchString = "^[a-zA-Z]{0,10}"
  let validationMessage = "Can only contain Alpha characters"
  var regExMatchingString: String {
    get {
      return regExFindMatchString + "$"
    }
  }
}
```

```
    func validateString(str: String) -> Bool {
      if let _ = str.range(of: regExMatchingString,
                           options: .regularExpression) {
        return true
      } else {
        return false
      }
    }
    func getMatchingString(str: String) -> String? {
      if let newMatch = str.range(of: regExFindMatchString,
                                  options:.regularExpression) {
        return str.substring(with:newMatch)
      } else {
        return nil
      }
    }
  }
}
```

In this implementation, the `regExFindMatchString` and `validationMessage` properties are stored properties, and the `regExMatchingString` property is a computed property. We also implement the `validateString()` and `getMatchingString()` methods within the structure.

Normally, we would have several different types that conform to the protocol where each one would validate a different type of input. As we can see from the `AlphaValidation1` structure, there is a bit of code involved with each validation type. A lot of the code would also be duplicated in each type. The code for both methods and the `regExMatchingString` property would probably be duplicated in every validation class. This is not ideal, but if we had wanted to avoid creating a class hierarchy with a superclass that contains the duplicate code (it is recommended that we prefer value types over reference types), prior to protocol extensions, we would have had no other choice. Now let's see how we would implement this using protocol extensions.

With protocol extensions, we need to think about the code a little differently. The big difference is that we neither need nor want to define everything in the protocol. With standard protocols, all the methods and properties that you would want to access using a protocol interface would have to be defined within the protocol.

With protocol extensions, it is preferable for us to not define a property or method in the protocol if we are going to be defining it within the protocol extension. Therefore, when we rewrite our text validation types with protocol extensions, TextValidating would be greatly simplified to look like this:

```
protocol TextValidating {
    var regExFindMatchString: String { get }
    var validationMessage: String { get }
}
```

In the original TextValidating protocol, we defined three properties and two methods. As we can see in this new protocol, we are only defining two properties. Now that we have our TextValidating protocol defined, let's create the protocol extension for it:

```
extension TextValidating {
    var regExMatchingString: String {
        get {
            return regExFindMatchString + "$"
        }
    }
    func validateString(str: String) -> Bool {
        if let _ = str.range(of:regExMatchingString,
                         options:.regularExpression){
            return true
        } else {
            return false
        }
    }
    func getMatchingString(str: String) -> String? {
        if let newMatch = str.range(of:regExFindMatchString,
                            options:.regularExpression) {
            return str.substring(with: newMatch)
        } else {
            return nil
        }
    }
}
```

In the TextValidating protocol extension, we define the two methods and the property that were defined in the original TextValidating protocol but were not defined in the new one. Now that we have created the protocol and protocol extension, we are able to define our new text validation types. In the following code, we define three structures that we will use to validate text as a user types it in:

```
struct AlphaValidation: TextValidating {
    static let sharedInstance = AlphaValidation()
    private init(){}
```

```
    let regExFindMatchString = "^[a-zA-Z]{0,10}"
    let validationMessage = "Can only contain Alpha characters"
}

struct AlphaNumericValidation: TextValidating {
  static let sharedInstance = AlphaNumericValidation()
  private init(){}
  let regExFindMatchString = "^[a-zA-Z0-9]{0,15}"
  let validationMessage = "Can only contain Alpha Numeric characters"
}

struct DisplayNameValidation: TextValidating {
  static let sharedInstance = DisplayNameValidation()
  privateinit(){}
  let regExFindMatchString = "^[\\s?[a-zA-Z0-9\\-_\\s]]{0,15}"
  let validationMessage = "Can only contain Alphanumeric Characters"
}
```

In each one of the text validation structures, we create a static constant and a private initializer so that we can use the structure as a singleton. For more information on the singleton pattern, please see *The singleton design pattern* section of Chapter 17, *Adopting Design Patterns in Swift*.

After we define the singleton pattern, all we do in each type is set the values for the regExFindMatchString and validationMessage properties. Now we have virtually no duplicate code. The only code that is duplicated is the code for the singleton pattern and that is not something we would want to put in the protocol extension because we would not want to force the singleton pattern on all the conforming types.

We can now use the text validation types as shown in the following code:

```
var testString = "abc123"

var alpha = AlphaValidation.sharedInstance
alpha.getMatchingString(str:testString)
alpha.validateString(str: testString)
```

In the previous code snippet, a new string is created to validate and get the shared instance of the AlphaValidation type. Then getMatchingString() is used to retrieve the longest matching prefix of the test string, which will be abc. Then, the validateString() method is used to validate the test string, but since the test string contains numbers, the method will return false.

Do I need to use protocols?

Do you need to use protocols and protocol extensions when you already know OOP? The short answer is no; however, it is highly recommended. In Chapter 7, *Protocol-Oriented Design*, we look at what makes protocol-oriented design so powerful to show you why you should prefer protocols with POP over OOP. By understanding protocols and protocol-oriented design, you will understand the Swift standard library better.

Swift's standard library

The Swift standard library defines a base layer of functionality for writing Swift applications. Everything we have used so far in this book is from the Swift standard library. The library defines the fundamental data types, such as the String, Int, and Double types. It also defines collections, optionals, global functions, and all the protocols that these types conform to.

One of the best sites to see everything that makes up the standard library is http://swiftdoc.org. This site lists all the types, protocols, operators, and globals that make up the standard library and contains documentation for all of it.

Let's look at how protocols are used in the standard library by looking at some of the http://swiftdoc.org/ documentation. When you first visit the home page, you will be greeted with a searchable list of everything that makes up the standard library. There is also a complete list of all Swift types that you can select from. Let's look at the Swift Array type by clicking on the Array link. This will take you to the documentation page for the Array type.

The http://swiftdoc.org/ documentation pages are extremely useful and contain a lot of information about the various types that make up the standard library, including samples of how to use them. For our discussion, here we are interested in the section labeled **Inheritance**:

Inheritance	BidirectionalCollection, Collection, CustomDebugStringConvertible, CustomReflectable, CustomStringConvertible, ExpressibleByArrayLiteral, MutableCollection, RandomAccessCollection, RangeReplaceableCollection, Sequence
	VIEW PROTOCOL HIERARCHY →

As we can see, the `Array` type conforms to 10 protocols, but this only shows us a small part of the picture. If we click on the view protocol hierarchy link, we can see the full protocol hierarchy that the array conforms to. This hierarchy looks like this:

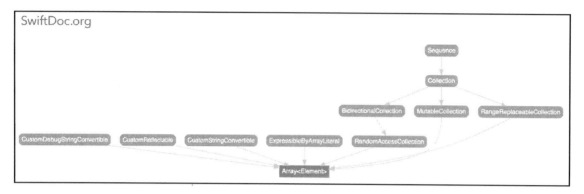

From what you have learned in this and previous chapters, you should be able to understand this diagram; however, you may not understand why the hierarchy is laid out like it is. In the next chapter, protocol-oriented design, we will look at how to design our applications and frameworks using a protocol-oriented approach. At the end of that chapter, we will take a closer look at this protocol hierarchy.

Summary

In this chapter, we saw that protocols are treated as full-fledged types by Swift. We also saw how polymorphism can be implemented in Swift with protocols. We concluded this chapter with an in-depth look at protocol extensions and saw how we would use them in Swift.

Protocols and protocol extensions are the backbone of Apple's new POP paradigm. This new model for programming has the potential to change the way we write and think about code. While we did not specifically cover POP in this chapter, getting to grips with the topics in this chapter gives us the solid understanding of protocols and protocol extensions needed to learn about this new programming model.

In the next chapter, we will look at how to use protocols and protocol extensions when we are designing our application.

Protocol-Oriented Design

When Apple announced Swift 2 at the **World Wide Developers Conference (WWDC)** in 2016, they also declared that Swift was the world's first **protocol-oriented programming (POP)** language. By its name, we might assume that protocol-oriented programming is all about the protocol; however, that would be a wrong assumption. Protocol-oriented programming is about so much more than just the protocol; it is actually a new way of not only writing applications, but also thinking about programming.

In this chapter, we will cover the following topics:

- What is the difference between OOP and POP design?
- What is protocol-oriented design?
- What is protocol composition?
- What is protocol inheritance?

Days after *Dave Abrahams* did his presentation on POP at WWDC 2016, there were numerous tutorials on the internet about POP that took a very object-oriented approach to it. By this statement, I mean the approach taken by these tutorials focused on replacing the superclass with protocols and protocol extensions. While protocols and protocol extensions are arguably two of the more important concepts of POP, these tutorials seem to be missing some very important concepts.

In this chapter, we will be comparing a protocol-oriented design with an object-oriented design to highlight some of the conceptual differences between the two. We will look at how we can use protocols and protocol extensions to replace superclasses, and how we can use POP to create a cleaner and easier-to-maintain code base. To do this, we will look at how to define animal types for a video game in both an object-oriented and a protocol-oriented way. Let's start off by defining the requirements for our animals.

Requirements

When we develop applications, we usually have a set of requirements that we need to develop toward. With that in mind, let's define the requirements for the animal types that we will be creating in this chapter:

- We will have three categories of animal: sea, land, and air.
- Animals may be members of multiple categories. For example, an alligator can be a member of both the land and sea categories.
- Animals may attack and/or move when they are on a tile that matches the categories they are in.
- Animals will start off with a certain number of hit points, and if those hit points reach 0 or less, then they will be considered dead.
- For our example here, we will define two animals, the `Lion` and `Alligator`, but we know that the number of animal types will grow as we develop the game.

We will start off by looking at how we would design our animal types using an object-oriented approach.

Object-oriented design

Before we start writing code, let's create a very basic diagram that shows how we would design the **Animal** class hierarchy. In this diagram, we will simply show the classes without much detail. This diagram will help us picture the class hierarchy in our mind. The following diagram shows the class hierarchy for the object-oriented design:

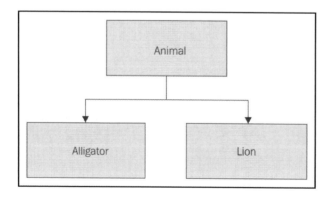

This diagram shows that we have one superclass named `Animal`, and two subclasses named `Alligator` and `Lion`. We may think with the three categories (land, air, and sea) that we would want to create a larger class hierarchy where the middle layer would contain the classes for the land, air, and sea animals. This would allow us to separate the code for each animal category; however, that is not possible with our requirements. The reason this is not possible is that any of the animal types can be members of multiple categories, and with a class hierarchy, each class can have one and only one superclass. This means that our `Animal` superclass will need to contain the code required for each of the three categories. Let's begin by looking at the code for the `Animal` superclass.

We will start the `Animal` superclass by defining 10 properties. These properties will define what type of animal it is and what type of attacks/movements it can do. We also define a property that will keep track of the hit points for the animal.

We defined these properties as `fileprivate` variables. We will need to set these properties in the subclasses that we defined in the same source file; however, we do not want external entities to change them. The preference is for these to be constants, but with an object-oriented approach; a subclass cannot set/change the value of a constant defined in a superclass. For this to work, the subclass will need to be defined in the same physical file as the superclass. You can read about `fileprivate` access control within the proposal at https://github.com/apple/swift-evolution/blob/master/proposals/25-scoped-access -level.md:

```
class Animal {
    fileprivate var landAnimal = false
    fileprivate var landAttack = false
    fileprivate var landMovement = false

    fileprivate var seaAnimal = false
    fileprivate var seaAttack = false
    fileprivate var seaMovement = false

    fileprivate var airAnimal = false
    fileprivate var airAttack = false
    fileprivate var airMovement = false

    fileprivate var hitPoints = 0
}
```

Next, we will define an initializer that will set the properties. We will set all the properties to `false` by default, and the hit points to zero. It will be up to the subclasses to set the appropriate properties that apply:

```
init() {
  landAnimal = false
  landAttack = false
  landMovement = false
  airAnimal = false
  airAttack = false
  airMovement = false
  seaAnimal = false
  seaAttack = false
  seaMovement = false
  hitPoints = 0
}
```

Since our properties are `fileprivate`, we need to create some getter methods so that we can retrieve their values. We will also create a couple of additional methods that will see if the animal is alive. We will need another method that will deduct hit points when the animal takes a hit:

```
func isLandAnimal() -> Bool {
  return landAnimal
}
func canLandAttack() -> Bool {
  return landAttack
}
func canLandMove() -> Bool {
  return landMovement
}
func isSeaAnimal() -> Bool {
  return seaAnimal
}
func canSeaAttack() -> Bool {
  return seaAttack
}
func canSeaMove() -> Bool {
  return seaMovement
}
func isAirAnimal() -> Bool {
  return airAnimal
}
func canAirAttack() -> Bool {
  return airAttack
}
func canAirMove() -> Bool {
```

```
      return airMovement
    }
    func doLandAttack() {}
    func doLandMovement() {}
    func doSeaAttack() {}
    func doSeaMovement() {}
    func doAirAttack() {}
    func doAirMovement() {}
    func takeHit(amount: Int) {
      hitPoints -= amount
    }
    func hitPointsRemaining() -> Int {
      return hitPoints
    }
    func isAlive() -> Bool {
      return hitPoints>0 ? true : false
    }
```

One big disadvantage of this design, as noted previously, is that all the subclasses need to be in the same physical file as the Animal superclass. Considering how large the animal classes can be once we get in all of the game logic, we probably do not want all of these types in the same file. To avoid this, we could set the properties to internal or public, but that would not prevent the values from being changed by instances of other types. This is a major drawback of our object-oriented design.

Now that we have our Animal superclass, we can create the Alligator and Lion classes, which will be subclasses of the Animal class:

```
    class Lion: Animal {
      override init() {
        super.init()
        landAnimal = true
        landAttack = true
        landMovement = true
        hitPoints = 20
      }
      override func doLandAttack() {
        print("Lion Attack")
      }
      override func doLandMovement() {
        print("Lion Move")
      }
    }

    class Alligator: Animal {
      override init() {
```

```
      super.init()
      landAnimal = true
      landAttack = true
      landMovement = true
      seaAnimal = true
      seaAttack = true
      seaMovement = true
      hitPoints = 35
    }
    override func doLandAttack() {
      print("Alligator Land Attack")
    }
    override func doLandMovement() {
      print("Alligator Land Move")
    }
    override func doSeaAttack() {
      print("Alligator Sea Attack")
    }
    override func doSeaMovement() {
      print("Alligator Sea Move")
    }

  }
```

As we can see, these classes set the functionality needed for each animal. The `Lion` class contains the functionality for a land animal and the `Alligator` class contains the functionality for both land and sea animals.

Another disadvantage of this object-oriented design is that we do not have a single point that defines what type of animal (air, land, or sea) this is. It is very easy to set the wrong flag or add the wrong function when we cut and paste, or type in the code. This may lead us to have an animal like this:

```
class landAnimal: Animal {
  override init() {
    super.init()
    landAnimal = true
    airAttack = true
    landMovement = true
    hitPoints = 20
  }
  override func doLandAttack() {
    print("Lion Attack")
  }
  override func doLandMovement() {
    print("Lion Move")
```

```
        }
    }
```

In the previous code, we set the `landAnimal` property to `true`; however, we accidentally set the `airAttack` to `true` as well. This will give us an animal that can move on land, but cannot attack, since the `landAttack` property is not set. Hopefully, we would catch these types of errors in testing; however, as we will see later in this chapter, a protocol-oriented approach would help prevent coding errors like this.

Since both classes have the same `Animal` superclass, we can use polymorphism to access them through the interface provided by the `Animal` superclass:

```
var animals = [Animal]()

animals.append(Alligator())
animals.append(Alligator())
animals.append(Lion())

for (index, animal) in animals.enumerated() {
  if animal.isAirAnimal() {
    print("Animal at \(index) is Air")
  }
  if animal.isLandAnimal() {
    print("Animal at \(index) is Land")
  }
  if animal.isSeaAnimal() {
    print("Animal at \(index) is Sea")
  }
}
```

The way we designed the animal types here would work; however, there are several drawbacks in this design. The first drawback is the large monolithic `Animal` superclass. Those who are familiar with designing characters for video games probably realize how much functionality is missing from this superclass and its subclasses. This is on purpose, so that we can focus on the design and not the functionality. For those who are not familiar with designing characters for video games, trust me when I say that this class may get very large.

Another drawback is not being able to define constants in the superclass that the subclasses can set. We could define various initializers for the superclass that would correctly set the constants for the different animal categories; however, these initializers will become pretty complex and hard to maintain as we add more animals. The builder pattern could help us with the initialization, but as we are about to see, a protocol-oriented design would be even better.

One final drawback that I am going to point out is the use of flags (`landAnimal`, `seaAnimal`, and `airAnimal` properties) to define the type of animal, and the type of attack and movements an animal can perform. If we do not correctly set these flags, then the animal will not behave correctly. As an example, if we set the `seaAnimal` flag rather than the `landAnimal` flag in the `Lion` class, then the lion will not be able to move or attack on land. Trust me, it is very easy, even for the most experienced developers, to set flags wrongly.

Now let's look at how we would define this same functionality in a protocol-oriented way.

Protocol-oriented design

Just like with our object-oriented design, we will start off with a diagram that shows the types needed and the relationships between them. The following diagram shows our protocol-oriented design:

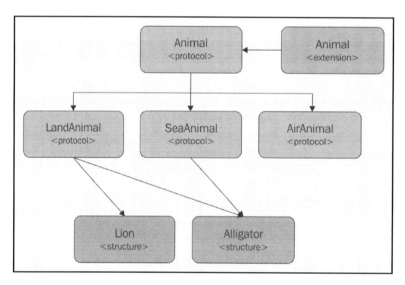

As we can see, the POP design is quite different from the OOP design. In this design, we use three techniques that make POP significantly different from OOP. These techniques are protocol inheritance, protocol composition, and protocol extensions. We looked at protocol extensions in the previous chapter, but we have not covered protocol inheritance or composition yet. It is important to understand these concepts, so before we go into the design, let's look at what protocol inheritance and protocol composition are.

Protocol inheritance

Protocol inheritance is where one protocol can inherit the requirements from one or more protocols. This is similar to class inheritance in OOP, but instead of inheriting functionality, we are inheriting requirements. We can also inherit requirements from multiple protocols, whereas a class in Swift can have only one superclass. Let's start off by defining four protocols, named Name, Age, Fur, and Hair:

```
protocol Name {
  var firstName: String { get set }
  var lastName: String { get set }
}

protocol Age {
  var age: Double { get set }
}

protocol Fur {
  var furColor: String { get set }
}

protocol Hair {
  var hairColor: String { get set }
}
```

Each of the four protocols has different requirements.

 There is one thing that I would like to point out. If you find yourself creating protocols with single requirements (as shown in this example), you probably want to reconsider your overall design. Protocols should not be this granular because we end up with too many protocols and they become hard to manage. We are using smaller protocols here as examples.

Now let's look at how we can use these protocols and protocol inheritance to create additional protocols. We will define two more protocols, named Person and Dog:

```
protocol Person: Name, Age, Hair {
  var height: Double { get set }
}

protocol Dog: Name, Age, Fur {
  var breed: String { get set }
}
```

In this example, any type that conforms to the `Person` protocol will need to fulfill the requirements of the `Name`, `Age`, and `Hair` protocols, as well as the requirements defined within the `Person` protocol itself. Any type that conforms to the `Dog` protocol will need to fulfill the requirements of the `Name`, `Age`, and `Fur` protocols as well as the requirements defined within the `Dog` protocol itself. This is the basis of protocol inheritance, where we can have one protocol inherit the requirements of one or more protocols.

Protocol inheritance is extremely powerful because we can define several smaller protocols and mix/match them to create larger protocols. You will want to be careful not to create protocols that are too granular because they will become hard to maintain and manage.

Protocol composition

Protocol composition allows types to conform to more than one protocol. This is one of the many advantages that protocol-oriented design has over object-oriented design. With object-oriented design, a class can have only one superclass. This can lead to very large, monolithic superclasses, as we saw in the *Object-oriented design* section of this chapter. With protocol-oriented design, we are encouraged to create multiple smaller protocols with very specific requirements. Let's look at how protocol composition works.

Let's add another protocol, named `Occupation`, to our example from the *Protocol inheritance* section:

```
protocol Occupation {
   var occupationName: String { get set }
   var yearlySalary:Double { get set }
   var experienceYears: Double { get set }
}
```

Next let's create a new type named `Programmer` that will conform to both the `Person` and `Occupation` protocols:

```
struct Programmer: Person, Occupation {
   var firstName: String
   var lastName: String
   var age: Double
   var hairColor: String
   var height: Double
   var occupationName: String
   var yearlySalary: Double
   var experienceYears: Double
}
```

In this example, the `Programmer` structure conforms to all the requirements from both the `Person` and `Occupation` protocols. Keep in mind that the `Person` protocol is a composite of the requirements from the `Name`, `Age`, `Hair`, and `Person` protocols; therefore, the `Programmer` type will need to conform to all those protocols plus the `Occupation` protocol.

Once again, I want to warn you not to make your protocols too granular. Protocol inheritance and composition are really powerful features, but can also cause problems if used wrongly.

Protocol composition and inheritance may not seem that powerful on their own; however, when we combine them with protocol extensions, we have a very powerful programming paradigm. Let's look at how powerful this paradigm is.

Protocol-oriented design

We will begin by rewriting the `Animal` superclass as a protocol:

```
protocol Animal {
  var hitPoints: Int { get set }
}
```

In the `Animal` protocol, the only item that we are defining is the `hitPoints` property. If we were putting in all the requirements for an animal in a video game, this protocol would contain all the requirements that would be common to every animal. To be consistent with our object-oriented design, we only need to add the `hitPoints` property to this protocol.

Next, we need to add an `Animal` protocol extension, which will contain the functionality that is common for all types that conform to the protocol. Our `Animal` protocol extension would contain the following code:

```
extension Animal {
  mutating func takeHit(amount: Int) {
  hitPoints -= amount
}
func hitPointsRemaining() -> Int {
  return hitPoints
}
func isAlive() -> Bool {
  return hitPoints> 0 ? true : false
  }
}
```

The `Animal` protocol extension contains the same `takeHit()`, `hitPointsRemaining()`, and `isAlive()` methods that we saw in the `Animal` superclass from the object-oriented example. Any type that conforms to the `Animal` protocol will automatically inherit these three methods.

Now let's define our `LandAnimal`, `SeaAnimal`, and `AirAnimal` protocols. These protocols will define the requirements for the land, sea, and air animals respectively:

```
protocol LandAnimal: Animal {
  var landAttack: Bool { get }
  var landMovement: Bool { get }

  func doLandAttack()
  func doLandMovement()
}

protocol SeaAnimal: Animal {
  var seaAttack: Bool { get }
  var seaMovement: Bool { get }

  func doSeaAttack()
  func doSeaMovement()
}

protocol AirAnimal: Animal {
  var airAttack: Bool { get }
  var airMovement: Bool { get }

  func doAirAttack()
  func doAirMovement()
}
```

Unlike the `Animal` superclass in the object-oriented design, these three protocols only contain the functionality needed for their particular type of animal. Each of these protocols only contains four lines of code, while the `Animal` superclass from the object-oriented example contains significantly more. This makes our protocol design much easier to read and manage. The protocol design is also much safer, because the functionality for the various animal types is isolated in their own protocol rather than being embedded in a giant superclass. We are also able to avoid the use of flags to define the animal category and, instead, define the category of the animal by the protocols it conforms to.

In a full design, we would probably need to add some protocol extensions for each of the animal types, but once again, to be consistent with our object-oriented design, we do not need them for our example here.

Now, let's look at how we would create our `Lion` and `Alligator` types using the protocol-oriented design:

```
struct Lion: LandAnimal {
  var hitPoints = 20
  let landAttack = true
  let landMovement = true

  func doLandAttack() {
    print("Lion Attack")
  }
  func doLandMovement() {
    print("Lion Move")
  }
}

struct Alligator: LandAnimal, SeaAnimal {
  var hitPoints = 35
  let landAttack = true
  let landMovement = true
  let seaAttack = true
  let seaMovement = true

  func doLandAttack() {
    print("Alligator Land Attack")
  }
  func doLandMovement() {
    print("Alligator Land Move")
  }
  func doSeaAttack() {
    print("Alligator Sea Attack")
  }
  func doSeaMovement() {
    print("Alligator Sea Move")
  }
}
```

Notice that we specify that the `Lion` type conforms to the `LandAnimal` protocol, while the `Alligator` type conforms to both the `LandAnimal` and `SeaAnimal` protocols. As we saw previously, having a single type that conforms to multiple protocols is called **protocol composition**, and is what allows us to use smaller protocols, rather than one giant monolithic superclass, as we did in the object-oriented example.

Both the `Lion` and `Alligator` types originate from the `Animal` protocol; therefore, they will inherit the functionality added with the `Animal` protocol extension. If our animal type protocols also had extensions, then they would also inherit the function added by those extensions as well. With protocol inheritance, composition, and extensions, our concrete types contain only the functionality needed by the particular animal types that they conform to, unlike in the object-oriented design, where each animal would contain all of the functionality from the huge, single superclass.

Since the `Lion` and `Alligator` types originate from the `Animal` protocol, we can still use polymorphism as we did in the object-oriented example. Let's look at how this works:

```
var animals = [Animal]()

animals.append(Alligator())
animals.append(Alligator())
animals.append(Lion())

for (index, animal) in animals.enumerated() {
  if let _ = animal as? AirAnimal {
    print("Animal at \(index) is Air")
  }
  if let _ = animal as? LandAnimal {
    print("Animal at \(index) is Land")
  }
  if let _ = animal as? SeaAnimal {
    print("Animal at \(index) is Sea")
  }
}
```

In this example, we create an array that will contain `Animal` types named `animals`. We then create two instances of the `Alligator` type and one instance of the `Lion` type that are added to the `animals` array. Finally, we use a `for-in` loop to loop through the array and print out the animal type based on the protocol that the instance conforms to.

Using the where statement with protocols

With protocols, we are able to use the `where` statement to filter the instances of our types. For example, if we only want to get the instances that conform to the `SeaAnimal` protocol, we can create a `for` loop as follows:

```
for (index, animal) in animals.enumerated() where animal is SeaAnimal {
  print("Only Sea Animal: \(index)")
}
```

This will retrieve only the animals that conform to the `SeaAnimal` protocol. This is a lot safer than using flags as we did in the object-oriented design.

Structures versus classes

You may have noticed that in the object-oriented design we used classes, while in protocol-oriented design we used structures. Classes, which are reference types, are one of the pillars of object-oriented programming and every major object-oriented programming language uses them. For Swift, Apple has said that we should prefer value types (structures) to reference types (classes). While this may seem odd for anyone who has extensive experience with object-oriented programming, there are several good reasons for this recommendation.

The biggest reason, in my opinion, for using structures (value types) over classes is the performance gain we get. Value types do not incur the additional overhead for reference counting that reference types incur. Value types are also stored on the stack, which provides better performance as compared to reference types, which are stored on the heap. It is also worth noting that copying values is relatively cheap in Swift.

Keep in mind that, as our value types get large, the performance cost of copying can negate the other performance gains of value types. In the Swift standard library, Apple has implemented copy-on-write behavior to reduce the overhead of copying large value types.

With copy-on-write behavior, we do not create a new copy of our value type when we assign it to a new variable. The copy is postponed until one of the instances changes the value. This means that, if we have an array of one million numbers, when we pass this array to another array we will not make a copy of the one million numbers until one of the arrays changes. This can greatly reduce the overhead incurred from copying instances of our value types.

Value types are also a lot safer than reference types, because we do not have multiple references pointing to the same instance, as we do with reference types. This really becomes apparent when we are dealing with a multithreaded environment. Value types are also safer because we do not have memory leaks caused by common programming errors, such as the strong reference cycles discussed in `Chapter 5`, *Classes and Structures*.

Don't worry if you do not understand some of the items discussed in this section. The thing to understand is that value types, like structures, are safer, and for the most part provide better performance in Swift, as compared to reference types, such as classes.

Now that we have a better understanding of protocol-oriented design, let's once again look at the array structure provided in the Swift standard library.

The array structure

At the end of Chapter 6, *Using Protocols and Protocol Extensions* we looked at the array structure provided in the Swift standard library. Now that we have a better understanding of protocol-oriented design, let's look at the protocol hierarchy for this structure again. The following figure shows the protocol hierarchy:

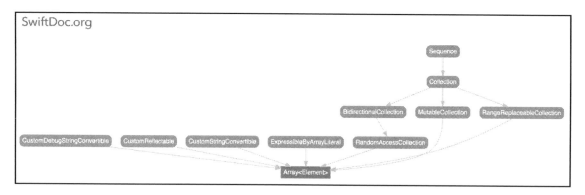

As we can see, the protocol hierarchy for the array structure uses protocol-oriented design. Protocol inheritance is used in several places within the array protocol hierarchy. For example, the Collection protocol inherits from the Sequence protocol, and the MutableCollection protocol inherits from the Collection protocol.

Protocol composition is used because the array protocol inherits directly from seven different protocols. When you add in the protocol inheritance and composition, the array actually conforms to all ten protocols shown in this diagram.

Summary

As we have read through this chapter and looked at some of the advantages that protocol-oriented design has over object-oriented design, we may think that protocol-oriented design is clearly superior to object-oriented design. However, this assumption would not be entirely correct.

Object-oriented design has been around since the 1970s and is a tried and true programming paradigm. Protocol-oriented design is the new kid on the block and was designed to correct some of the issues with object-oriented design.

Object-oriented and protocol-oriented design have similar philosophies, such as creating custom types that model real-world objects, and polymorphism to use a single interface to interact with multiple types. The difference is how these philosophies are implemented.

To me, the code base in a project that uses protocol-oriented design is much safer, easier to read, and easier to maintain as compared to a project that uses an object-oriented design. This does not mean that I am going to stop using object-oriented design altogether. I can still see a need for class hierarchy in certain instances.

Remember that, when we are designing our application, we should always use the right tool for the job. We would not want to use a chainsaw to cut a piece of 2 x 4 lumber, but we also would not want to use a skill saw to cut down a tree. Therefore, the winner is the programmer who has the choice of using different programming paradigms rather than being limited to only one.

In the next chapter, we will look at how to write safer code with error handling.

8
Writing Safer Code with Availability and Error Handling

When I first started writing applications with Objective-C, one of the most noticeable deficiencies was the lack of exception handling. Most modern programming languages, such as Java and C#, use `try...catch` blocks, or something similar, for exception handling. While Objective-C did have the `try...catch` block, it wasn't used within the Cocoa framework itself, and it never really felt like a true part of the language. I have significant experience in C, so I was able to understand how Apple's frameworks received and responded to errors. To be honest, I sometimes preferred this method, even though I had grown accustomed to exception handling with Java and C#. When Swift was first introduced, I was hoping that Apple would put true error handling into the language so we would have the option of using it; however, it was not in the initial release of Swift. When Swift 2 was released, Apple added error handling to Swift. While this error handling may look similar to exception handling in Java and C#, there are some very significant differences.

We will cover the following topics in this chapter:

- How to use the `do-catch` block in Swift?
- How to represent errors?
- How to use the `defer` statement?
- How to use the availability attribute?

Native error handling

Languages such as Java and C# generally refer to the error handling process as exception handling. Within the Swift documentation, Apple refers to this process as error handling. While on the outside, Java and C# exception handling may look somewhat similar to Swift's error handling, there are some significant differences that those familiar with exception handling in other languages will notice throughout this chapter.

Representing errors

Before we can really understand how error handling works in Swift, we must see how we would represent an error. In Swift, errors are represented by values of types that conform to the `Error` protocol. Swift's enumerations are very well suited to modeling error conditions because we have a finite number of error conditions to represent.

Let's look at how we would use an enumeration to represent an error. For this, we will define a fictitious error named `MyError` with three error conditions: `Minor`, `Bad`, and `Terrible`:

```
enum MyError: Error {
  case Minor
  case Bad
  case Terrible
}
```

In this example, we define that the `MyError` enumeration conforms to the `Error` protocol. We then define the three error conditions: `Minor`, `Bad`, and `Terrible`. That is all there is to defining a basic error condition.

We can also use the associated values with our error conditions to allow us to add more details about the error condition. Let's say that we want to add a description to the `Terrible` error condition. We would do it like this:

```
enum MyError: Error {
  case Minor
  case Bad
  case Terrible(description:String)
}
```

Those who are familiar with exception handling in Java and C# can see that representing errors in Swift is a lot cleaner and easier, because we do not need to create a lot of boilerplate code or create a full class. With Swift, it can be as simple as defining an enumeration with our error conditions. Another advantage that we have is that it is very easy to define multiple error conditions and group them together so that all related error conditions are of one type.

Now let's see how we can model errors in Swift. For this example, let's look at how we would assign numbers to players on a baseball team. For a baseball team, every new player who is called up is assigned a unique number. This number must also be within a certain range, because only two numbers fit on a baseball jersey. Therefore, we would have three error conditions: number is too large, number is too small, and number is not unique. The following example shows how we might represent these error conditions:

```
enum PlayerNumberError: Error {
  case NumberTooHigh(description: String)
  case NumberTooLow(description: String)
  case NumberAlreadyAssigned
}
```

With the `PlayerNumberError` type, we define three very specific error conditions that tell us exactly what went wrong. These error conditions are also grouped together in one type since they are all related to assigning the players' numbers.

This method of defining errors allows us to define very specific errors that let our code know exactly what went wrong if an error condition occurs. It also lets us group the errors so that all related errors can be defined in the same type.

Now that we know how to represent errors, let's look at how we would throw errors.

Throwing errors

When an error occurs in a function, the code that called the function must be made aware of it; this is called **throwing the error**. When a function throws an error, it assumes that the code that called the function, or some code further up the chain, will catch and recover appropriately from the error.

To throw an error from a function, we use the `throws` keyword. This keyword lets the code that called it know that an error may be thrown from the function. Unlike exception handling in other languages, we do not list the specific error types that may be thrown.

Since we do not list the specific error types that may be thrown from a function within the function's definition, it would be good practice to list them in the documentation and comments for the function, so that other developers who use the function know what error types to catch.

Soon we will look at how we can throw errors. But first, let's add a fourth error to our `PlayerNumberError` type that we defined earlier. This error condition is thrown if we are trying to retrieve a player by their number, but no player has been assigned that number. The new `PlayerNumberError` type will now look similar to this:

```
enum PlayerNumberError: Error {
   case NumberTooHigh(description: String)
   case NumberTooLow(description: String)
   case NumberAlreadyAssigned
   case NumberDoesNotExist
}
```

To demonstrate how to throw errors, let's create a `BaseballTeam` structure that will contain a list of players for a given team. These players will be stored in a dictionary object named `players`, and will use the player's number as the key, because we know that each player must have a unique number. The `BaseballPlayer` type, which will be used to represent a single player, will be a `typealias` for a tuple type, and is defined like this:

```
typealias BaseballPlayer = (firstName: String, lastName: String, number:
Int)
```

In this `BaseballTeam` structure, we will have two methods. The first one will be named `addPlayer()`. This method will accept one parameter of the `BaseballPlayer` type and will attempt to add the player to the team. This method can also throw one of three error conditions: `NumberTooHigh`, `NumberTooLow`, or `NumberAlreadyExists`. Here is how we would write this method:

```
mutating func addPlayer(player: BaseballPlayer) throws {
   guard player.number < maxNumber else {
     throw PlayerNumberError.NumberTooHigh(description: "Max number is
\ (maxNumber)")
   }
   guard player.number > minNumber else {
     throw PlayerNumberError.NumberTooLow(description: "Min number is
\ (minNumber)")
   }
   guard players[player.number] == nil else {
     throw PlayerNumberError.NumberDoesNotExist
```

```
    }
    players[player.number] = player
  }
```

We can see that the `throws` keyword is added to the method's definition. The `throws` keyword lets any code that calls this method know that it may throw an error and the error must be handled. We then use the three guard statements to verify that the number is not too large, not too small, and is unique in the `players` dictionary. If any of the conditions are not met, we throw the appropriate error using the `throws` keyword. If we make it through all three checks, the player is then added to the `players` dictionary.

The second method that we will be adding to the `BaseballTeam` structure is the `getPlayerByNumber()` method. This method will attempt to retrieve the baseball player that is assigned a given number. If no player is assigned that number, this method will throw a `NumberDoesNotExist` error. The `getPlayerByNumber()` method will look similar to this:

```
func getPlayerByNumber(number: Int) throws -> BaseballPlayer {
  if let player = players[number] {
    return player
  } else {
    throw PlayerNumberError.NumberDoesNotExist
  }
}
```

We have added the `throws` keyword to this method definition as well; however, this method also has a return type. When we use the `throws` keyword with a return type, it must be placed before the return type in the method's definition.

Within the method, we attempt to retrieve the baseball player with the number that is passed into the method. If we are able to retrieve the player, we return it; otherwise, we throw the `NumberDoesNotExist` error. Note that if we throw an error from a method that has a return type, a return value is not required.

Now let's see how we would catch an error with Swift.

Catching errors

When an error is thrown from a function, we need to catch it in the code that called it; this is done using the do-catch block. The do-catch block takes the following syntax:

```
do {
  try [Some function that throws]
  [code if no error was thrown]
} catch [pattern] {
  [Code if function threw error]
}
```

If an error is thrown, it is propagated out until it is handled by a catch clause. The catch clause consists of the catch keyword, followed by a pattern to match the error against. If the error matches the pattern, the code within the catch block is executed.

Let's look at how we can use the do-catch block by calling both the getPlayerByNumber() and addPlayer() methods of the BaseballTeam structure. Let's look at the getPlayerByNumber() method first, since it only throws one error condition:

```
do {
  let player = try myTeam.getPlayerByNumber(number: 34)
  print("Player is \(player.firstName) \(player.lastName)")
} catch PlayerNumberError.NumberDoesNotExist {
  print("No player has that number")
}
```

Within this example, the do-catch block calls the getPlayerByNumber() method of the BaseballTeam structure. This method will throw the NumberDoesNotExist error condition if no player on the team has been assigned this number; therefore, we attempt to match this error in the catch statement.

Anytime an error is thrown within a do-catch block, the remainder of the code within the block is skipped and the code within the catch block, which matches the error, is executed. Therefore, in our example, if the NumberDoesNotExist error is thrown by the getPlayerByNumber() method, then the print statement is never reached.

We do not have to include a pattern after the catch statement. If a pattern is not included after the catch statement, or if we put in an underscore, the catch statement will match all error conditions. For example, either one of the following two catch statements will catch all errors:

```
do {
  // our statements
} catch {
```

```
  // our error conditions
}

do {
  // our statements
} catch _ {
  // our error conditions
}
```

If we want to capture the error, we can use the `let` keyword, as shown in the following example:

```
do {
  // our statements
} catch let error {
  print("Error:\(error)")
}
```

Now, let's look at how we can use the `catch` statement, similar to a `switch` statement, to catch different error conditions. To do this, we will call the `addPlayer()` method of the `BaseballTeam` struct:

```
do {
  try myTeam.addPlayer(player:("David", "Ortiz", 34))
} catch PlayerNumberError.NumberTooHigh(let description) {
  print("Error: \(description)")
} catch PlayerNumberError.NumberTooLow(let description) {
  print("Error: \(description)")
} catch PlayerNumberError.NumberAlreadyAssigned {
  print("Error: Number already assigned")
}
```

In this example, we have three catch statements. Each catch statement has a different pattern to match; therefore, they will each match a different error condition. If you recall, the `NumberToHigh` and `NumberToLow` error conditions have associated values. To retrieve the associated value, we use the let statement within the parentheses, as shown in the example.

It is always good practice to make your last `catch` statement an empty `catch` statement so that it will catch any error that did not match any of the patterns in the previous `catch` statements. Therefore, the previous example should be rewritten like this:

```
do {
  try myTeam.addPlayer(player:("David", "Ortiz", 34))
} catch PlayerNumberError.NumberTooHigh(let description) {
  print("Error: \(description)")
} catch PlayerNumberError.NumberTooLow(let description) {
```

```
  print("Error: \(description)")
} catch PlayerNumberError.NumberAlreadyAssigned {
  print("Error: Number already assigned")
} catch {
  print("Error: Unknown Error")
}
```

We can also let the errors propagate out rather than immediately catch them. To do this, we just need to add the `throws` keyword to the function definition. For instance, in the following example, rather than catching the error, we could let it propagate out to the code that called the function, like this:

```
func myFunc() throws {
  try myTeam.addPlayer(player:("David", "Ortiz", 34))
}
```

If we are certain that an error will not be thrown, we can call the function using a forced-try expression, which is written as `try!`. The forced-try expression disables error propagation and wraps the function call in a runtime assertion that no error will be thrown from this call. If an error is thrown, you will get a runtime error, so be very careful when using this expression.

It is highly recommended that you avoid using the forced-`try` expression in production code since it can cause a runtime error and cause your application to crash.

When I work with exceptions in languages such as Java and C#, I see a lot of empty `catch` blocks. This is where we need to catch the exception, because one might be thrown; however, we do not want to do anything with it. In Swift, the code would look something like this:

```
do {
  let player = try myTeam.getPlayerByNumber(number: 34)
  print("Player is \(player.firstName) \(player.lastName)")
} catch {}
```

Seeing code like this is one of the things that I dislike about exception handling. Well, the Swift developers have an answer for this: the `try?`. The `try?` attempts to perform an operation that may throw an error and converts it to an optional value; therefore, the results of the operation will be nil if an error was thrown, or the result of the operation if there was no error thrown.

Since the results of `try?` are returned in the form of an optional, we would normally use this with optional binding. We could rewrite the previous example like this:

```
if let player = try? myTeam.getPlayerByNumber(number: 34) {
  print("Player is \(player.firstName) \(player.lastName)")
}
```

As we can see, this makes our code much cleaner and easier to read.

If we need to perform some cleanup action, regardless of whether or not we had any errors, we can use a `defer` statement. We use `defer` statements to execute a block of code just before the code execution leaves the current scope. The following example shows how we can use the `defer` statement:

```
func deferFunction(){
  print("Function started")
  var str: String?

  defer {
    print("In defer block")
    if let s = str {
      print("str is \(s)")
    }
  }
  str = "Jon"
  print("Function finished")
}
```

If we called this function, the first line that is printed to the console is `Function started`. The execution of the code would skip over the `defer` block, and `Function finished` would then be printed to the console. Finally, the `defer` block of code would be executed just before we leave the function's scope, and we would see the message `In defer block`. The following is the output from this function:

```
Function started
Function finished
In defer block
str is Jon
```

The `defer` block will always be called before the execution leaves the current scope, even if an error is thrown. The defer statement is very useful when we want to make sure we perform all the necessary cleanup, even if an error is thrown. For example, if we successfully open a file to write to, we will always want to make sure we close that file, even if we have an error during the write operation.

In this case, we could put the file closed functionality in a `defer` block to make sure that the file is always closed prior to leaving the current scope.

Next, let's look at how we would use the new availability attribute with Swift.

The availability attribute

Using the latest SDK gives us access to all the latest features for the platform that we are developing for; however, there are times when we want to also target older platforms. Swift allows us to use the availability attribute to safely wrap code to run only when the correct version of the operating system is available. The availability was first introduced in Swift 2.

 The availability attribute is only available when we use Swift on Apple platforms.

The availability blocks essentially let us, if we are running the specified version of the operating system or higher, run this code or otherwise run some other code. There are two ways in which we can use the availability attribute. The first way allows us to execute a specific block of code that can be used with an `if` or a `guard` statement. The second way allows us to mark a method or type as available only on certain platforms.

The availability attribute accepts up to six comma-separated arguments that allow us to define the minimum version of the operating system or application extension needed to execute our code. These arguments are as follows:

- **iOS**: This is the minimum iOS version that is compatible with our code
- **OSX**: This is the minimum OS X version that is compatible with our code
- **watchOS**: This is the minimum watchOS version that is compatible with our code
- **tvOS**: This is the minimum tvOS version that is compatible with our code
- **iOSApplicationExtension**: This is the minimum iOS application extension that is compatible with our code
- **OSXApplicationExtension**: This is the minimum OS X application extension that is compatible with our code

After the argument, we specify the minimum version that is required. We only need to include the arguments that are compatible with our code. As an example, if we are writing an iOS application, we only need to include the iOS argument in the availability attribute. We end the argument list with an * (asterisk). Let's look at how we would execute a specific block of code only if we meet the minimum requirements:

```
if #available(iOS 9.0, OSX 10.10, watchOS 2, *) {
  //Available for iOS 9, OSX 10.10, watchOS 2 or above print("Minimum
requirements met")
} else {
  //Block on anything below the above minimum requirements print("Minimum
requirements not met")
}
```

In this example, the `if #available(iOS 9.0, OSX 10.10, watchOS 2, *)` line of code prevents the block of code from executing when the application is run on a system that does not meet the specified minimum operating system version. In this example, we also use the `else` statement to execute a separate block of code if the operating system did not meet the minimum requirements.

We can also restrict access to a function or a type. In the previous code, the available attribute was prefixed with the # (pound, also known as octothorpe and hash) character. To restrict access to a function or type, we prefix the available attribute with an @ (at) character. The following example shows how we could restrict access to a type and function:

```
@available(iOS 9.0, *)
func testAvailability() {
  // Function only available for iOS 9 or above
}

@available(iOS 9.0, *)
struct TestStruct {
  // Type only available for iOS 9 or above
}
```

In the previous example, we specified that the `testAvailability()` function and the `testStruct()` type can only be accessed if the code is run on a device that has iOS version 9 or newer. In order to use the `@available` attribute to block access to a function or type, we must wrap the code that calls that function or type with the `#available` attribute.

The following example shows how we could call the `testAvailability()` function:

```
if #available(iOS 9.0, *) {
  testAvailability()
} else {
  // Fallback on earlier versions
}
```

In this example, the `testAvailability()` function is only called if the application is running on a device that has iOS version 9 or later.

Summary

In this chapter, we looked at Swift's error handling features. While we are not required to use this feature in our custom types, it does give us a uniform manner in which to handle and respond to errors. Apple has also started to use this error handling in their frameworks. It is recommended that we use error handling in our code.

We also looked at the availability attribute, which allows us to develop applications that take advantage of the latest features of our target operating systems, while still allowing our applications to run on older versions.

In the next chapter, we will be looking at how to add subscripts to our custom types.

9

Custom Subscripting

Custom subscripts were added to Objective-C in 2012. At that time, *Chris Lattner* was already two years into developing Swift, and like other good features, subscripts were added to the Swift language. I have not used custom subscripts in many other languages; however, I do find myself using subscripts extensively when I am developing in Swift. The syntax for using subscripts in Swift seems like a natural part of the language, possibly because they were part of the language when it was released and not added in later. Once you start using subscripts in Swift, you may find them indispensable.

In this chapter, you will learn the following topics:

- What custom subscripts are?
- How to add custom subscripts to classes, structures, or enumerations?
- How to create read/write and read-only subscripts?
- How to use external names without custom subscripts?
- How to use multidimensional subscripts?

Introducing subscripts

Subscripts, in the Swift language, are used as shortcuts for accessing elements of a collection, list, or sequence. We can use them in our custom types to set or retrieve the values by index rather than using getter and setter methods. Subscripts, if used correctly, can significantly enhance the usability and readability of our custom types.

We can define multiple subscripts for a single type. When types have multiple subscripts, the appropriate subscript will be chosen based on the type of index passed in with the subscript. We can also set external parameter names for our subscripts that can help distinguish between subscripts that have the same types.

We use custom subscripts just like we use subscripts for arrays and dictionaries. For example, to access an element in an array, we use the an `Array[index]` syntax. When we define a custom subscript for our custom types, we also access them with the same syntax, `ourType[key]`.

When creating custom subscripts, we should try to make them feel like a natural part of the class, structure, or enumeration. As mentioned previously, subscripts can significantly enhance the usability and readability of our code, but if we try to overuse them, they will not feel natural and will be hard to use and understand.

In this chapter, we will look at several examples of how we can create and use custom subscripts. We will also show an example of how not to use a subscript. Before we show how to use custom subscripts, let's review how subscripts are used with Swift arrays to understand how subscripts are used within the Swift language itself. We should use subscripts in a similar manner to how Apple uses them within the language, to make our custom subscripts easy to understand and use.

Subscripts with Swift arrays

The following example shows how to use subscripts to access and change the values of an array:

```
var arrayOne = [1, 2, 3, 4, 5, 6]
print(arrayOne[3])   //Displays '4'
arrayOne[3] = 10
print(arrayOne[3])   //Displays '10'
```

In the preceding example, we create an array of integers and then use the subscript syntax to display and change the element at index 3. Subscripts are mainly used to get or retrieve information from a collection. We generally do not use subscripts when specific logic needs to be applied to determine which item to select. As an example, we would not want to use subscripts to append an item to the end of the array or to retrieve the number of items in the array. To append an item to the end of an array or to get the number of items in an array, we will use functions or properties, such as the following:

```
arrayOne.append(7)   //append 7 to the end of the array
arrayOne.count   //returns the number of items in an array
```

Subscripts in our custom types should follow the same standard set by the Swift language itself, so other developers that use our types are not confused by the implementation. The key to knowing when to use subscripts, and when not to, is to understand how the subscript will be used.

Creating and using custom subscripts

Let's look at how to define a subscript that is used to read and write to a backend array. Reading and writing to a backend storage class is one of the most common uses of custom subscripts, but as we will see in this chapter, we do not need to have a backend storage class. The following code shows how to use a subscript to read and write to an array:

```
class MyNames {
  private var names = ["Jon", "Kim", "Kailey", "Kara"]
  subscript(index: Int) -> String {
    get {
      return names[index]
    }
    set {
      names[index] = newValue
    }
  }
}
```

As we can see, the syntax for subscripts is similar to how we define properties within a class using the get and set keywords. The difference is that we declare the subscript using the subscript keyword. We then specify one or more inputs and the return type.

We can now use the custom subscript just like we used subscripts with arrays and dictionaries. The following code shows how to use the subscript in the preceding example:

```
var nam = MyNames()
print(nam[0])   //Displays 'Jon'
nam[0] = "Buddy"
print(nam[0])   //Displays 'Buddy'
```

In the preceding code, we create an instance of the MyNames class and display the original name at index 0. We then change the name at index 0 and redisplay it. In this example, we use the subscript that we defined in the MyNames class to retrieve and set elements of the names array within the class.

While we could make the `names` array available for external code to read and write directly, this would lock our code into using an array to store the data. In the future, if we wanted to change the backend storage mechanism to a dictionary object, or even a SQLite database, we would have a hard time doing so because all of the external code would also have to be changed. Subscripts are very good at hiding how we store information within our custom types; therefore, external code that uses these custom types does not rely on the specific storage implementations.

If we gave direct access to the `names` array, we would also be unable to verify that the external code was inserting valid information into the array. With subscripts, we can add validation to our setters to verify that the data being passed in is correct before adding it to the array. This can be very useful when we are creating a framework or a library.

Read-only custom subscripts

We can also make the subscript read-only by either not declaring a setter method within the subscript or by not implicitly declaring a getter or setter method. The following code shows how to declare a read-only property by not declaring a getter or setter method:

```
//No getter/setters implicitly declared
subscript(index: Int) -> String {
  return names[index]
}
```

The following example shows how to declare a read-only property by only declaring a getter method:

```
//Declaring only a getter
subscript(index: Int) -> String {
  get {
    return names[index]
  }
}
```

In the first example, we do not define either a getter or setter method; therefore, Swift sets the subscript as read-only, and the code acts as if it was in a getter definition. In the second example, we specifically set the code in a getter definition. Both examples are valid read-only subscripts. One thing to note is that write-only subscripts are not valid in Swift.

Calculated subscripts

While the preceding example is very similar to using the stored properties in a class or structure, we can also use subscripts in a similar manner to the computed properties. Let's look at how to do this:

```
struct MathTable {
  var num: Int
  subscript(index: Int) -> Int {
    return num * index
  }
}
```

In the preceding example, we used an array as the backend storage mechanism for the subscript. In this example, we use the value of the subscript to calculate the return value. We would use this subscript as follows:

```
var table = MathTable(num: 5)
print(table[4])
```

This example will display the calculated value of 5 (the number defined in the initialization) multiplied by 4 (the subscript value), which is equal to 20.

Subscript values

In the preceding subscript examples, all of the subscripts accepted integers as the value for the subscript; however, we are not limited to integers. In the following example, we will use a String type as the value for the subscript. The subscript will also return a String type:

```
struct Hello {
  subscript (name: String) -> String {
    return "Hello \(name)"
  }
}
```

In this example, the subscript takes a string as the value within the subscript and returns a message saying Hello. Let's look at how to use this subscript:

```
var hello = Hello()
print(hello["Jon"])
```

This example will display a Hello Jon message to the console.

External names for subscripts

As mentioned earlier in this chapter, we can have multiple subscript signatures for our custom types. The appropriate subscript will be chosen based on the type of index passed into the subscript. There are times when we may wish to define multiple subscripts that have the same type. For this, we could use external names similar to how we define external names for the parameters of a function.

Let's rewrite the original `MathTable` structure to include two subscripts that each accept an integer as the subscript type; however, one will perform a multiplication operation, and the other will perform an addition operation:

```
struct MathTable {
  var num: Int
  subscript(multiply index: Int) -> Int {
    return num * index
  }
  subscript(addition index: Int) -> Int {
    return num + index
  }
}
```

As we can see, in this example we define two subscripts, and each subscript accepts an integer type. The difference between the two subscripts is the external name within the definition. In the first subscript, we define an external name of `multiply` because we multiply the value of the subscript by the `num` property within this subscript. In the second subscript, we define an external name of `addition` because we add the value of the subscript to the `num` property within the subscript.

Let's look at how to use these two subscripts:

```
var table = MathTable(num: 5)
print(table[multiply: 4])  //Displays 20 because 5*4=20
print(table[addition: 4])  //Displays 9 because 5+4=9
```

If we run this example, we will see that the correct subscript is used, based on the external name within the subscript.

Using external names within our subscript is very useful if we need multiple subscripts of the same type. I would not recommend using external names unless they are needed to distinguish between multiple subscripts.

Multidimensional subscripts

While the most common subscripts are the ones that take a single parameter, subscripts are not limited to single parameters. They can take any number of input parameters, and these parameters can be of any type.

Let's look at how we could use a multidimensional subscript to implement a Tic-Tac-Toe board. A Tic-Tac-Toe board looks similar to the following figure:

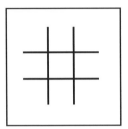

The board can be represented by a two-dimensional array, where each dimension has three elements. Each player will then take a turn placing his/her pieces (typically x or o) onto the board until one player has three pieces in a row or the board is full.

Let's look at how we could implement a Tic-Tac-Toe board using a multidimensional array and multidimensional subscripts:

```
struct TicTacToe {
  var board = [["","",""],["","",""],["","",""]]
  subscript(x: Int, y: Int) -> String {
    get {
      return board[x][y]
    }
    set {
      board[x][y] = newValue
    }
  }
}
```

We start the Tic-Tac-Toe structure by defining a 3×3 array, also known as a matrix, which will represent the game board. We then define a subscript that can be used to set and retrieve player pieces on the board. The subscript will accept two integer values. We define multiple parameters for our subscripts by putting the parameters between parentheses. In this example, we are defining the subscript with the parameters, (x: Int, y: Int). We can then use the x and y variable names within our subscripts to access the values that are passed in.

Let's look at how to use this subscript to set the user's pieces on the board:

```
var board = TicTacToe()
board[1,1] = "x"
board[0,0] = "o"
```

If we run this code, we will see that we added the **x** piece to the center square and the **o** piece to the upper-left square, so our game board will look similar to the following:

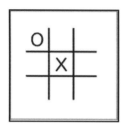

We are not limited to using only one type for our multidimensional subscripts. For example, we could have a subscript of the `(x: Int, y: Double, z: String)`.

We can also add external names for our multidimensional subscript types to help identify what values are used for and to distinguish between the subscripts that have the same types. Let's take a look at how to use multiple types and external names with subscripts, by creating a subscript that will return an array of string instances based on the values of the subscript:

```
struct SayHello {
   subscript(messageText message: String, messageName name: String, number
number: Int) -> [String]{
     var retArray: [String] = []
     for _ in 0..<number {
       retArray.append("\(message) \(name)")
     }
     return retArray
   }
}
```

In the `SayHello` structure, we define our subscript as follows:

```
subscript(messageText message: String,messageName name: String, number
number: Int) -> [String]
```

This defines a subscript with three elements. Each element has an external name (messageText, messageName, and number) and an internal name (message, name, and number). The first two elements are of the string type and the last one is an integer type. We use the first two elements to create a message for the user that will repeat the number of times defined by the last (number) element. We will use this subscript as follows:

```
var message = SayHello()
var ret = message[messageText:"Bonjour",messageName:"Jon",number:5]
```

If we run this code, we will see that the ret variable contains an array of five strings, where each string equals Bonjour Jon.

When not to use a custom subscript

As we have seen in this chapter, creating custom subscripts can really enhance our code; however, we should avoid overusing them or using them in a way that is not consistent with the standard subscript usage. The way to avoid overusing subscripts is to examine how subscripts are used in Swift's standard libraries.

Let's look at the following example:

```
class MyNames {
  private var names:[String] = ["Jon", "Kim", "Kailey", "Kara"]
  var number: Int {
    get {
      return names.count
    }
  }
  subscript(add name: String) -> String {
    names.append(name)
    return name
  }
  subscript(index: Int) -> String {
    get {
      return names[index]
    }
    set {
      names[index] = newValue
    }
  }
}
```

In the preceding example, within the `MyNames` class, we define an array of names that is used within our application. As an example, let's say that within our application we display this list of names and allow users to add names to it. Within the `MyNames` class, we then define the following subscript, which allows us to append a new name to the array:

```
subscript(add name: String) -> String {
  names.append(name)
  return name
}
```

This would be a poor use of subscripts because its usage is not consistent with how subscripts are used within the Swift language itself. This might cause confusion when the class is used. It would be more appropriate to rewrite this subscript as a function, such as the following:

```
func append(name: String) {
  names.append(name)
}
```

 Remember, when you are using custom subscripts, make sure that you are using them appropriately.

Summary

As we saw in this chapter, adding support for subscripts to our custom types can greatly enhance their readability and usability. We saw that subscripts can be used to add an abstraction layer between our backend storage class and external code. Subscripts can also be used in a similar manner to computed properties, where the subscript is used to calculate a value. As we noted, the key with subscripts is to use them appropriately and in a manner that is consistent with subscripts in the Swift language.

In the next chapter, we will take an in-depth look at optional types.

10
Using Optional Types

When I first started using Swift, the concept that I had the most trouble learning was optional types. Coming from an Objective-C, C, Java, and Python background, I was able to relate most of Swift's features to how things worked in one of the other languages that I knew, but optionals were different. There really was nothing like optionals in the other languages that I used, so it took a lot of reading to fully understand them. While we briefly covered optionals in Chapter 2, *Learning About Variables, Constants, Strings, and Operators*, we really need to cover them in more detail to really understand what optionals are, how to properly use them, and why they are so important in the Swift language.

In this chapter, we will cover the following topics:

- What are optional types?
- Why do we need optional types in Swift?
- How to unwrap an optional?
- What is optional binding?
- What is optional chaining?

Introducing optionals

When we declare variables in Swift, they are by default non-optional, which means that they must contain a valid, non-nil value. If we try to set a non-optional variable to nil, it will result in an error.

For example, the following code will throw an error when we attempt to set the message variable to nil because it is a non-optional type:

```
var message: String = "My String"
message = nil
```

It is very important to understand that `nil` in Swift is very different from `nil` in Objective-C or other C-based languages. In these languages, `nil` is a pointer to a non-existent object; however, in Swift `nil` is the absence of a value. This concept is very important to fully understand optionals in Swift.

A variable defined as an optional can contain a valid value or it can indicate the absence of a value. We indicate the absence of a value by assigning it a special `nil` value. Optionals of any type can be set to `nil`, whereas in Objective-C, only objects can be set to `nil`.

To really understand the concept behind optionals, let's look at a line of code that defines an optional:

```
var myString: String?
```

The question mark at the end indicates that the `myString` variable is an optional. We read this line of code as saying that the `myString` variable is an optional type, which may contain a value of the string type or may contain no value. The subtle difference between the two lines actually makes a big difference in understanding how optionals work.

Optionals are a special type in Swift. When we defined the `myString` variable, we actually defined it as an optional type. To understand this, let's look at some more code:

```
var myString1: String?
var myString2: Optional<String>
```

These two declarations are equivalent. Both lines declare an optional type that may contain a string type or may lack a value. In Swift, we can think of the absence of a value as being set to `nil`, but always remember that this is different than setting something to nil in Objective-C. In this book, when we refer to `nil`, we are referring to how Swift uses nil and not how Objective-C uses nil.

The optional type is an enumeration with two possible values, None and Some(T), where T is the generic associated value of the appropriate type. If we set the optional to `nil`, then it will have a value of None, and if we set a value, then the optional will have a value of Some with an associated value of the appropriate type. In Chapter 2, *Learning About Variables, Constants, Strings, and Operators*, we explained that an enumeration in Swift may have associated values. Associated values allow us to store additional information along with the enumeration's member values.

Internally, an optional is defined as follows:

```
enum Optional<T> {
  case None
  case Some(T)
}
```

Here, T is the type to associate with the optional. The T symbol is used to define a generic. We can read more about generics in Chapter 11, *Working with Generics*. For now, just remember that the T symbol represents any type.

The need for optional types in Swift

Now, the burning question is, Why does Swift need optionals? To understand this question, we should examine what problems optionals are designed to solve.

In most languages, it is possible to create a variable without giving it an initialized value. For example, in Objective-C, both of these lines of code are valid:

```
int i;
MyObject *m;
```

Now, let's say that the MyObject class, written in Objective-C, has the following method:

```
-(int)myMethodWithValue:(int)i {
  return i*2;
}
```

This method takes the value passed in from the i parameter, multiplies it by 2, and returns the results. Let's try to call this method using the following code:

```
MyObject *m;
NSLog(@"Value: %d",[m myMethodWithValue:5]);
```

Our first thought might be that this code would display Value: 10, since we are passing the value of 5 to a method that doubles the value passed in; however, this would be incorrect. In reality, this code would display Value: 0 because we did not initialize the m object prior to using it.

When we forget to initialize an object or set a value for a variable, we can get unexpected results at runtime, as we just demonstrated. The unexpected results can be, at times, very difficult to track down.

With optionals, Swift is able to detect problems like this at compile time and alert us before it becomes a runtime issue. If we expect a variable or object to always contain a value prior to using it, we will declare the variable as a non-optional (this is the default declaration). Then we will receive an error if we try to use it prior to initializing it. Let's look at an example of this. The following code would display an error because we are attempting to use a non-optional variable prior to initializing it:

```
var myString: String
print(myString)
```

If a variable is declared as an optional, it is good programming practice to verify that it contains a valid value before attempting to use it. We should only declare a variable as an optional if there is a valid reason for the variable to contain no value. This is the reason Swift declares variables as non-optional by default.

Now that we have a better understanding of what optionals are and what types of problem they are designed to solve, let's look at how to use them.

Defining an optional

One thing to keep in mind is that the type we define in the variable's declaration is actually the associated value in the optional enumeration. The following code shows us how we would typically declare an optional:

```
var myOptional: String?
```

This code declares an optional variable that might contain a string or might contain no value (nil). When a variable such as this is declared, by default it is set to nil.

Using optionals

The key to using optionals is to always verify that they contain a valid value prior to accessing them. We use the term **unwrapping** to refer to the process of retrieving a value from an optional.

Forced unwrapping of an optional

To unwrap or retrieve the value of an optional, we place an exclamation mark (!) after the variable name. This is called forced unwrapping. Forced unwrapping, in this manner, is very dangerous and should be used only if we are certain that the variable contains a non-nil value. Otherwise, if it does contain a `nil` value, we will get a runtime error and the application will crash.

When we use the exclamation point to unwrap an optional, we are telling the compiler that we know the optional contains a value, so go ahead and give it to us. Let's look at how to do this:

```
var myString1: String?
myString1 = "test"
var test: String = myString1!
```

This code will work as we expect it to, where the `test` variable will contain the `test` string; however, if the line that set the `myString1` optional to `test` were removed, we would receive a runtime error when we run the application. Note that the compiler will not alert us to an issue because we are using the exclamation point to unwrap the optional, therefore, the compiler assumes that we know what we are doing and will happily compile the code for us. We should verify that the `myString1` optional; contains a valid value prior to unwrapping it. The following example is one way to do this:

```
var myString1: String?
myString1 = "test"
if myString1 != nil {
  var test = myString1!
}
```

Now, if the line that sets the `myString1` optional to `test` were removed, we would not receive a runtime error because we only unwrap the `myString` optional if it contains a valid (non-nil) value.

Unwrapping optionals, as we just described, is not the optimal way, and it is not recommended that we unwrap optionals in this manner. We can combine verification and unwrapping in one step, called **optional binding**.

Optional binding

Optional binding is the recommended way to unwrap an optional. With optional binding, we perform a check to see whether the optional contains a valid value and, if so, unwrap it into a temporary variable or constant. This is all performed in one step.

Optional binding is performed with the `if` or `while` conditional statements. It takes the following format if we want to put the value of the optional in a constant:

```
if let constantName = optional {
   statements
}
```

If we need to put the value in a variable, instead of a constant, we can use the `var` keyword, as shown in the following example:

```
if var variableName = optional {
   statements
}
```

The following example shows how to perform optional binding:

```
var myString3: String?
myString3 = "Space"
if let tempVar = myString3 {
   print(tempVar)
} else {
   print("No value")
}
```

In the example, we define the `myString3` variable as an optional type. If the `myString3` optional contains a valid value, then we set the new variable named `tempvar` to that value and print it to the console. If the `myString3` optional does not contain a value, then we print `No value` to the console.

We are able to use optional binding to unwrap multiple optionals within the same optional binding line. For example, if we had three optionals named `optional1`, `optional2`, and `optional3`, we could use the following code to attempt to unwrap all three at once:

```
if let tmp1 = optional1, let tmp2 = optional2, let tmp3 = optional3 {
}
```

If any of the three optionals are `nil`, the whole optional binding statement fails. It is also perfectly acceptable with optional binding to assign the value to a variable of the same name. The following code illustrates this:

```
if let myOptional = myOptional {
  print(myOptional)
} else {
  print("myOptional was nil")
}
```

One thing to note is that the temporary variable is scoped only for the conditional block and cannot be used outside it. To illustrate the scope of the temporary variable, let's take a look at the following code:

```
var myOptional: String?
myOptional = "test"
if var tmp = myOptional {
  print("Inside:\(tmp)")
}
// This next line will cause a compile time error
print("Outside: \(tmp)")
```

This code would not compile because the `tmp` variable is only valid within the conditional block and we are attempting to use it outside it.

Using optional binding is a lot cleaner and easier than manually verifying that the optional has a value and using forced unwrapping to retrieve the value of the optional.

Returning optionals from functions and methods

We can set the return type of a function or a method to an optional type. This allows us to return a `nil` (no value) from the function or method. To set the return type to an optional type, we insert a question mark after the name of the type in the function or method declaration.

The following example shows us how we would return an optional from a function or method:

```
func getName(index: Int) -> String? {
  let names = ["Jon", "Kim", "Kailey", "Kara"]
  if index >= names.count || index < 0 {
    return nil
  } else {
```

```
        return names[index]
    }
}
```

In the example, we defined the return type as an optional that can be either a string value or no value. Inside the function, we will return the name if the index is within the bounds of the array, or `nil` if it is outside the bounds of the array.

The following code shows how to call this function where the return value is an optional:

```
var name = getName(index: 2)
var name2 = getName(index: 5)
```

In the previous code, the `name` variable will contain `Kailey`, while the `name2` variable will contain `nil`. Note that we do not have to define the variable as an optional since Swift knows it is an optional type because the return type, defined by the function is an optional.

We can also define a subscript that returns an optional type. We define a subscript as an optional exactly like we defined functions. Here is an example template of a subscript that returns an optional:

```
subscript(index: Int) -> String? {
    //some statements
}
```

With this definition, we are able to return a `nil` from our subscript.

Using an optional as a parameter in a function or method

We can also accept an optional as a parameter to a function or a method. This allows us to have the option of passing a `nil` into a function or method if required. The following example shows how to define an optional parameter for a function:

```
func optionalParam(myString: String?) {
    if let temp = myString {
        print("Contains value \(temp)")
    }else {
        print("Does not contain value")
    }
}
```

To define a parameter as an optional type, we use the question mark within the parameter definition. Within this example, we use optional binding to check whether the optional contains a value or not. If it contains a value, we print `Contains value` to the console; otherwise, we print `Does not contain value`.

Optional binding with the guard statement

We can use the `guard` statement with optional binding to verify that an optional has a valid value. The following example illustrates this:

```
func sayHello(name: String?) {
  guard let internalName = name else {
    print("Name has not value")
    return
  }
  print("Hello \(internalName)")
}
```

In the `sayHello(name:)` function, we use the `guard` statement to verify that the name parameter contains a valid value, and if not, we print out the message `Name has no value`. If the name parameter does have a valid value, we then print out a `hello` message. The one thing to note from this example is that the `internalName` constant is scoped for the function; therefore, we can use it throughout the function. This is different from normal optional binding where the constant or variable is scoped to the conditional block. The difference in scope between the standard optional binding statement and the `guard` statement makes using the `guard` statement preferable when verifying optional parameters, as shown in this example.

Optional types with tuples

We can define a whole tuple as an optional or any of the elements within a tuple as an optional. It is especially useful to use optionals with tuples when we return a tuple from a function or method. This allows us to return part (or all) of the tuple as `nil`. The following example shows how to define a tuple as an optional, and also how to define individual elements of a tuple as optional types:

```
var tuple1: (one: String, two: Int)?
var tuple2: (one: String, two: Int?)
```

The first line defines the whole tuple as an optional type. The second line defines the second value within the tuple as an optional, while the first value is a non-optional.

Optional chaining

Optional binding allows us to unwrap one optional at a time, but what would happen if we had optional types embedded within other optional types? This would force us to have optional binding statements embedded within other optional binding statements. There is a better way to handle this, by using optional chaining. Before we look at optional chaining, let's see how this would work with optional binding. We will start off by defining three types that we will be using for our examples in this section:

```
class Collar {
  var color: String
  init(color: String) {
    self.color = color
  }
}

class Pet {
  var name: String
  var collar: Collar?
  init(name: String) {
    self.name = name
  }
}

class Person {
  var name: String
  var pet: Pet?
  init(name: String) {
    self.name = name
  }
}
```

In this example, we begin by defining a `Collar` class, which has one property defined. This property is named `color`, which is of type string. We can see that the `color` property is not an optional; therefore, we can safely assume that it will always have a valid value.

Next, we define a `Pet` class that has two properties defined. These properties are named `name` and `collar`. The `name` property is of the string type and the `collar` property is an optional that may contain an instance of the `Collar` type or may contain no value.

Finally, we define a `Person` class, which also has two properties. These properties are named `name` and `pet`. The `name` property is of the string type and the `pet` property is an optional that may contain an instance of the `Pet` type or may contain no value.

For the examples that follow, let's use the following code to initialize the classes:

```
var jon = Person(name: "Jon")
var buddy = Pet(name: "Buddy")
jon.pet = buddy
var collar = Collar(color: "red")
buddy.collar = collar
```

Now, let's say that we want to get the `color` of the `collar` for a person's pet; however, the person may not have a pet (the `pet` property may be `nil`) or the pet may not have a collar (the `collar` property may be `nil`). We could use optional binding to drill down through each layer, as shown in the following example:

```
if let tmpPet = jon.pet, let tmpCollar = tmpPet.collar {
    print("The color of the collar is \(tmpCollar.color)")
}else {
    print("Cannot retrieve color")
}
```

While this example is perfectly valid and would print out the message `The color of the collar is red`, the code is rather messy and hard to follow because we have multiple optional binding statements on the same line, where the second optional binding statement is dependent on the first one.

Optional chaining allows us to drill down through multiple optional type layers of properties, methods, and subscripts in one line of code. These layers can be chained together and if any layer returns a `nil`, the entire chain gracefully fails and returns `nil`. If none of the values return `nil`, the last value of the chain is returned. Since the results of optional chaining may be a `nil` value, the results are always returned as an optional type, even if the final value we are retrieving is a non-optional type.

To specify optional chaining, we place a question mark (?) after each of the optional values within the chain. The following example shows how to use optional chaining to make the preceding example much cleaner and easier to read:

```
if let color = jon.pet?.collar?.color {
    print("The color of the collar is \(color)")
} else {
    print("Cannot retrieve color")
}
```

In this example, we put a question mark after the `pet` and `collar` properties to signify that they are of the optional type and that, if either value is `nil`, the whole chain will return `nil`. This code would also print out the message, `The color of the collar is red`; however, it is much easier to read than the preceding example because it clearly shows us what optionals we are dependent on.

The nil coalescing operator

The nil coalescing operator is similar to the ternary operator that we discussed in `Chapter 2`, *Learning About Variables, Constants, Strings, and Operators*. The ternary operator assigns a value to a variable, based on the evaluation of a comparison operator or a `Boolean` value. The nil coalescing operator attempts to unwrap an optional, and if it contains a value, it will return that value, or a default value if the optional is `nil`.

Let's look at a prototype for the `nil` coalescing operator:

```
optionalA ?? defaultValue
```

In this example, we demonstrate the `nil` coalescing operator when the optional contains a `nil` and also when it contains a value:

```
var defaultName = "Jon"

var optionalA: String?
var optionalB: String?

optionalB = "Buddy"

var nameA = optionalA ?? defaultName
var nameB = optionalB ?? defaultName
```

In this example, we begin by initializing our `defaultName` variable to `Jon`. We then define two optionals named `optionalA` and `optionalB`. The `optionalA` variable will be set to `nil`, while the `optionalB` variable is set to `Buddy`.

The nil coalescing operator is used in the final two lines. Since the `optionalA` variable contains a `nil`, the `nameA` variable will be set to the value of the `defaultName` variable, which is `Jon`. The `nameB` variable will be set to the value of the `optionalB` variable since it contains a value.

The nil coalescing operator is shorthand for using the ternary operator as follows:

```
var nameC = optionalA != nil ? optionalA! :defaultName
```

As we can see, the `nil` coalescing operator is much cleaner and easier to read than the equivalent ternary operator.

Summary

While the concept of optional types, as used in the Swift language, might seem a little foreign at first, the more you use them the more they will make sense. One of the biggest advantages with optional types is we get additional compile time checks that alert us if we forget to initialize non-optionals prior to using them.

These two paragraphs give examples of what optionals actually are and how they are defined in Swift. It is import to understand this concept because optionals are used a lot in Swift.

In the next chapter we will be looking at Generics in Swift.

11
Working with Generics

My first experience with generics was back in 2004, when they were first introduced in the Java programming language. I can still remember picking up my copy of *The Java Programming Language, Fourth Edition*, which covered Java 5, and reading about Java's implementation of generics. Since then, I have used generics in several projects, not only in Java, but in other languages as well. If you are familiar with generics in other languages, such as Java, the syntax that Swift uses will be very familiar to you. Generics allow us to write very flexible and reusable code; however, just like with subscripts, we need to make sure that we use them properly and do not overuse them.

In this chapter, we will cover the following topics:

- What are generics?
- How to create and use generic functions?
- How to create and use generic types?
- How to use associated types with protocols?

An introduction to generics

The concept of generics has been around for a while, so it should not be a new concept to developers coming from languages such as Java or C#. The Swift implementation of generics is very similar to these languages. For those developers coming from languages such as Objective-C, which do not have generics, they might seem a bit foreign at first, but once you start using them you will realize how powerful they are.

Generics allow us to write very flexible and reusable code that avoids duplication. With a type-safe language, such as Swift, we often need to write functions or types that are valid for multiple types. For example, we might need to write a function that swaps the values of two variables; however, we may also use this function to swap two String types, two integer types, and two Double types. Without generics, we will need to write three separate functions; however, with generics, we can write one generic function to provide the swap functionality for multiple types. Generics allow us to tell a function or type *I know Swift is a type-safe language, but I do not know the type that will be needed yet. I will give you a placeholder for now and will let you know what type to enforce later.*

In Swift, we have the ability to define both generic functions and generic types. Let's look at generic functions first.

Generic functions

Let's begin by examining the problem that generics try to solve, and then we will see how generics solve this problem. Let's say that we wanted to create functions that swapped the values of two variables (as described in the first part of this chapter); however, for our application, we need to swap two integer types, two Double types, and two String types. The following code shows what these functions could look like:

```swift
func swapInts(a: inout Int,b: inout Int) {
  let tmp = a
  a = b
  b = tmp
}

func swapDoubles(a: inout Double,b: inout Double) {
  let tmp = a
  a = b
  b = tmp
}

func swapStrings(a: inout String, b: inout String) {
  let tmp = a
  a = b
  b = tmp
}
```

With these three functions, we can swap the original values of two `Integer` types, two `Double` types, and two `String` types. Now, let's say, as we develop our application further, that we find out that we also need to swap the values of two unsigned `Integer` types, two `Float` types, and even a couple of custom types. We might easily end up with eight or more swap functions. The worst part is that each of these functions contains duplicate code. The only difference between these functions is that the parameter types change. While this solution does work, generics offer a much more elegant and simple solution that eliminates all the duplicate code. Let's see how we would condense all three of the preceding functions into a single generic function:

```
func swapGeneric<T>(a: inout T, b: inout T) {
   let tmp = a
   a = b
   b = tmp
}
```

Let's look at how we defined the `swapGeneric` function. The function itself looks pretty similar to a normal function, except for the capital `T`. The capital `T`, as used in the `swapGeneric` function, is a placeholder type, and tells Swift that we will be defining the type later. When a type is defined it will be used in place of all the placeholders.

To define a generic function, we include the placeholder type between two angular brackets (`<T>`) after the function's name. We can then use that placeholder type in place of any type definition within the parameter definitions, the return type, or the function itself. The big thing to keep in mind is that, once the placeholder is defined as a type, all the other placeholders assume that type. Therefore, any variable or constant defined with that placeholder must conform to that type.

There is nothing special about the capital `T`; we could use any valid identifier in place of `T`. The following definitions are perfectly valid:

```
func swapGeneric<G>(a: inout G, b: inout G) {
   //Statements
}

func swapGeneric<xyz>(a: inout xyz, b: inout xyz) {
   //Statements
}
```

In most documentation, generic placeholders are defined with either `T` (for type) or `E` (for element). We will, for the purposes of this chapter, use the capital `T` to define generic placeholders. It is also good practice to use capital `T` to define a generic placeholder within our code so that the placeholder is easily recognized when we are looking at the code at a later time.

If you do not like using the capital T or capital E to define generics, then try to be consistent. I would recommend that you avoid the use of different identifiers to define generics throughout your code.

If we need to use multiple generic types, we can create multiple placeholders by separating them with commas. The following example shows how to define multiple placeholders for a single function:

```
func testGeneric<T,E>(a: T, b: E) {
   //Statements
}
```

In this example, we are defining two generic placeholders, T and E. In this case, we can set the T placeholder to one type and the E placeholder to a different type.

Let's look at how to call a generic function. The following code will swap two integers using the swapGeneric<T>(inout a: T, inout b: T) function:

```
var a = 5
var b = 10
swapGeneric(a: &a, b: &b)
print("a:\(a) b:\(b)")
```

If we run this code, the output will be a: 10 b: 5. We can see that we do not have to do anything special to call a generic function. The function infers the type from the first parameter and then sets all the remaining placeholders to that type. Now, if we need to swap the values of two strings, we will call the same function, as follows:

```
var c = "My String 1"
var d = "My String 2"
swapGeneric(a: &c, b: &d)
print("c:\(c) d:\(d)")
```

We can see that the function is called in exactly the same way as we called it when we wanted to swap two integers. One thing that we cannot do is pass two different types into the swap function because we defined only one generic placeholder. If we attempt to run the following code, we will receive an error:

```
var a = 5
var c = "My String 1"swapGeneric(a: &a, b: &c)
```

The error that we will receive is error cannot convert value of type 'String' to expected argument type 'Int', which tells us that we are attempting to use a String value when an Int value is expected. The reason the function is looking for an Int value is that the first parameter that we pass into the function is an Int value, and, therefore, all the generic types in the function became Int types.

Now, let's say we have the following function, which has multiple generic types defined:

```
func testGeneric<T,E>(a: T, b: E) {
  print("\(a)\(b)")
}
```

This function would accept parameters of different types; however, since they are of different types, we would be unable to swap the values because they are different. There are also other limitations to generics. For example, we may think that the following generic function would be valid; however, we would receive an error if we tried to implement it:

```
func genericEqual<T>(a: T, b: T) -> Bool{
  return a == b
}
```

The error that we receive is due to the fact that the binary operator == cannot be applied to two T operands. Since the type of the arguments is unknown at the time the code is compiled, Swift does not know if it is able to use the equal operator on the types, and, therefore, the error is thrown. We might think that this is a limit that will make generics hard to use; however, we have a way to tell Swift that we expect the type, represented by the placeholder, will have a certain functionality. This is done with type constraints.

A type constraint specifies that a generic type must inherit from a specific class or conform to a particular protocol. This allows us to use the methods or properties defined by the parent class or protocol within the generic function. Let's look at how to use type constraints by rewriting the genericEqual function to use the comparable protocol:

```
func testGenericComparable<T: Comparable>(a: T, b: T) -> Bool{
  return a == b
}
```

To specify the type constraint, we put the class or protocol constraint after the generic placeholder, where the generic placeholder and the constraint are separated by a colon. This new function works as we might expect, and it will compare the values of the two parameters and return true if they are equal or false if they are not.

We can declare multiple constraints just like we declare multiple generic types. The following example shows how to declare two generic types with different constraints:

```
func testFunction<T: MyClass, E: MyProtocol>(a: T, b: E) {
  //Statements
}
```

In this function, the type defined by the T placeholder must inherit from the MyClass class, and the type defined by the E placeholder must conform to the MyProtocol protocol. Now that we have looked at generic functions, let's look at generic types.

Generic types

We have already had a general introduction to how generic types work when we looked at Swift arrays and dictionaries. A generic type is a class, structure, or enumeration that can work with any type, just like the way Swift arrays and dictionaries work. As we recall, Swift arrays and dictionaries are written so that they can contain any type. The catch is that we cannot mix and match different types within an array or dictionary. When we create an instance of our generic type, we define the type that the instance will work with. After we define that type, we cannot change the type for that instance.

To demonstrate how to create a generic type, let's create a simple List class. This class will use a Swift array as the backend storage for the list and will let us add items to the list or retrieve values from the list.

Let's begin by seeing how to define our generic list type:

```
class List<T> {
}
```

The preceding code defines the generic list type. We can see that we use the <T> tag to define a generic placeholder, just like we did when we defined a generic function. This T placeholder can then be used anywhere within the type instead of a concrete type definition.

To create an instance of this type, we would need to define the type of items that our list will hold. The following example shows how to create instances of the generic list type for various types:

```
var stringList = List<String>()
var intList = List<Int>()
var customList = List<MyObject>()
```

The preceding example creates three instances of the `List` class. The `stringList` instance can be used with instances of the `String` type, the `intList` instance can be used with instances of the integer type, and the `customList` instance can be used with instances of the `MyObject` type.

We are not limited to using generics only with classes. We can also define structures and enumerations as generics. The following example shows how to define a generic structure and a generic enumeration:

```
struct GenericStruct<T> {
}

enum GenericEnum<T> {
}
```

The next step in our `List` class is to add the backend storage array. The items that are stored in this array need to be of the same type that we define when we initiate the class; therefore, we will use the `T` placeholder for the array's definition. The following code shows the `List` class with an array named items. The `items` array will be defined using the `T` placeholder, so it will hold the same types that we defined for the class:

```
class List<T> {
   var items = [T]()
}
```

This code defines our generic `List` type and uses `T` as the type placeholder. We can then use this `T` placeholder anywhere in the class to define the type of an item. That item will then be of the same type that we defined when we created the instance of the `List` class. Therefore, if we create an instance of the list type such as `var stringList = List<String>()`, the `items` array will be an array of string instances. If we created an instance of the `List` type such as `var intList = List<Int>()`, the `item` array will be an array of integer instances.

Now, we will need to create the `add()` method, which will be used to add an item to the list. We will use the `T` placeholder within the method declaration to define that the `item` parameter will be of the same type that we declared when we initiated the class. Therefore, if we create an instance of the list type to use the string type, we will be required to use an instance of the string type as the parameter for the `add()` method. However, if we create an instance of the list type to use the integer type, we will be required to use an instance of the integer type as the parameter for the `add()` method.

Here is the code for the `add()` function:

```
func add(item: T) {
    items.append(item)
}
```

To create a standalone generic function, we add the `<T>` declaration after the function name to declare that it is a generic function; however, when we use a generic method within a generic type, we do not need the `<T>` declaration. Instead, all we need to do is to use the type that we defined in the class declaration. If we wanted to introduce another generic type, we could define it with the method declaration.

Now, let's add the `getItemAtIndex()` method, which will return the item from the backend array, at the specified index:

```
func getItemAtIndex(index: Int) -> T? {
    if items.count>index {
        return items[index]
    } else {
        return nil
    }
}
```

The `getItemAtIndex()` method accepts one argument, which is the index of the item we want to retrieve. We then use the `T` placeholder to specify that our return type is an optional that might be of type `T` or that might be `nil`. If the backend storage array contains an item at the specified index, we will return that item; otherwise, we return `nil`.

Now, let's look at our entire generic list class:

```
class List<T> {
    var items = [T]()
    func add(item: T) {
        items.append(item)
    }
    func getItemAtIndex(index: Int) -> T? {
        if items.count > index {
            return items[index]
        } else {
            return nil
        }
    }
}
```

As we can see, we initially defined the generic `T` placeholder type in the class declaration. We then used this placeholder type within our class. In our `List` class, we use this placeholder in three places. We use it as the type for our items array, as the parameter type for our `add()` method, and as the optional return type in the `getItemAtIndex()` method.

Now, let's look at how to use the `List` class. When we use a generic type, we define the type to be used within the class between angle brackets, such as `<type>`. The following code shows how to use the `List` class to store instances of the `String` types:

```
var list = List<String>()
list.add(item: "Hello")
list.add(item: "World")
print(list.getItemAtIndex(index: 1))
```

In this code, we start off by creating an instance of the `List` type called `list` and specify that it will store instances of the `String` type. We then use the `add()` method twice to store two items in the `list` instance. Finally, we use the `getItemAtIndex()` method to retrieve the item at index number 1, which will display `Optional(World)` to the console.

We can also define our generic types with multiple placeholder types, similarly to how we use multiple placeholders in our generic methods. To use multiple placeholder types, we separate them with commas. The following example shows how to define multiple placeholder types:

```
class MyClass<T,E>{
  //Code
}
```

We then create an instance of the `MyClass` type that uses instances of the `String` and `Integer` types, like this:

```
var mc = MyClass<String, Int>()
```

We can also use type constraints with generic types. Once again, using a type constraint for a generic type is exactly the same as using one with a generic function. The following code shows how to use a type constraint to ensure that the generic type conforms to the comparable protocol:

```
class MyClass<T: Comparable>{}
```

So far, in this chapter, we have seen how to use placeholder types with functions and types. Now let's see how we can add generic subscripts to a non-generic type.

Generic subscripts

Starting with Swift 4, we can create generic subscripts, where either the subscript's return type or its parameters may be generic. Let's look at how we can create a generic subscript. In this first example, we will create a subscript that will accept one generic parameter:

```
subscript<T: Hashable>(item: T) -> Int {
    return item.hashValue
}
```

When we create a generic subscript, we define the placeholder type after the subscript keyword. In the previous example, we define the T placeholder type and use a type constraint to ensure that the type conforms to the Hashable protocol. This will allow us to pass in an instance of any type that conforms to the Hashable protocol.

As we mentioned at the start of this section, we can also use generics for the return type of a subscript. We define the generic placeholder for the return type exactly as we did for the generic parameter. The following example illustrates this.

```
subscript<T>(key: String) -> T? {
    return dictionary[key] as? T
}
```

In this example, we define the T placeholder type after the subscript keyword, as we did in the previous example. We then use this type as our return type for the subscript.

Associated types

An associated type declares a placeholder name that can be used instead of a type within a protocol. The actual type to be used is not specified until the protocol is adopted. While creating generic functions and types, we used a very similar syntax, as we have seen throughout this chapter so far. Defining associated types for a protocol, however, is very different. We specify an associated type using the associatedtype keyword.

Let's see how to use associated types when we define a protocol. In this example, we will define the QueueProtocol protocol that will define the capabilities that need to be implemented by the queue that implements it:

```
protocol QueueProtocol {
    associatedtype QueueType
    mutating func add(item: QueueType)
```

```
    mutating func getItem() -> QueueType?
    func count() -> Int
}
```

In this protocol, we defined one associated type named QueueType. We then used this associated type twice within the protocol-once as the parameter type for the add() method and once when we defined the return type of the getItem() method as an optional type that might return an associated type of QueueType or nil.

Any type that implements the QueueProtocol protocol must be able to specify the type to use for the QueueType placeholder, and must also ensure that only items of that type are used where the protocol uses the QueueType placeholder.

Let's look at how to implement QueueProtocol in a nongeneric class called IntQueue. This class will implement the QueueProtocol protocol using the Integer type:

```
class IntQueue: QueueProtocol {
    var items = [Int]()
    func add(item: Int) {
        items.append(item)
    }
    func getItem() -> Int? {
        return items.count > 0 ? items.remove(at: 0) : nil
    }
    func count() -> Int {
        return items.count
    }
}
```

In the IntQueue class, we begin by defining our backend storage mechanism as an array of integer types. We then implement each of the methods defined in the QueueProtocol protocol, replacing the QueueType placeholder defined in the protocol with the Integer type. In the add() method, the parameter type is defined as an instance of the integer type, and in the getItem() method the return type is defined as an optional that might return an instance of the integer type or nil.

We use the IntQueue class as we would use any other class. The following code shows this:

```
var intQ = IntQueue()
int Q.add(item: 2)
int Q.add(item: 4)
print(intQ.getItem())
int Q.add(item: 6)
```

We begin by creating an instance of the `IntQueue` class named `intQ`. We then call the `add()` method twice to add two values of the integer type to the `intQ` instance. We then retrieve the first item in the `intQ` instance by calling the `getItem()` method. This line will print `Optional(2)` to the console. The final line of code adds another instance of the integer type to the `intQ` instance.

In the preceding example, we implemented the `QueueProtocol` protocol in a nongeneric way. This means that we replaced the placeholder types with an actual type. `QueueType` was replaced by the `Integer` type. We can also implement the `QueueProtocol` with a generic type. Let's see how we would do this:

```
class GenericQueue<T>: QueueProtocol {
  var items = [T]()
  func add(item: T) {
    items.append(item)
  }
  func getItem() -> T? {
    return items.count > 0 ? items.remove(at:0) : nil
  }
  func count() -> Int {
    return items.count
  }
}
```

As we can see, the `GenericQueue` implementation is very similar to the `IntQueue` implementation, except that we define the type to use as the generic placeholder `T`. We can then use the `GenericQueue` class as we would use any generic class. Let's look at how to use the `GenericQueue` class:

```
var intQ2 = GenericQueue<Int>()
intQ2.add(item: 2)
intQ2.add(item: 4)
print(intQ2.getItem())
intQ2.add(item: 6)
```

We begin by creating an instance of the `GenericQueue` class that will use the `integer` type and name it `intQ2`. Next, we call the `add()` method twice to add two instances of the `integer` type to the `intQ2` instance. We then retrieve the first item in the queue that was added using the `getItem()` method and print the value to the console. This line will print `Optional(2)` to the console.

We can also use type constraints with associated types. When the protocol is adapted, the type defined for the associated type must inherit from the class or conform to the protocol defined by the type constraint. The following line defines an associated type with a type constraint:

```
associatedtype QueueType: Hashable
```

In this example, we specify that, when the protocol is implemented, the type defined for the associated type must conform to the `Hashable` protocol.

Summary

Generic types can be incredibly useful, and they are also the basis of the Swift standard collection types (array and dictionary); however, as mentioned in the introduction to this chapter, we have to be careful to use them correctly.

We have seen a couple of examples in this chapter that show how generics can make our lives easier. The `swapGeneric()` function that was shown at the beginning of the chapter is a good use of a generic function because it allows us to swap two values of any type we choose, while only implementing the swap code once.

The generic `List` type is also a good example of how to make custom collection types that can be used to hold any type. How we implemented the generic `List` type in this chapter is similar to how Swift implements an array and dictionary with generics.

In the next chapter, we will look at how to use closures.

12
Working with Closures

Today, most major programming languages have functionalities similar to those of closures in Swift. Some of these implementations are really hard to use (Objective-C blocks), while others are easy (Java lambdas and C# delegates). I have found that the functionality closures provide is especially useful when developing frameworks. I have also used them extensively when communicating with remote services over a network connection. While blocks in Objective-C are incredibly useful, the syntax used to declare a block was absolutely horrible. Luckily, when Apple was developing the Swift language, they made the syntax of closures much easier to use and understand.

In this chapter, we will cover the following topics:

- What are closures?
- How to create a closure?
- How to use a closure?
- What are examples of useful closures?
- How to avoid strong reference cycles within closures?

An introduction to closures

Closures are self-contained blocks of code that can be passed around and used throughout our application. We can think of the `Int` type as a type that stores an integer and a `String` type as a type that stores a string. In this context, a closure can be thought of as a type that contains a block of code. What this means is that we can assign closures to a variable, pass them as arguments to functions, and return them from a function.

Closures have the ability to capture and store references to any variable or constant from the context in which they were defined. This is known as closing over the variables or constants and, for the most part, Swift will handle the memory management for us. The only exception is in creating a strong reference cycle, and we will look at how to resolve this in the *Creating strong reference cycles with closures* section of this chapter.

Closures in Swift are similar to blocks in Objective-C; however, closures in Swift are a lot easier to use and understand. Let's look at the syntax used to define a closure in Swift:

```
{
   (parameters) -> return-type in
   statements
}
```

The syntax used to create a closure looks very similar to the syntax we use to create functions and, in Swift, global and nested functions are closures. The biggest difference in the format between closures and functions is the `in` keyword. The `in` keyword is used in place of curly brackets to separate the definition of the closure's parameter and return types from the body of the closure.

There are many uses for closures, and we will go over a number of them later in this chapter, but first we need to understand the basics of closures. Let's start by looking at some very basic closures so that we can get a better understanding of what they are, how to define them, and how to use them.

Simple closures

We will begin by creating a very simple closure that does not accept any arguments and does not return any value. All it does is print `Hello World` to the console. Let's look at the following code:

```
let clos1 = { () -> Void in
   print("Hello World")
}
```

In this example, we create a closure and assign it to the constant `clos1`. Since there are no parameters defined between the parentheses, this closure will not accept any parameters. Also, the return type is defined as `Void`; therefore, this closure will not return any value. The body of the closure contains one line, which prints `Hello World` to the console.

There are many ways to use closures; in this example, all we want to do is execute it. We can execute the closure as follows:

```
clos1()
```

When we execute the closure, we will see that Hello World is printed to the console. At this point, closures may not seem that useful, but as we get further along in this chapter, we will see how useful and powerful they can be.

Let's look at another simple example. This closure will accept one string parameter named name, but will not return a value. Within the body of the closure, we will print out a greeting to the name passed into the closure through the name parameter. Here is the code for this second closure:

```
let clos2 = {
   (name: String) -> Void in
   print("Hello \(name)")
}
```

The big difference between the clos2 closure and the clos1 closure is that we define a single string parameter between the parentheses. As we can see, we define parameters for closures just like we define parameters for functions.

We can execute this closure in the same way in which we executed the clos1 closure. The following code shows how this is done:

```
clos2( "Jon")
```

This example, when executed, will print the message Hello Jon to the console. Let's look at another way we can use the clos2 closure.

Our original definition of closures stated: *Closures are self-contained blocks of code that can be passed around and used throughout our application code.* What this tells us is that we can pass our closure from the context that they were created in to other parts of our code. Let's look at how to pass our clos2 closure into a function. We will define a function that accepts our clos2 closure, as follows:

```
func testClosure(handler: (String) -> Void) {
   handler("Dasher")
}
```

We define the function just like we would any other function; however, in the parameter list, we define a parameter named `handler`, and the type defined for the handler parameter is `(String) -> Void`. If we look closely, we can see that the `(String) -> Void` definition of the `handler` parameter matches the parameter and return types that we defined for the `clos2` closure. This means that we can pass the `clos2` closure into the function. Let's look at how to do this:

```
testClosure(handler: clos2)
```

We call the `testClosure()` function just like any other function, and the closure that is being passed in looks like any other variable. Since the `clos2` closure is executed in the `testClosure()` function, we will see the message, `Hello Dasher`, printed to the console when this code is executed.

As we will see a little later in this chapter, the ability to pass closures to functions is what makes closures so exciting and powerful.

As the final piece to the closure puzzle, let's look at how to return a value from a closure. The following example shows this:

```
let clos3 = {
    (name: String) -> String in
    return "Hello \(name)"
}
```

The definition of the `clos3` closure looks very similar to how we defined the `clos2` closure. The difference is that we changed the `Void` return type to a `String` type. Then, in the body of the closure, instead of printing the message to the console, we used the return statement to return the message. We can now execute the `clos3` closure just like the previous two closures, or pass the closure to a function like we did with the `clos2` closure. The following example shows how to execute the `clos3` closure:

```
var message = clos3("Buddy")
```

After this line of code is executed, the message variable will contain the `Hello Buddy` string.

The previous three examples of closures demonstrate the format and how to define a typical closure. Those who are familiar with Objective-C can see that the format of closures in Swift is a lot cleaner and easier to use. The syntax for creating closures that we have shown so far in this chapter is pretty short; however, we can shorten it even more. In this next section, we will look at how to do this.

Shorthand syntax for closures

In this section, we will look at a couple of ways to shorten the definition of closures.

 Using the shorthand syntax for closures is really a matter of personal preference. There are a lot of developers that like to make their code as small and compact as possible, and they take great pride in doing so. However, at times this can make code hard to read and understand for other developers.

The first shorthand syntax for closures that we are going to look at is one of the most popular, and is the syntax we saw when we were using algorithms with arrays in Chapter 3, *Using Swift Collections and the Tuple Type*. This format is mainly used when we want to send a really small (usually one line) closure to a function, like we did with the algorithms for arrays. Before we look at this shorthand syntax, we need to write a function that will accept a closure as a parameter:

```
func testFunction(num: Int, handler:() -> Void) {
  for _ in 0..<num {
    handler()
  }
}
```

This function accepts two parameters--the first parameter is an integer named num, and the second parameter is a closure named handler that does not have any parameters and does not return any value. Within the function, we create a for loop that will use the num integer to define how many times it loops. Within the for loop, we call the handler closure that was passed into the function.

Now let's create a closure and pass it to the testFunction() as follows:

```
let clos = {
  () -> Void in
  print("Hello from standard syntax")
}
testFunction(num: 5, handler: clos)
```

This code is very easy to read and understand; however, it does take five lines of code. Now let's look at how to shorten this code by writing the closure inline within the function call:

```
testFunction(num: 5,handler: {print("Hello from Shorthand closure")})
```

In this example, we created the closure inline within the function call, using the same syntax that we used with the algorithms for arrays. The closure is placed in between two curly brackets ({}), which means the code to create the closure is {print("Hello from Shorthand closure")}. When this code is executed, it will print out the message Hello from Shorthand closure five times on the screen.

The ideal way to call the testFunction() with a closure, for both compactness and readability, would be as follows:

```
testFunction(num: 5) {
  print("Hello from Shorthand closure")
}
```

Having the closure as the final parameter allows us to leave off the label when calling the function. This example gives us both compact and readable code.

In Chapter 3, *Using Swift Collections and the Tuple Type,* we saw that we were able to pass parameters to the array algorithms using the $0, $1, $2, and so on, parameters. Let's look at how to use parameters with this shorthand syntax. We will begin by creating a new function that will accept a closure with a single parameter. We will name this function testFunction2. The following example shows what the new testFunction2 function does:

```
func testFunction2(num: Int, handler: (_ : String)->Void) {
  for _ in 0..<num {
    handler("Me")
  }
}
```

In testFunction2, we define the closure like this: (_ : String)->Void. This definition means that the closure accepts one parameter and does not return any value. Now let's look at how to use the same shorthand syntax to call this function:

```
testFunction2(num: 5){
  print("Hello from \($0)")
}
```

The difference between this closure definition and the previous one is $0. The $0 parameter is shorthand for the first parameter passed into the function. If we execute this code, it prints out the message Hello from Me five times.

Using the dollar sign ($) followed by a number with inline closures allows us to define the closure without having to create a parameter list in the definition. The number after the dollar sign defines the position of the parameter in the parameter list. Let's examine this format a bit more, because we are not limited to only using the dollar sign ($) and number shorthand format with inline closures. This shorthand syntax can also be used to shorten the closure definition by allowing us to leave the parameter names off. The following example demonstrates this:

```
let clos5: (String, String) -> Void = {
    print("\($0) \($1)")
}
```

In this example, the closure has two string parameters defined; however, we do not give them names. The parameters are defined like this: `(String, String)`. We can then access the parameters within the body of the closure using `$0` and `$1`. Also, note that the closure definition is after the colon (`:`), using the same syntax that we use to define a variable type rather than inside the curly brackets. When we use anonymous arguments, this is how we would define the closure. It will not be valid to define the closure as follows:

```
let clos5b = {
    (String, String) in
    print("\($0) \($1)")
}
```

In this example, we will receive an error letting us know that this format is not valid. Next, let's look at how we would use the `clos5` closure as follows:

```
clos5("Hello", "Kara")
```

Since `Hello` is the first string in the parameter list, it is accessed with `$0`, and as `Kara` is the second string in the parameter list, it is accessed with `$1`. When we execute this code, we will see the message `Hello Kara` printed to the console.

This next example is used when the closure doesn't return any value. Rather than defining the return type as `Void`, we can use parentheses, as the following example shows:

```
let clos6: () -> () = {
    print("Howdy")
}
```

In this example, we define the closure as `()  -> ()`. This tells Swift that the closure does not accept any parameters and also does not return a value. We will execute this closure as follows:

```
clos6()
```

As a personal preference, I am not very fond of this shorthand syntax. I think the code is much easier to read when the `void` keyword is used rather than the parentheses.

We have one more shorthand closure example to demonstrate before we begin showing some really useful examples of closures. In this last example, we will demonstrate how we can return a value from the closure without the need to include the `return` keyword.

If the entire closure body consists of only a single statement, then we can omit the `return` keyword, and the results of the statement will be returned. Let's look at an example of this:

```
let clos7 = {(first: Int, second: Int) -> Int in first + second }
```

In this example, the closure accepts two parameters of the integer type and will return an instance of the integer type. The only statement within the body of the closure adds the first parameter to the second parameter. However, if you notice, we do not include the `return` keyword before the additional statement. Swift will see that this is a single statement closure and will automatically return the results, just as if we put the `return` keyword before the addition statement. We do need to make sure the result type of our statement matches the return type of the closure.

All of the examples shown in the previous two sections were designed to show how to define and use closures. On their own, these examples did not really show off the power of closures and they did not show how incredibly useful closures are. The remainder of this chapter is written to demonstrate the power and usefulness of closures in Swift.

Using closures with Swift's array algorithms

In Chapter 3, *Using Swift Collections and the Tuple Type*, we looked at several built-in algorithms that we could use with Swift's arrays. In that chapter, we briefly looked at how to add simple rules to each of these algorithms with very basic closures. Now that we have a better understanding of closures, let's look at how we can expand on these algorithms using more advanced closures.

In this section, we will primarily be using the map algorithm for consistency purposes; however, we can use the basic ideas demonstrated with any of the algorithms. We will start by defining an array to use:

```
let guests = ["Jon", "Kim", "Kailey", "Kara"]
```

This array contains a list of names and the array is named `guests`. This array will be used for the majority of examples in this section.

Now that we have our `guests` array, let's add a closure that will print a greeting to each of the names in the array:

```
guests.map { name in
  print("Hello \(name)")
}
```

Since the map algorithm applies the closure to each item of the array, this example will print out a greeting for each name within the array. After the first section in this chapter, we should have a pretty good understanding of how this closure works. Using the shorthand syntax that we looked at in the last section, we could reduce the preceding example down to the following single line of code:

```
guests.map {print("Hello \($0)")}
```

This is one of the few times, in my opinion, where the shorthand syntax may be easier to read than the standard syntax.

Now, let's say that rather than printing the greeting to the console, we wanted to return a new array that contained the greetings. For this, we would return a `String` type from our closure, as shown in the following example:

```
var messages = guests.map {
  (name:String) -> String in
  return "Welcome \(name)"
}
```

When this code is executed, the `messages` array will contain a greeting to each of the names in the `guests` array, while the `guests` array will remain unchanged. We could access the greetings as follows:

```
for message in messages {
  print("\(message)")
}
```

The preceding examples in this section showed how to add a closure to the map algorithm inline. This is good if we only had one closure that we wanted to use with the map algorithm, but what if we had more than one closure that we wanted to use, or if we wanted to use the closure multiple times or reuse it with different arrays? For this, we could assign the closure to a constant or variable and then pass in the closure, using its constant or variable name, as needed. Let's look at how to do this. We will begin by defining two closures. One of the closures will print a greeting for each element in the array, and the other closure will print a goodbye message for each element in the array:

```
let greetGuest = {
  (name:String) -> Void in
  print("Hello guest named \(name)")
}

let sayGoodbye = {
  (name:String) -> Void in
  print("Goodbye \(name)")
}
```

Now that we have two closures, we can use them with the map algorithm as needed. The following code shows how to use these closures interchangeably with the guests array:

```
guests.map(greetGuest)
guests.map(sayGoodbye)
```

When we use the greetGuest closure with the guests array, the greetings message is printed to the console, and when we use the sayGoodbye closure with the guests array, the goodbye message is printed to the console. If we had another array named guests2, we could use the same closures for that array, as shown in the following example:

```
guests.map(greetGuest)
guests2.map(greetGuest)
guests.map(sayGoodbye)
guests2.map(sayGoodbye)
```

All of the examples in this section so far have either printed a message to the console or returned a new array from the closure. We are not limited to such basic functionality in our closures. For example, we can filter the array within the closure, as shown in the following example:

```
let greetGuest2 = {
  (name:String) -> Void in
  if (name.hasPrefix("K")) {
    print("\(name) is on the guest list")
  } else {
```

```
         print("\(name) was not invited")

    }
}
```

In this example, we print out a different message depending on whether the name starts with the letter K or not.

As mentioned earlier in the chapter, closures have the ability to capture and store references to any variable or constant from the context in which they were defined. Let's look at an example of this. Let's say that we have a function that contains the highest temperature for the last seven days at a given location and this function accepts a closure as a parameter. This function will execute the closure on the array of temperatures. The function can be written as follows:

```
func temperatures(calculate:(Int)->Void) {
  var tempArray = [72,74,76,68,70,72,66]
  tempArray.map(calculate)

}
```

This function accepts a closure defined as (Int)-> Void. We then use the map algorithm to execute this closure for each item of the tempArray array. The key to using a closure correctly in this situation is to understand that the temperatures function does not know or care what goes on inside the calculate closure. Also, be aware that the closure is also unable to update or change the items within the function's context, which means that the closure cannot change any other variable within the temperature's function; however, it can update variables in the context that it was created in.

Let's look at the function that we will create the closure in. We will name this function testFunction:

```
func testFunction() {
  var total = 0
  var count = 0
  let addTemps = {
    (num: Int) -> Void in
    total += num
    count += 1
  }
  temperatures(calculate: addTemps)
  print("Total: \(total)")
  print("Count: \(count)")
  print("Average: \(total/count)")
}
```

In this function, we begin by defining two variables named `total` and `count`, where both variables are of the integer type. We then create a closure named `addTemps` that will be used to add all the temperatures from the `temperatures` function together. The `addTemps` closure will also count how many temperatures there are in the array. To do this, the `addTemps` closure calculates the sum of each item in the array and keeps the total in the `total` variable that was defined at the beginning of the function. The `addTemps` closure also keeps track of the number of items in the array by incrementing the `count` variable for each item. Notice that neither the `total` nor `count` variables are defined within the closure; however, we are able to use them within the closure because they were defined in the same context as the closure.

We then call the `temperatures` function and pass it the `addTemps` closure. Finally, we print the total, count, and average temperature to the console. When the `testFunction` is executed, we will see the following output to the console:

```
Total: 498
Count: 7
Average: 71
```

As we can see from the output, the `addTemps` closure is able to update and use items that are defined within the context that it was created in, even when the closure is used in a different context.

Now that we have looked at using closures with the array map algorithm, let's look at using closures by themselves. We will also look at the ways we can clean up our code to make it easier to read and use.

Standalone closures and good style guidelines

Closures give us the ability to truly separate the data portions of our code from the user interface and business logic portions. This gives us the ability to create reusable classes that focus solely on retrieving the data. This is especially good for developing types and frameworks that are designed to retrieve data from external services, such as web services, databases, or files. In this section, I will show you how to develop a type that will execute a closure once our data is returned.

Let's begin by creating a class that will contain the data portion of our code. In this example, the class will be named `Guests`, and it will contain an array of guest's names. Let's look at the following code:

```
class Guests {
  var guestNames = ["Jon", "Kim", "Kailey", "Kara", "Buddy", "Lily",
                    "Dash"]
  typealias UseArrayClosure = ([String]) -> Void

  func getGuest(handler: UseArrayClosure) {
    handler(guestNames)
  }

}
```

The first line in the `Guests` class defines an array named `guestNames` that contains seven names. We then create a `typealias`. A `typealias` defines a named alias for an existing type. Just like a function, closures have types that consist of the parameter and return types, which can be aliased. This allows us to define the closure once, and then use the alias anywhere within our code. Using a `typealias` can reduce the amount of typing we have to do, and also prevents errors; therefore, it is recommended that we use them rather than trying to retype the closure definition multiple times in our code. It also allows us to change the definition in one location and it will then update throughout the code.

In this example, our `typealias` is named `UseArrayClosure`, and it is defined as a closure that accepts an array of strings as the only parameter, and does not return a value. We can now use this `typealias` throughout our code as shorthand for the closure definition.

Finally, we define a `getGuest()` method that accepts a closure named `handler` as its only parameter. Within this method, the only thing we do is execute the `handler` closure. Normally, in this method, we will have the logic to retrieve the data from our external data source. In this example, we have an array that is hardcoded with our guest's' names; therefore, all we need to do is to execute the closure with the `guestsNames` array as the only parameter.

Now, let's say that we want to display this array of names in a `UITableView`. A `UITableView` is an iOS view that is designed for displaying lists of information. In the view controller, we will need to create an array to hold the data to display in the `UITableView` and a variable that will link to `UITableView` in our display. These will both be class variables defined in our view controller, and they are defined as follows:

```
@IBOutlet var tableView:UITableView!
var tableData: [String]?
```

Now, let's create a function called getData() that will be used to retrieve the list of guests and update the table view:

```
func getData() {
  let dataClosure; Guests.UseArrayClosure = {
    self.tableData = $0
    self.tableView.reloadData()
  }
  let guests = Guests() guests.getGuest(dataClosure)
}
```

We begin the getData() function by defining a closure named dataClosure. This closure uses the UseArrayClosure type alias that we defined in the Guests class for the closure definition. Within the closure definition, we set the tableData array, which is defined within the view controller itself (not in the closure), equal to the string array that is passed into the closure. We then verify whether the tableView variable contains an instance of the UITableView class, and if so, we reload its data. Finally, we create an instance of the Guests class and call the getGuest() method, passing it the dataClosure closure.

When the dataClosure closure is passed to the getGuests() method, it will load the array of names from the Guests class into the tableData array. The tableData array is then used within the view controller class as the data elements for the UITableView. The key items to note in this example is that we are able to load data from one context (the Guests class) into a variable that was defined within the same context as the closure (the view controller), and also have the ability to call methods on instances of classes (tableView and UITableView) defined within the same context as the closure.

We could have very easily created a method in the Guest class that returned the guestNames array. With a hardcoded array, such as the one we have in the Guest class, this method would have worked very well. However, if we were loading the data from a web service that takes a little time to load, this would not work as well because our UI would freeze while waiting for the data to load. By using a closure as shown in this example, we can make the web service call asynchronously, and then when the data is returned, the closure will be executed, and the UI updates automatically without our UI freezing.

This book is primarily written to teach the Swift language and not specifically iOS development; therefore, we are not covering how the UI elements from the Cocoa Touch framework work in this example.

Changing functionality

Closures also give us the ability to change the functionality of types on the fly. We saw, in Chapter 11, *Working with Generics*, that generics give us the ability to write functions that are valid for multiple types. With closures, we are able to write functions and types whose functionality can change, based on the closure that is passed in. In this section, we will show how to write a function whose functionality can be changed with a closure.

Let's begin by defining a type that will be used to demonstrate how to swap out functionality. We will name this type `TestType`:

```
struct TestType {
  typealias getNumClosure = ((Int, Int) -> Int)

  var numOne = 5
  var numTwo = 8

  var results = 0;

  mutating func getNum(handler: getNumClosure) -> Int {
    results = handler(numOne,numTwo)
    print("Results: \(results)")
    return results
  }
}
```

We begin this type by defining a `typealias` for our closure that is named `getNumClosure`. Any closure that is defined as a `getNumClosure` closure will take two integers and return a single integer. Within this closure, we assume that it does something with the integers that we pass in to get the value to return, but it really doesn't have to. To be honest, this class doesn't really care what the closure does as long as it conforms to the `getNumClosure` type. Next, we define three integers named `numOne`, `numTwo`, and `results`.

We also define a method named `getNum()`. This method accepts a closure that conforms to the `getNumClosure` type as its only parameter. Within the `getNum()` method, we execute the closure by passing in the `numOne` and `numTwo` variables, and the integer that is returned is put into the `results` class variable.

Now let's look at several closures that conform to the `getNumClosure` type that we can use with the `getNum()` method:

```
var max: TestType.getNumClosure = {
  if $0 > $1 {
    return $0
  } else {
```

```
    return $1
    }
}

var min: TestType.getNumClosure = {
  if $0 < $1 {
    return $0
  } else {
    return $1
  }
}

var multiply: TestType.getNumClosure = {
  return $0 * $1
}

var second: TestType.getNumClosure = {
  return $1
}

var answer: TestType.getNumClosure = {
  var tmp = $0 + $1
  return 42
}
```

In this code, we define five closures that conform to the getNumClosure type:

- max: This returns the maximum value of the two integers that are passed
- in min: This returns the minimum value of the two integers that are passed
- in multiply: This multiplies both the values that are passed in and returns the product
- second: This returns the second parameter that was passed in
- answer: This returns the answer to life, the universe, and everything

In the answer closure, we have an extra line that looks like it does not have a purpose: _= $0 + $1. We do this purposely because the following code is not valid:

```
var answer: TestClass.getNumClosure = {
  return 42
}
```

This type gives us the error: `contextual type for closure argument list expects 2 arguments, which cannot be implicitly ignored`. As we can see by the error, Swift will not let us ignore the expected parameters within the body of the closure. In the closure named second, Swift assumes that there are two parameters because `$1` specifies the second parameter.

We can now pass each one of these closures to the `getNum()` method to change the functionality of the function to suit our needs. The following code illustrates this:

```
var myType = TestType()

myType.getNum(handler: max)
myType.getNum(handler: min)
myType.getNum(handler: multiply)
myType.getNum(handler: second)
myType.getNum(handler: answer)
```

When this code is run, we will receive the following results for each of the closures:

```
For Max:        Results: 8
For Min:        Results: 5
For Multiply:   Results: 40
For Second:     Results: 8
For Answer:     Results: 42
```

The last example we are going to show you in this chapter is one that is used a lot in frameworks, especially ones that have a functionality that is designed to be run asynchronously.

Selecting a closure based on results

In the final example, we will pass two closures to a method, and then, depending on some logic, one or possibly both of the closures will be executed. Generally, one of the closures is called if the method was successfully executed and the other closure is called if the method failed.

Let's start off by creating a type that will contain a method that will accept two closures and then execute one of the closures based on the defined logic. We will name this type `TestType`. Here is the code for the `TestType` type:

```
class TestType {
    typealias ResultsClosure = ((String) -> Void)

    func isGreater(numOne: Int, numTwo: Int, successHandler: ResultsClosure,
```

```
                    failureHandler: ResultsClosure) {
      if numOne > numTwo {
        successHandler("\(numOne) is greater than \(numTwo)")
      }
      else {
        failureHandler("\(numOne) is not greater than \(numTwo)")
      }

    }
  }
```

We begin this type by creating a `typealias` that defines the closure that we will use for both the successful and failure closures. We will name this `typealias ResultsClosure`. This example also illustrates why you should use a `typealias` rather than retyping the closure definition. It saves us a lot of typing and prevents us from making mistakes. In this example, if we did not use a `typealias`, we would need to retype the closure definition four times, and if we needed to change the closure definition, we would need to change it in four spots. With the type alias, we only need to type the closure definition once and then use the alias throughout the remaining code.

We then create a method named `isGreater`, which takes two integers as the first two parameters, and two closures as the next two parameters. The first closure is named `successHandler`, and the second closure is named `failureHandler`. Within this method, we check whether the first integer parameter is greater than the second one. If the first integer is greater, the `successHandler` closure is executed, otherwise, the `failureHandler` closure is executed.

Now, let's create two closures outside of the `TestType` structure. The code for these two closures is as follows:

```
var success: TestType.ResultsClosure = {
  print("Success: \($0)")
}

var failure: TestType.ResultsClosure = {
  print("Failure: \($0)")
}
```

Note that both closures are defined as the `TestClass.ResultsClosure` type. In each closure, we simply print a message to the console to let us know which closure was executed. Normally, we would put some functionality in the closure.

We will then call the method with both the closures, as follows:

```
var test = TestType()
test.isGreater(numOne: 8, numTwo: 6, successHandler: success,
failureHandler: failure)
```

Note that in the method call, we are sending both the success closure and the failure closure. In this example, we will see the message `Success: 8 is greater than 6`. If we reversed the numbers, we would see the message `Failure: 6 is not greater than 8`. This use case is really good when we call asynchronous methods, such as loading data from a web service. If the web service call was successful, the success closure is called; otherwise, the failure closure is called.

One big advantage of using closures like this is that the UI does not freeze while we wait for the asynchronous call to complete. This also involves a concurrency piece, which we will be covering in `Chapter 14`, *Concurrency and Parallelism in Swift*, later in this book. As an example, if we tried to retrieve data from a web service as follows:

```
var data = myWebClass.myWebServiceCall(someParameter)
```

Our UI would freeze while we wait for the response to come back, or we would have to make the call in a separate thread so that the UI would not hang. With closures, we pass the closures to the networking framework and rely on the framework to execute the appropriate closure when it is done. This does rely on the framework to implement concurrency correctly, to make the calls asynchronously, but a decent framework should handle that for us.

Creating strong reference cycles with closures

Earlier in this chapter, we said that: *for the most part, Swift will handle memory management for us*. The *for the most part* section of the quote means that if everything is written correctly, Swift will handle the memory management of the closures for us. However, there are times where memory management fails. Memory management will work correctly for all of the examples that we have seen in this chapter so far. It is possible to create a strong reference cycle that would prevent Swift's memory management from working correctly. Let's look at what happens if we create a strong reference cycle with closures.

A strong reference cycle will happen if we assign a closure to a property of a class instance and within that closure, we capture the instance of the class. This capture occurs because we access a property of that particular instance using self, such as `self.someProperty`, or we assign self to a variable or constant, such as `let c = self`. By capturing a property of the instance, we are actually capturing the instance itself, thereby creating a strong reference cycle where the memory manager will not know when to release the instance. As a result, the memory will not be freed.

Let's begin by creating a class that has a closure and an instance of the `String` type as its two properties. We will also create a `typealias` for the closure type in this class, and define a `deinit()` method that prints a message to the console. The `deinit()` method is called when the class gets released and the memory is freed. We will know when the class gets released when the message from the `deinit()` method is printed to the console. This class will be named `TestClassOne`. Let's look at the following code:

```
class TestClassOne {
  typealias nameClosure = (() -> String)
  var name = "Jon"
  lazy var myClosure: nameClosure = {
    return self.name
  }
  deinit {
    print("TestClassOne deinitialized")
  }
}
```

Now, let's create a second class that will contain a method that accepts a closure that is of the `nameClosure` type, which was defined in the `TestClassOne` class. This class will also have a `deinit()` method, so we can also see when it gets released. We will name this class `TestClassTwo`. Let's look at the following code:

```
class TestClassTwo {
  func closureExample(handler: TestClassOne.nameClosure) {
    print(handler())
  }
  deinit {
    print("TestClassTwo deinitialized")
  }
}
```

Now, let's look at this code in action, by creating instances of each class and then trying to manually release the instance by setting them to `nil`:

```
var testClassOne: TestClassOne? = TestClassOne()
var testClassTwo: TestClassTwo? = TestClassTwo()
```

```
testClassTwo?.closureExample(handler: testClassOne!.myClosure)
testClassOne = nil
print("testClassOne is gone")
testClassTwo = nil
print("testClassTwo is gone")
```

What we do in this code is create two optionals, which may contain an instance of our two test classes or `nil`. We need to create these variables as optionals because we will be setting them to `nil` later in the code so that we can see whether the instances are released properly.

We then call the `closureExample()` method of the `TestClassTwo` instance and pass it the `myClosure` property from the `TestClassOne` instance. We now try to compare both instances by setting them to `nil`. Keep in mind that when an instance of a class is released, it attempts to call the `deinit()` method of the class if it exists. In our case, both classes have a `deinit()` method that prints a message to the console, so we know when the instances are actually released.

If we run this project, we will see the following messages printed to the console:

```
testClassOne is gone
TestClassTwo deinitialized
testClassTwo is gone
```

As we can see, we do attempt to release the `TestClassOne` instances, but the `deinit()` method of the class is never called, indicating that it was not actually released; however, the `TestClassTwo` instance was properly released because the `deinit()` method of that class was called.

To see how this is supposed to work without the strong reference cycle, change the `myClosure` closure to return a string type that is defined within the closure itself, as shown in the following code:

```
lazy var myClosure: nameClosure = {
    return "Just Me"
}
```

Now, if we run the project, we should see the following output:

```
TestClassOne deinitialized
testClassOne is gone
TestClassTwo deinitialized
testClassTwo is gone
```

This shows that the `deinit()` methods from both the `TestClassOne` and `TestClassTwo` instances were properly called, indicating that they were both released properly.

In the first example, we capture an instance of the `TestClassOne` class within the closure because we accessed a property of the `TestClassOne` class using `self.name`. This created a strong reference from the closure to the instance of the `TestClassOne` class, preventing memory management from releasing the instance.

Swift does provide a very easy and elegant way to resolve strong reference cycles in closures. We simply need to tell Swift not to create a strong reference by creating a capture list. A capture list defines the rules to use when capturing reference types within a closure. We can declare each reference to be a weak or unowned reference rather than a strong reference.

A `weak` keyword is used when there is the possibility that the reference will become nil during its lifetime; therefore, the type must be an optional. The `unowned` keyword is used when there is no possibility of the reference becoming nil.

We define the capture list by pairing the `weak` or `unowned` keywords with a reference to a class instance. These pairings are written within square brackets (`[ ]`). Therefore, if we update the `myClosure` closure and define an `unowned` reference to self, we should eliminate the strong reference cycle. The following code shows what the new `myClosure` closure will look like:

```
lazy var myClosure: nameClosure = { [unowned self] in
    return self.name
}
```

Notice the new line, `[unowned self]` in, this line says that we do not want to create a strong reference to the instance of `self`. If we run the project now, we should see the following output:

```
TestClassOne deinitialized
testClassOne is gone
TestClassTwo deinitialized
testClassTwo is gone
```

This shows that both the `TestClassOne` and `TestClassTwo` instances were properly released.

Summary

In this chapter, we saw that we can define a closure just like we can define an `Integer` or `String` type. We can assign closures to a variable, pass them as an argument to functions, and return them from functions.

Closures capture strong references to any constants or variables from the context in which the closure was defined. We do have to be careful with this functionality, to make sure that we do not create a strong reference cycle, which would lead to memory leaks in our applications.

Swift closures are very similar to blocks in Objective-C, but they have a much cleaner and more eloquent syntax. This makes them a lot easier to use and understand.

Having a good understanding of closures is vital to mastering the Swift programming language, and will make it easier to develop great applications that are easy to maintain. They are also essential for creating first-class frameworks that are easy both to use and maintain.

The three use cases that we looked at in this chapter are by no means the only three useful uses for closures. I can promise you that the more you use closures in Swift, the more uses you will find for them. Closures are definitely one of the most powerful and useful features of the Swift language, and Apple did a great job by implementing them in the language.

In the next chapter, we will look at how to use Swift and Objective-C together.

13
Using Mix and Match

When Apple first introduced Swift at WWDC 2014, my first thought was how much work it would be for developers to rewrite their apps in Swift. Somewhere in the Swift presentation, Apple spoke about mix and match, which enables Swift and Objective-C to interact within the same project. Mix and match sure sounded like the ideal solution because developers could rewrite sections of their code in Swift as they needed to do updates, instead of having to rewrite their whole application. My big question was around the functionality of mix and match, and how it would work in the real world, because I definitely had my doubts. I must confess that I was very surprised. Not only did mix and match work as advertised, it was also very easy to implement.

In this chapter, we will cover the following topics:

- What is mix and match?
- How to use Swift and Objective-C together in the same project?
- How to add Swift to an Objective-C project?
- How to use Objective-C in a Swift project?

What is mix and match?

Mix and match allows us to create a project in either Objective-C or Swift and include code from either language. This feature is arguably one of the most important features that came out with Swift.

 If you do not plan on using Objective-C and Swift together, you can skip this chapter. You can always come back to this chapter if, at a later time, you find you need to use the languages together.

The reason why this feature is so important is that there are over a million apps written in Objective-C in Apple's App Store, and it would not be feasible for developers to spend the resources required for converting all of these apps from Objective-C to Swift. Without mix and match, the adoption of the Swift language would be very slow. With mix and match, developers can begin to use Swift in any of their present apps that are written in Objective-C without having to convert the entire code base to Swift.

When to use mix and match

With mix and match, we can update a current Objective-C project using Swift. We can also use any framework written in Objective-C within our Swift projects and use newer frameworks written in Swift in our Objective-C projects.

Developers that have been using Apple products for a long time might find a similarity between mix and match and Rosetta, which Apple started including with OS X Tiger. OS X 10.4.4 Tiger was the first version of Apple's operating system that was released with Apple's first Intel-based machines. Rosetta was written to allow many PowerPC applications to run seamlessly on the new Intel-based machines.

For those developers who are new to Apple products, you might not have heard of Rosetta. This is because Rosetta was not included or supported as of OS X 10.7 Lion. The reason this is mentioned here is because, if mix and match takes a similar path as Rosetta, it might not be a part of the language forever, and we can infer from what Apple has said in the past that Swift is the future. It also makes sense from a technological standpoint that as the Swift language evolves and matures, Apple will not want to maintain compatibility with Objective-C.

If you maintain legacy apps written in Objective-C, it might be a good idea to take advantage of mix and match to slowly upgrade your code base to Swift.

Let's look at how Swift and Objective-C can interact together. For this, we will be creating a very basic iOS project whose language will be Objective-C, and then we will add some Swift code to the project. In the downloadable code for this book, we have included an Objective-C project that includes Swift code, and a Swift project that includes Objective-C code. One thing to keep in mind is that it does not matter if our project is an Objective-C or a Swift project; interaction between Swift and Objective-C works the same way.

Using Swift and Objective-C together in the same project

In this section, we will be walking through how to add Swift to an Objective-C project. As we just mentioned, the same steps can also be used to add the Objective-C code to a Swift project.

Creating the project

Let's begin by creating an iOS project to work with. When we first start Xcode, we should see a screen that looks similar to the following screenshot:

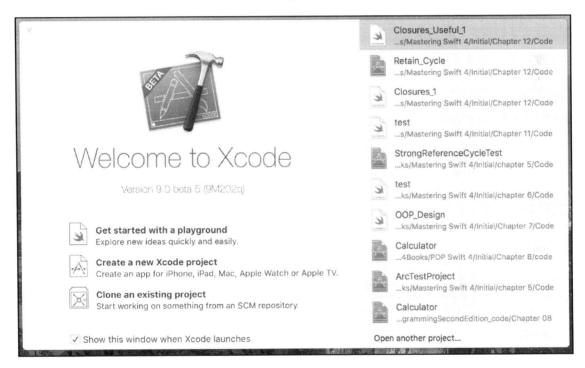

From this menu, we will want to select the **Create a new Xcode project** option. This option will walk us though creating a new Xcode project. Once this option is selected, Xcode will start up and we will see a menu. As a shortcut, if we do not see this menu, we can also navigate to **File | New | Project** in the top menu bar, which will display the following menus:

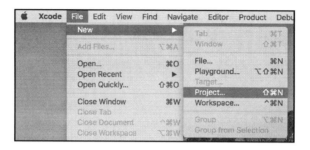

This menu lets us select the type of project we will be creating and also what platform we are targeting (iOS or OS X). For this example, we will be targeting the iOS platform and creating a simple single view application. Once we make the selection, we should see the following menu:

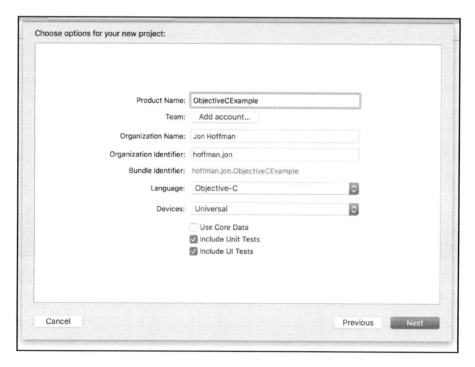

In this menu, we will define several properties about the project. The two properties we need to focus on are the language of the project and the **Product Name**. For this particular project, we will select Objective-C as the language and name it `ObjectiveCExample`. Once we have all of the properties defined, we can click on the **Next** button. In the last menu, we select where we wish to save the project files, and once we have done that, Xcode creates the project template files for us, and we can begin.

The application that we will be creating will let the user enter a name and will then respond with a personal message to them. The user interface will consist of a `UITextField` field that the user can enter their name into, a `UIButton` that the user will press after they have entered their name, and a `UITextView` that will display the personalized message. Since this book is about Swift programming, we will not go into how the user interface is laid out. Full working applications are available as part of this book's downloadable source code.

Since we are walking through the Objective-C project, the user interface and the messages class, which will generate a message, will be written in Objective-C. The message builder, which will personalize the message, will be written in Swift. This will show us how to access a Swift class from the Objective-C code, as well as Objective-C resources from our Swift code within an Objective-C project.

Let's summarize how Objective-C as Swift will interact. The backend of the user interface, which is written in Objective-C, will call a `getPersonalizedMessage()` method from the `MessageBuilder` class written in Swift. This method will call a `getMessage()` function of the `Messages` class written in Objective-C.

Adding Swift files to the Objective-C project

Let's begin by creating the Swift `MessageBuilder` class. This class will be used to build the personalized message for the user. Within Objective-C projects, I usually create a separate group called **SwiftFiles** to hold the Swift files in. This allows me to very easily see which files are written in Swift and which files are written in Objective-C. To add a Swift file to our project, right-click on the group icon that we want to add the file to and we should see the following menu:

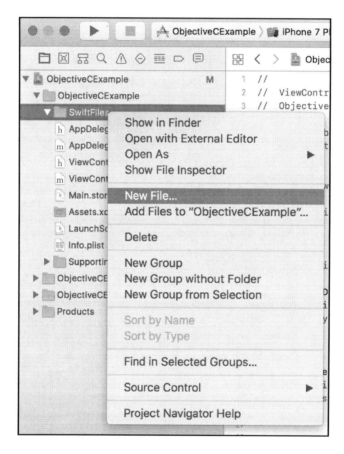

From this menu, select the **New File...** option. This option will walk us through creating a new file for our project. Once you select that option, you should see the following menu:

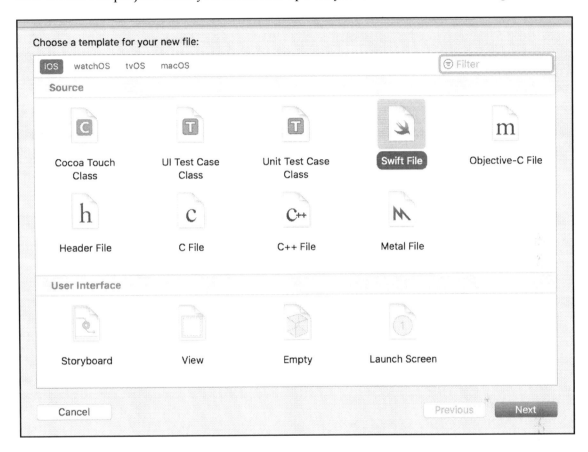

This menu lets us choose what type of file we will be adding to our project. In our case, we will want to add a Swift file to the project, and, therefore, we will select the **SwiftFiles** option. Once we select this option, we should see the following menu:

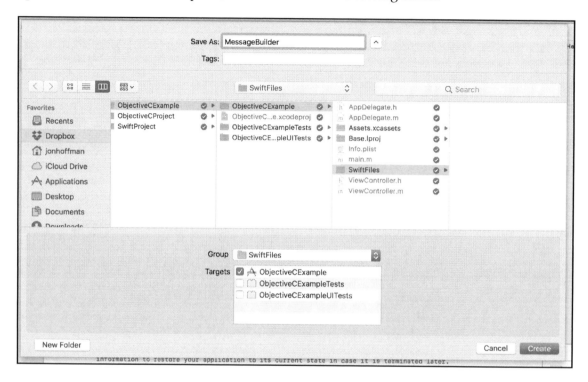

This menu lets us name the file and define some of the properties, such as where we want to save the file and what group it will be in. In this case, we name the file MessageBuilder. Once we have finished, we will click on the **Create** button. If this is the first Swift file added to an Objective-C project (or the first Objective-C file added to a Swift project), we should see the following menu pop up:

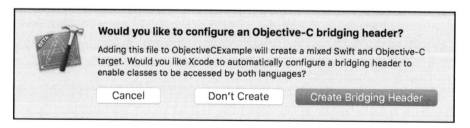

This popup offers to create the bridging header file that will be used in our code. Select **Create Bridging Header** to create the file.

The Objective-C bridging header file - part 1

In order to expose our Objective-C files to our Swift code, we rely on an Objective-C header file. The first time we add an Objective-C file to a Swift project or a Swift file to an Objective-C project, Xcode will offer to create this file for us. It is easier to let Xcode create and configure this file rather than doing it manually, so it is recommended to select **Create Bridging Header** when Xcode offers to create it.

If, for some reason, we need to create the Objective-C bridging header file manually, we would take the following steps:

1. Create an Objective-C header file in our project using the **New File...** option we saw earlier. The recommended naming convention for this file is [MyProjectName]-Bridging-Header.h, where [MyProjectName] is the name of our project. This will be the header file where we import the Objective-C header files for any Objective-C classes that we want our Swift code to access.
2. In the project's **Build Settings**, find the **Swift Compiler| General** section. In this section, locate the setting titled **Objective-C Bridging Header**. We will want to set this to the path for the bridging header we created in step 1. The path will be from the project root.

The **Objective-C Bridging Header** setting for the present project that we are working on looks similar to the following screenshot:

The bridging header is located at the root of the project. If we want to put the header file in another directory within the project, all we would need to do is change the path in this setting.

Adding the Objective-C file to the project

Now that we have our Objective-C bridging header file and the `MessageBuilder` Swift file, let's create the Objective-C class that will generate a generic message to the user. We will name this class `Messages`. To create this file, right-click on the group folder that we want to add the file to, and we should see the following menu:

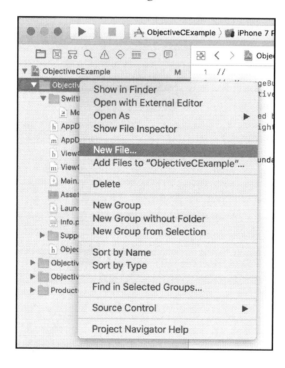

From this menu, select the **New File...**option. This option will walk us through creating a new file for our project. Once you select that option, you should see the following menu:

Previously, when we added the `MessageBuilder` Swift file, we selected **Swift File** on this menu. This time, we will be adding an Objective-C file, so we will select the **Cocoa Touch Class** option. Once we select that option, we should see a screen similar to this:

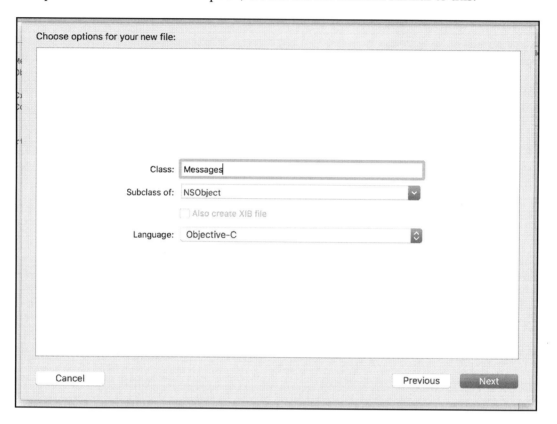

In this menu, we can enter the class name and also the language for the class. Make sure that the language is set to Objective-C. Finally, we click on the **Next** button, which will take us to a menu that will let us select where we want to save our Objective-C files. Once we select the location to save our files, both the header and implementation files will be added to our project.

Now that all of our files have been created, let's begin writing the code and getting Swift and Objective-C to work together. We will begin by adding the code to the Objective-C messages header and implementation files.

The Messages Objective-C class

The `Messages` Objective-C class will contain an array of messages and will expose one method named `getMessage`, which will return one randomly picked message from the array.

The following code shows the `Messages` header file:

```
#import <Foundation/Foundation.h>

@interface Messages : NSObject

-(NSString *)getMessage;
@end
```

In this header file, we expose one method named `getMessage`, which will return a message when called. The following code shows the implementation file for the `Messages` class:

```
#import "Messages.h"

@implementation Messages
NSMutableArray *theMessages;
-(id)init {
  if ( self = [super init] ) {
    theMessages = [NSMutableArray new];
    [theMessages addObject:@"You should learn from your mistakes"];
    [theMessages addObject:@"It is in the now that we must live"];
    [theMessages addObject:@"The greatest risk is not taking one"];
    [theMessages addObject:@"You will be a Swift programmer"];
  }
  return self;
}

-(NSString *)getMessage {
  int num = arc4random() % theMessages.count;
  return theMessages[num];
}
@end
```

In this code, we created the `NSArray` object, which contains several messages. We also created the `getMessage` method, which randomly picks one of the messages from the `NSArray` object and returns it.

The `Messages` class that we just created in Objective-C will need to be accessed by the `MessageBuilder` class that we are going to write in Swift. To access an Objective-C class from the Swift code, we need to edit the `Objective-C Bridging Header` file.

The Objective-C bridging header file - part 2

Now that we have created the Messages Objective-C class, we will need to expose it to our Swift code. Those who are familiar with Objective-C (or any C-based language), will know that we need to import the class header using the #import or #include directive prior to using it within another class. In that same context, we need to import the header file of any Objective-C class in the Objective-C bridging header file prior to using that class in our Swift code. Therefore, to allow our Swift code to access the Messages Objective-C class, we need to add the following line to the Objective-C bridging header file that Xcode created for us:

```
#import "Messages.h"
```

Yep, that's it. Pretty simple. Now, let's look at how we would write the MessageBuilder Swift class that will use the Objective-C Messages class.

The MessageBuilder Swift class - accessing Objective-C code from Swift

The Swift MessageBuilder class will contain one method named getPersonalizedMessage(). This method will use the getMessage() method from the Objective-C Messages class to retrieve a message and will then customize that message prior to returning it to the function that called it. Here is the code for the Swift MessageBuiler class:

```
import Foundation

class MessageBuilder: NSObject {
  func getPersonalizedMessage(name: String) -> String {
    let messages = Messages()
    let retMessage = "To: " + name + ", " + messages.getMessage()
    return retMessage;
  }
}
```

When we define this class, we create it as a subclass of the NSObject class. If a Swift class will be accessed from the Objective-C code, this class needs to be a subclass of the NSObject class. If we forget to do this, we will receive an error.

Now, let's look at how we will create an instance of the Objective-C `Messages` class in our Swift code. The code phrase `let messages = Messages()` creates the instance. As we can see, we create the instance of the Objective-C `Messages` class exactly as we would create an instance of any Swift class. We then access the `getMessages()` method like we would access a method of any Swift class.

As we can see from this code, Objective-C classes are both initiated and used as if they were written in Swift when we access them from a Swift type. This allows us to access our Objective-C and Swift types in a consistent way.

Now that we have created the Swift `MessageBuilder` class, we need a way to call the `getPersonalizedMessage()` method from the Objective-C `ViewController` class.

The Objective-C class - accessing Swift code from Objective-C

Once the user enters their name and presses the **Get Message** button, we will create an instance of the Swift `MessageBuilder` class in the Objective-C code and call the `getPersonlizedMessage()` method to generate the message to be displayed.

When we access Swift code from Objective-C, we rely on an Xcode-generated header file to expose the Swift classes. This automatically generated header file declares the interface for the Swift classes. The name of this header file is the name of your project followed by -`Swift.h`, so the name of the header file for our project is `ObjectiveCExample-Swift.h`. Therefore, the first step to access the Swift code from Objective-C is to import this header file, as shown in the following line of code:

```
#import "ObjectiveCProject-Swift.h"
```

Now that we have imported the header file to expose our Swift classes, we can use the Swift `MessageBuilder` class within the Objective-C code. We create an instance of the Swift `MessageBuilder` class exactly like we would create an instance of any standard Objective-C class. We also call the method and properties of a Swift class exactly like we would call the method and properties from an Objective-C class. The following example shows how we would create an instance of the Swift `MessageBuilder` class, and also how we would call the `getPersonalizedMessage()` method of that class:

```
MessageBuilder *mb = [[MessageBuilder alloc] init];
self.messageView.text = [mb getPersonalizedMessageWithName:@"Jon"];
```

As we can see from this code sample, Swift classes are treated as if they were Objective-C classes when we access them from Objective-C code. Once again, this allows us to access both our Objective-C and Swift types in a consistent manner.

The noticeable difference is that when we access our `getPersonalizedMessage()` method in our Swift code, we access it like this:

```
getPersonalizedMessage(name: "Jon")
```

When we access it from the Objective-C code, we access it like this:

```
[mb getPersonalizedMessageWithName:@"Jon"];
```

Note how the message name changed to include the `name` parameter.

Summary

As we saw in this chapter, Apple has made mix and match very easy and convenient to use. In order to access Swift classes from our Objective-C code, all we need to do is import the Xcode-generated header file that exposes the Swift classes. While we do not see this header file as part of our code, Xcode automatically creates it for mixed language projects. The name of this header file takes the format of `{Project Name}-Swift.h`, where `{Project Name}` is the name of our project.

It is also very easy to use Objective-C classes within our Swift code. To expose Objective-C classes to our Swift code, all we need to do is add the Objective-C header file to the `Objective-C Bridging Header` file. Xcode can create this bridging header file for us the first time we add an Objective-C file to a Swift project, or the first time we add a Swift file to an Objective-C project.

While Apple has said that the future of application development for iOS and OS X platforms is in Swift, mix and match can be used to slowly migrate our current Objective-C code base to Swift. Mix and match also lets us use Objective-C frameworks in our Swift projects or Swift frameworks in our Objective-C projects.

In the next chapter, we will look at how to add concurrency to our application.

14

Concurrency and Parallelism in Swift

When I first started learning Objective-C, I already had a good understanding of concurrency and multitasking with my background in other languages, such as C and Java. This background made it very easy for me to create multithreaded applications using threads. Then, Apple changed everything when they released **Grand Central Dispatch (GCD)** with OS X 10.6 and iOS 4. At first, I went into denial; there was no way GCD could manage my application's threads better than I could. Then I entered the anger phase; GCD was hard to use and understand. Next was the bargaining phase; maybe I can use GCD with my threading code, so I could still control how the threading worked. Then there was the depression phase; maybe GCD does handle threading better than I could. Finally, I entered the wow phase; this GCD thing is really easy to use and works amazingly well. After using GCD and operation queues with Objective-C, I do not see a reason for using manual threads with Swift.

In this chapter, we will learn the following topics:

- What are basics of concurrency and parallelism?
- How to use GCD to create and manage concurrent dispatch queues?
- How to use GCD to create and manage serial dispatch queues?
- How to use various GCD functions to add tasks to the dispatch queues?
- How to use `Operation` and `OperationQueues` to add concurrency to our applications?

Concurrency and parallelism

Concurrency is the concept of multiple tasks starting, running, and completing within the same time period. This does not necessarily mean that the tasks are executing simultaneously. In fact, in order for tasks to be run simultaneously, our application needs to be running on a multicore or multiprocessor system. Concurrency allows us to share the processor or cores for multiple tasks; however, a single core can only execute one task at a given time.

Parallelism is the concept of two or more tasks running simultaneously. Since each core of our processor can only execute one task at a time, the number of tasks executing simultaneously is limited to the number of cores within our processors and the number of processors that we have. As an example, if we have a four-core processor, then we are limited to running four tasks simultaneously. Today's processors can execute tasks so quickly that it may appear that larger tasks are executing simultaneously. However, within the system, the larger tasks are actually taking turns executing subtasks on the cores.

In order to understand the difference between concurrency and parallelism, let's look at how a juggler juggles balls. If you watch a juggler, it seems they are catching and throwing multiple balls at any given time, however, a closer look reveals that they are, in fact, only catching and throwing one ball at a time. The other balls are in the air waiting to be caught and thrown. If we want to be able to catch and throw multiple balls simultaneously, we need to have multiple jugglers.

This example is really good because we can think of jugglers as the cores of a processer. A system with a single core processor (one juggler), regardless of how it seems, can only execute one task (catch and throw one ball) at a time. If we want to execute more than one task at a time, we need to use a multicore processor (more than one juggler).

Back in the old days when all the processors were single-core, the only way to have a system that executed tasks simultaneously was to have multiple processors in the system. This also required specialized software to take advantage of the multiple processors. In today's world, just about every device has a processor that has multiple cores, and both the iOS and macOS operating systems are designed to take advantage of the multiple cores to run tasks simultaneously.

Traditionally, the way applications added concurrency was to create multiple threads; however, this model does not scale well to an arbitrary number of cores. The biggest problem with using threads was that our applications ran on a variety of systems (and processors), and in order to optimize our code, we needed to know how many cores/processors could be efficiently used at a given time, which is usually not known at the time of development.

To solve this problem, many operating systems, including iOS and macOS, started relying on asynchronous functions. These functions are often used to initiate tasks that could possibly take a long time to complete, such as making an HTTP request or writing data to disk. An asynchronous function typically starts the long running task and then returns prior to the task's completion. Usually, this task runs in the background and uses a callback function (such as closure in Swift) when the task completes.

These asynchronous functions work great for the tasks that the OS provides them for, but what if we need to create our own asynchronous functions and do not want to manage the threads ourselves? For this, Apple provides a couple of technologies. In this chapter, we will be covering two of these technologies: GCD and operation queues.

GCD is a low-level, C-based API that allows specific tasks to be queued up for execution, and schedules the execution on any of the available processor cores. Operation queues are similar to GCD; however, they are Foundation objects and are internally implemented using GCD.

Let's begin by looking at GCD.

Grand Central Dispatch

Prior to Swift 3, using GCD felt like writing low-level C code. The API was a little cumbersome, and sometimes, hard to understand because it did not use any of the Swift language design features. This all changed with Swift 3 because Apple took up the task of rewriting the API so it would meet the Swift 3 API guidelines.

Grand Central Dispatch provides what is known as dispatch queues to manage submitted tasks. The queues manage these submitted tasks and execute them in a **first-in, first-out (FIFO)** order. This ensures that the tasks are started in the order they were submitted.

A task is simply some work that our application needs to perform. For example, we can create tasks that perform simple calculations, read/write data to disk, make an HTTP request, or anything else that our application needs to do. We define these tasks by placing the code inside either a function or a closure and adding it to a dispatch queue.

GCD provides three types of queues:

- **Serial queues**: Tasks in a serial queue (also known as a **private queue**) are executed one at a time in the order they were submitted. Each task is started only after the preceding task is completed. Serial queues are often used to synchronize access to specific resources because we are guaranteed that no two tasks in a serial queue will ever run simultaneously. Therefore, if the only way to access the specific resource is through the tasks in the serial queue, then no two tasks will attempt to access the resource at the same time or out of order.
- **Concurrent queues**: Tasks in a concurrent queue (also known as a **global dispatch queue**) execute concurrently; however, the tasks are still started in the order that they were added to the queue. The exact number of tasks that can be executed at any given instance is variable and is dependent on the system's current conditions and resources. The decision on when to start a task is up to GCD and is not something that we can control within our application.
- **Main dispatch queue**: The main dispatch queue is a globally available serial queue that executes tasks on the application's main thread. Since tasks put into the main dispatch queue run on the main thread, it is usually called from a background queue when some background processing has finished and the user interface needs to be updated.

Dispatch queues offer several advantages over traditional threads. The first and foremost advantage is that, with dispatch queues, the system handles the creation and management of threads rather than the application itself. The system can scale the number of threads dynamically, based on the overall available resources of the system and the current system conditions. This means that dispatch queues can manage the threads with greater efficiency than we could.

Another advantage of dispatch queues is that we are able to control the order in which the tasks are started. With serial queues, not only do we control the order in which tasks are started, but we also ensure that one task does not start before the preceding one is complete. With traditional threads, this can be very cumbersome and brittle to implement, but with dispatch queues, as we will see later in this chapter, it is quite easy.

Calculation type

Before we look at how to use the dispatch queues, let's create a class that will help us demonstrate how the various types of queues work. This class will contain two basic functions and we will name the class DoCalculations. The first function will simply perform some basic calculations and then return a value. Here is the code for this function, which is named doCalc():

```
func doCalc() {
  var x = 100
  var y = x*x
  _ = y/x
}
```

The other function, which we will name performCalculation(), accepts two parameters. One is an integer named iterations and the other is a string named tag. The performCalculation() function calls the doCalc() function repeatedly until it calls the function the same number of times as defined by the iterations parameter. We also use the CFAbsoluteTimeGetCurrent() function to calculate the elapsed time it took to perform all of the iterations, and then print the elapsed time with the tag string to the console. This will let us know when the function completes and how long it took to complete it. Here is the code for this function:

```
func performCalculation(iterations: Int, tag: String) {
  let start = CFAbsoluteTimeGetCurrent()
  for _ in 0 ..< iterations {
    self.doCalc()
  }
  let end = CFAbsoluteTimeGetCurrent()
  print("time for \(tag):\(end-start)")
}
```

These functions will be used together to keep our queues busy, so we can see how they work. Let's begin by looking at how we would create a dispatch queue.

Creating queues

We use the DispatchQueue initializer to create a new dispatch queue. The following code shows how we would create a new dispatch queue:

```
let concurrentQueue = DispatchQueue(label: "cqueue.hoffman.jon",
                                    attributes: .concurrent)
let serialQueue = DispatchQueue(label: "squeue.hoffman.jon")
```

The first line would create a concurrent queue with the label of `cqueue.hoffman.jon`, while the second line would create a serial queue with the label of `squeue.hoffman.jon`.

The `DispatchQueue` initializer takes the following parameters:

- **label**: This is a string label that is attached to the queue to uniquely identify it in debugging tools, such as instruments and crash reports. It is recommended that we use a reverse DNS naming convention. This parameter is optional and can be nil.
- **attributes**: This specifies the type of queue to make. This can be `DISPATCH_QUEUE_SERIAL`, `DISPATCH_QUEUE_CONCURRENT`, or `nil`. If the this parameter is nil, a serial queue is created.

> Some programming languages use the reverse DNS naming convention to name certain components. This convention is based on a registered domain name that is reversed. As an example, if we worked for a company that had a domain name `mycompany.com` with a product called widget, the reverse DNS name will be `com.mycompany.widget`.

Creating and using a concurrent queue

A concurrent queue will execute the tasks in a FIFO order; however, the tasks will execute concurrently and finish in any order. Let's see how we would create and use a concurrent queue. The following line will create the concurrent queue that we will be using for this section and will also create an instance of the `DoCalculations` type that will be used to test the queue:

```
let cqueue = DispatchQueue(label: "cqueue.hoffman.jon",
                           attributes:.concurrent)
let calculation = DoCalculations()
```

The first line will create a new dispatch queue that we will name `cqueue`, and the second line creates an instance of the `DoCalculations` type. Now let's see how we would use our concurrent queue by using the `performCalculation()` method from the `DoCalculations` type to perform some calculations:

```
let c = {calculation.performCalculation(1000, tag: "async1")}
cqueue.async(execute: c)
```

In the preceding code, we created a closure, which represents our task and simply calls the `performCalculation()` function of the `DoCalculation` instance, requesting that it runs through 1000 iterations of the `doCalc()` function. Finally, we use the `async(execute:)` method of our queue to execute it. This code will execute the task in a concurrent dispatch queue, which is separate from the main thread.

While the preceding example works perfectly, we can actually shorten the code a little bit. The next example shows that we do not need to create a separate closure as we did in the preceding example. We can also submit the task to execute as follows:

```
cqueue.async {
    calculation.performCalculation(1000, tag: "async1")
}
```

This shorthand version is how we usually submit small code blocks to our queues. If we have larger tasks or tasks that we need to submit multiple times, we will generally want to create a closure and submit the closure to the queue as we showed in the first example.

Let's see how a concurrent queue works by adding several items to the queue and looking at the order and time that they return. The following code will add three tasks to the queue. Each task will call the `performCalculation()` function with various iteration counts. Remember that the `performCalculation()` function will execute the calculation routine continuously until it is executed the number of times defined by the iteration count passed in. Therefore, the larger the iteration count we pass into the function, the longer it should take to execute. Let's look at the following code:

```
cqueue.async {
    calculation.performCalculation(10000000, tag: "async1")
}

cqueue.async {
    calculation.performCalculation(1000, tag: "async2")
}

cqueue.async {
    calculation.performCalculation(100000, tag: "async3")
}
```

Note that each of the functions is called with a different value in the `tag` parameter. Since the `performCalculation()` function prints out the `tag` variable with the elapsed time, we can see the order in which the tasks complete and the time they took to execute. If we execute the preceding code, we should see results similar to this:

```
time for async2:  0.000200986862182617
time for async3:  0.00800204277038574
time for async1:  0.461670994758606
```

 The elapsed time will vary from one run to the next and from system to system.

Since the queues function in a FIFO order, the task that had the tag of `async1` was executed first. However, as we can see from the results, it was the last task to finish. Since this is a concurrent queue, if it is possible (if the system has the available resources), the blocks of code will execute concurrently. This is why tasks with the tags of `async2` and `async3` completed prior to the task that had the `async1` tag, even though the execution of the `async1` task began before the other two.

Now, let's see how a serial queue executes tasks.

Creating and using a serial queue

A serial queue functions a little different than a concurrent queue. A serial queue will only execute one task at a time and will wait for one task to complete before starting the next one. This queue, like the concurrent dispatch queue, follows the FIFO order. The following line of code will create a serial queue that we will be using for this section and will also create an instance of the `DoCalculations` type:

```
let squeue = DispatchQueue(label: "squeue.hoffman.jon")
let calculation = DoCalculations()
```

The first line will create a new serial dispatch queue that we name `squeue`, and the second line creates the instance of the `DoCalculations` type. Now let's see how we would use our serial queue by using the `performCalculation()` method from the `DoCalculations` type to perform some calculations:

```
let s = {calculation.performCalculation(1000, tag: "sync1")}
squeue.async (execute: s)
```

In the preceding code, we created a closure, which represents our task, that simply calls the `performCalculation()` function of the `DoCalculation` instance, requesting that it runs through 1000 iterations of the `doCalc()` function. Finally, we use the `async(execute:)` method of our queue to execute it. This code will execute the task in a serial dispatch queue, which is separate from the main thread. As we can see from this code, we use the serial queue exactly like we use the concurrent queue.

We can shorten this code a little bit, just like we did with the concurrent queue. The following example shows how we would do this with a serial queue:

```
squeue.async {
    calculation.performCalculation(1000, tag: "sync2")
}
```

Let's see how the serial queue works by adding several items to the queue and looking at the order in which they complete. The following code will add three tasks, which will call the `performCalculation()` function with various iteration counts, to the queue:

```
squeue.async {
    calculation.performCalculation(100000, tag: "sync1")
}

squeue.async {
    calculation.performCalculation(1000, tag: "sync2")
}

squeue.async {
    calculation.performCalculation(100000, tag: "sync3")
}
```

Just as we did in the concurrent queue example, we call the `performCalculation()` function with various iteration counts and different values in the `tag` parameter. Since the `performCalculation()` function prints out the tag string with the elapsed time, we can see the order that the tasks complete in and the time it takes to execute. If we execute this code, we should see the following results:

```
time for sync1: 0.00648999214172363
time for sync2: 0.00009602308273315
time for sync3: 0.00515800714492798
```

The elapsed time will vary from one run to the next and from system to system.

Unlike the concurrent queues, we can see that the tasks completed in the same order that they were submitted in, even though the sync2 and sync3 tasks took considerably less time to complete. This demonstrates that a serial queue only executes one task at a time and that the queue waits for each task to complete before starting the next one.

In the previous examples, we used the async method to execute the code blocks. We could also use the sync method.

async versus sync

In the previous examples, we used the async method to execute the code blocks. When we use the async method, the call will not block the current thread. This means that the method returns and the code block is executed asynchronously.

Rather than using the async method, we could use the sync method to execute the code blocks. The sync method will block the current thread, which means it will not return until the execution of the code has completed. Generally, we use the async method, but there are use cases where the sync method is useful. This use case is usually when we have a separate thread and we want that thread to wait for some work to finish.

Executing code on the main queue function

The DispatchQueue.main.async(execute:) function will execute code on the application's main queue. We generally use this function when we want to update our code from another thread or queue.

The main queue is automatically created for the main thread when the application starts. This main queue is a serial queue; therefore, items in this queue are executed one at a time, in the order that they were submitted. We will generally want to avoid using this queue unless we have a need to update the user interface from a background thread.

The following code example shows how we would use this function:

```
let squeue = DispatchQueue(label: "squeue.hoffman.jon")
squeue.async{
  let resizedImage = image.resize(to: rect)
  DispatchQueue.main.async {
    picView.image = resizedImage
  }
}
```

In the previous code, we assume that we have added a method to the `UIImage` type that will resize the image. In this code, we create a new serial queue and in that queue we resize an image. This is a good example of how to use a dispatch queue because we would not want to resize an image on the main queue since it would freeze the UI while the image is being resized. Once the image is resized, we then need to update a `UIImageView` with the new image; however, all updates to the UI need to occur on the main thread. Therefore we will use the `DispatchQueue.main.async` function to perform the update on the main queue.

There will be times when we need to execute tasks after a delay. If we were using a threading model, we would need to create a new thread, perform some sort of `delay` or `sleep` function, and execute our task. With GCD, we can use the `asyncAfter` function.

Using asyncAfter

The `asyncAfter` function will execute a block of code asynchronously after a given delay. This is very useful when we need to pause the execution of our code. The following code sample shows how we would use the `asyncAfter` function:

```
let queue2 = DispatchQueue(label: "squeue.hoffman.jon")
let delayInSeconds = 2.0
let pTime = DispatchTime.now() + Double(Int64(delayInSeconds *
Double(NSEC_PER_SEC))) / Double(NSEC_PER_SEC)
queue2.asyncAfter(deadline: pTime) {
  print("Times Up")
}
```

In this code, we begin by creating a serial dispatch queue. We then create an instance of the `DispatchTime` type and calculate the time to execute the block of code based on the current time. We then use the `asyncAfter` function to execute the code block after the delay.

Now that we have looked at GCD, let's look at operation queues.

Using the Operation and OperationQueue types

The `Operation` and `OperationQueue` types, working together, provide us with an alternative to GCD for adding concurrency to our applications. Operation queues are part of the Foundation framework and function like dispatch queues as they are a higher-level of abstraction over GCD.

We define the tasks (Operations) that we wish to execute and then add the tasks to the operation queue. The operation queue will then handle the scheduling and execution of tasks. Operation queues are instances of the OperationQueue class and operations are instances of the Operation class.

An operation represents a single unit of work or task. The Operation type is an abstract class that provides a thread-safe structure for modeling the state, priority, and dependencies. This class must be subclassed to perform any useful work; we will look at how to subclass this class in the *Subclassing the Operation class* section of this chapter.

Apple does provide a concrete implementation of the Operation type that we can use as-is for situations where it does not make sense to build a custom subclass. This subclass is BlockOperation.

More than one operation queue can exist at the same time, and, in fact, there is always at least one operation queue running. This operation queue is known as the **main queue**. The main queue is automatically created for the main thread when the application starts and is where all the UI operations are performed.

There are several ways that we can use the Operation and OperationQueue classes to add concurrency to our application. In this chapter, we will look at three of these ways. The first one we will look at is the use of the BlockOperation implementation of the Operation abstract class.

Using BlockOperation

In this section, we will be using the same DoCalculation class that we used in the *Grand Central Dispatch* section to keep our queues busy with work so that we could see how the OpererationQueue class works.

The BlockOperation class is a concrete implementation of the Operation type that can manage the execution of one or more blocks. This class can be used to execute several tasks at once without the need to create separate operations for each task.

Let's see how we can use the BlockOperation class to add concurrency to our application. The following code shows how to add three tasks to an operation queue using a single BlockOperation instance:

```
let calculation = DoCalculations()
let blockOperation1: BlockOperation = BlockOperation.init(
  block: {
    calculation.performCalculation(10000000, tag: "Operation 1")
  }
```

```
)
blockOperation1.addExecutionBlock({
    calculation.performCalculation(10000, tag: "Operation 2")
})
blockOperation1.addExecutionBlock({
    calculation.performCalculation(1000000, tag: "Operation 3")
})
let operationQueue = OperationQueue()
operationQueue.addOperation(blockOperation1)
```

In this code, we begin by creating an instance of the `DoCalculation` class and an instance of the `OperationQueue` class. Next, we created an instance of the `BlockOperation` class using the `init` constructor. This constructor takes a single parameter, which is a block of code that represents one of the tasks we want to execute in the queue. Next, we add two additional tasks using the `addExecutionBlock()` method.

One of the differences between dispatch queues and operations is that, with dispatch queues, if resources are available, the tasks are executed as they are added to the queue. With operations, the individual tasks are not executed until the operation itself is submitted to an operation queue. This allows us to initiate all of the operations into a single block operation prior to executing them.

Once we add all the tasks to the `BlockOperation` instance, we then add the operation to the `OperationQueue` instance that we created at the beginning of the code. At this point, the individual tasks within the operation start to execute.

This example shows how to use `BlockOperation` to queue up multiple tasks and then pass the tasks to the operation queue. The tasks are executed in a FIFO order; therefore, the first task that is added will be the first task executed. However, the tasks can be executed concurrently if we have the available resources. The output from this code should look similar to this:

```
time for Operation 2:   0.00546294450759888
time for Operation 3:   0.0800899863243103
time for Operation 1:   0.484337985515594
```

What if we do not want the tasks to run concurrently? What if we wanted them to run serially like the serial dispatch queue? We can set a property in the operation queue that defines the number of tasks that can be run concurrently in the queue. The property is named `maxConcurrentOperationCount`, and is used like this:

```
operationQueue.maxConcurrentOperationCount = 1
```

However, if we add this line to our previous example, it will not work as expected. To see why this is, we need to understand what the property actually defines. If we look at Apple's OperationQueue class reference, the definition of the property is, *the maximum number of queued operations that can execute at the same time.*

What this tells us is that this property defines the number of operations (this is the keyword) that can be executed at the same time. The BlockOperation instance, which we added all of the tasks to, represents a single operation, therefore, no other BlockOperation added to the queue will execute until the first one is complete, but the individual tasks within the operation will execute concurrently. To run the tasks serially, we would need to create a separate instance of BlockOperation for each task.

Using an instance of the BlockOperation class is good if we have several tasks that we want to execute concurrently, but they will not start executing until we add the operation to an operation queue. Let's look at a simpler way of adding tasks to an operation queue using the addOperationWithBlock() method.

Using the addOperation() method of the operation queue

The OperationQueue class has a method named addOperation(), which makes it easy to add a block of code to the queue. This method automatically wraps the block of code in an operation object and then passes that operation to the queue. Let's see how to use this method to add tasks to a queue:

```
let operationQueue = OperationQueue()
let calculation = DoCalculations()
operationQueue.addOperation() {
  calculation.performCalculation(10000000, tag: "Operation1")
}
operationQueue.addOperation() {
  calculation.performCalculation(10000, tag: "Operation2")
}
operationQueue.addOperation() {
  calculation.performCalculation(1000000, tag: "Operation3")
}
```

In the BlockOperation example, earlier in this chapter, we added the tasks that we wished to execute into a BlockOperation instance. In this example, we are adding the tasks directly to the operation queue, and each task represents one complete operation. Once we create the instance of the operation queue, we then use the addOperation() method to add the tasks to the queue.

Also, in the `BlockOperation` example, the individual tasks did not execute until all of the tasks were added, and then that operation was added to the queue. This example is similar to the GCD example where the tasks began executing as soon as they were added to the operation queue.

If we run the preceding code, the output should be similar to this:

```
time for Operation2: 0.0115870237350464
time for Operation3: 0.0790849924087524
time for Operation1:  0.520610988140106
```

You will notice that the operations are executed concurrently. With this example, we can execute the tasks serially by using the `maxConcurrentOperationCount` property that we mentioned earlier. Let's try this by initializing the `OperationQueue` instance as follows:

```
var operationQueue = OperationQueue()
operationQueue.maxConcurrentOperationCount = 1
```

Now, if we run the example, the output should be similar to this:

```
time for Operation1:  0.418763995170593
time for Operation2:  0.000427007675170898
time for Operation3:  0.0441589951515198
```

In this example, we can see that each task waited for the previous task to complete prior to starting.

Using the `addOperation()` method to add tasks to the operation queue is generally easier than using the `BlockOperation` method; however, the tasks will begin as soon as they are added to the queue. This is usually the desired behavior, although there are use cases where we do not want the tasks executing until all operations are added to the queue, as we saw in the `BlockOperation` example.

Now, let's look at how we can subclass the `Operation` class to create an operation that we can add directly to an operation queue.

Subclassing the Operation class

The previous two examples showed how to add small blocks of code to our operation queues. In these examples, we called the `performCalculations` method in the `DoCalculation` class to perform our tasks. These examples illustrate two really good ways to add concurrency for functionality that is already written, but what if, at design time, we want to design our `DoCalculation` class itself for concurrency? For this, we can subclass the `Operation` class.

The Operation abstract class provides a significant amount of infrastructure. This allows us to very easily create a subclass without a lot of work. We will need to provide at least an initialization method and a main method. The main method will be called when the queue begins executing the operation.

Let's see how to implement the DoCalculation class as a subclass of the Operation class; we will call this new class, MyOperation:

```
class MyOperation: Operation {
  let iterations: Int
  let tag: String
  init(iterations: Int, tag: String) {
    self.iterations = iterations
    self.tag = tag
  }

  override func main() {
    performCalculation()
  }

  func performCalculation() {
    let start = CFAbsoluteTimeGetCurrent()
    for _ in 0 ..< iterations {
      self.doCalc()
    }

    let end = CFAbsoluteTimeGetCurrent()
    print("time for \(tag):\(end-start)")
  }

  func doCalc() {
    let x=100
    let y = x*x
    _ = y/x
  }
}
```

We begin by defining that the MyOperation class is a subclass of the Operation class. Within the implementation of the class, we define two class constants, which represent the iteration count and the tag that the performCalculations() method uses. Keep in mind that when the operation queue begins executing the operation, it will call the main() method with no parameters; therefore, any parameters that we need to pass in must be passed in through the initializer.

In this example, our initializer takes two parameters that are used to set the `iterations` and `tag` class constants. Then the `main()` method, which the operation queue is going to call to begin execution of the operation, simply calls the `performCalculation()` method.

We can now very easily add instances of our `MyOperation` class to an operation queue, as follows:

```
let operationQueue = NSOperationQueue()
operationQueue.addOperation(
  MyOperation(iterations: 10000000, tag:"Operation 1")
)
operationQueue.addOperation(
  MyOperation(iterations: 10000, tag:"Operation 2")
)
operationQueue.addOperation(
  MyOperation(iterations: 1000000, tag:"Operation 3")
)
```

If we run this code, we will see the following results:

```
time for Operation 2:   0.00187397003173828
time for Operation 3:   0.104826986789703
time for Operation 1:   0.866684019565582
```

As we saw earlier, we can also execute the tasks serially by setting the `maxConcurrentOperationCount` property of the operation queue to 1.

If we know that we need to execute some functionality concurrently prior to writing the code, I would recommend subclassing the `Operation` class, as shown in this example, rather than using the previous examples. This gives us the cleanest implementation; however, there is nothing wrong with using the `BlockOperation` class or the `addOperation()` methods described earlier in this section.

Summary

Before we consider adding concurrency to our application, we should make sure that we understand why we are adding it and ask ourselves whether it is necessary. While concurrency can make our application more responsive by offloading work from our main application thread to a background thread, it also adds extra overhead and complexity to our code. I have even seen numerous applications, in various languages, which actually run better after we pulled out some of the concurrency code. This is because the concurrency was not well thought out or planned. With this in mind, it is always a good idea to think and talk about concurrency while we are discussing the application's expected behavior.

At the start of this chapter, we had a discussion about running tasks concurrently compared to running tasks in parallel. We also discussed the hardware limitations that restrict how many tasks can run in parallel on a given device. Having a good understanding of those concepts is very important to understanding how and when to add concurrency to our projects.

While GCD is not limited to system-level applications, before we use it in our application, we should consider whether operation queues would be easier and more appropriate for our needs. In general, we should use the highest level of abstraction that meets our needs. This will usually point us to using operation queues; however, there really is nothing preventing us from using GCD, and it may be more appropriate for our needs.

One thing to keep in mind with operation queues is that they do add additional overhead because they are Foundation objects. For the large majority of applications, this little extra overhead should not be an issue or even noticed; however, for some projects, such as games that need every last resource that they can get, this extra overhead might very well be an issue.

In the next chapter, we will look at how to properly format and style our Swift code.

15
Swift Formatting and Style Guide

Throughout my development experience, every time I learned a new programming language, there was usually some mention of how the code for that language should be written and formatted. Early in my development career (which was a long time ago), these recommendations were very basic formatting recommendations, such as how to indent your code, or having one statement per line. It really wasn't until the last 10 to 12 years that I started to see complex and detailed formatting and style guides for different programming languages. Today, you will be hard pressed to find a development shop with more than two or three developers that does not have a style/formatting guides for each language that they use. Even companies that do not create their own style guides generally refer back to some standard guide published by other companies, such as Google, Oracle, or Microsoft. These style guides help teams to write consistent and easy-to-maintain code.

What is a programming style guide?

Coding styles are very personal, and every developer has his or her own preferred style. These styles can vary from language to language, person to person, and also over time. The personal nature of coding styles can make it difficult to have a consistent and readable code base when numerous individuals are contributing to the code.

While most developers might have their own preferred styles, the recommended or preferred style between languages can vary. As an example, in C#, when we name a method or function, it is preferred that we use PascalCase, which is similar to CamelCase except the first letter is capitalized. While in most other languages, such as C, Objective-C, and Java, it is also recommended that we use CamelCase, where the first letter is lowercase.

The best applications are coded so they are easy to maintain and the code is easy to read. It is hard for large projects and companies with many developers to have code that is easy to maintain and read if every developer uses their own coding style. This is why companies and projects with multiple developers usually adopt programming style guides for each language that they use.

A programming style guide defines a set of rules and guidelines that a developer should follow while writing applications with a specific language within a project or company. These style guides can differ greatly between companies or projects and reflect how a company or project expects code to be written. These guides can also change over time. It is important to follow these style guides to maintain a consistent code base.

A lot of developers do not like the idea of being told how they should write code, and claim that as long as their code functions correctly, it shouldn't matter how they format their code. This type of philosophy doesn't work in a coding team or sports team, like a basketball team. What do you think would happen if all the players on a basketball team believed that they could all play the way they wanted to and the team was better when they did their own thing? That team would probably lose the majority of its games. It is impossible for a basketball team (or any sports team, for that matter) to win most of its games unless its members are working together. It is up to the coach to make sure that everyone is working together and executing the same game plan, just like it is up to the team leader of the development project to make sure all the developers are writing code according to the adopted style guide.

Your style guide

The style guide that we define in this book is just a guide. It reflects the author's opinion on how Swift code should be written and is meant to be a good starting point for creating your own style guide. If you really like this guide and adopt it as - is, great. If there are parts that you do not agree with and you change them within your guide, that is great as well. The appropriate style for you and your team is the one that you and your team feel comfortable with, and it may or may not be different from the guide in this book. Don't be afraid to adjust your style guide as needed.

One thing that is noticeable in the style guide within this chapter, and most good style guides, is that there is very little explanation about why each item is preferred or not preferred. Style guides should give enough details so that the reader understands the preferred and non-preferred methods for each item, but should also be small and compact to make them easy and quick to read.

If a developer has questions about why a particular method is preferred, they should bring that concern up with the development group. With that in mind, let's get started with the guide.

Do not use semicolons at the end of statements

Unlike a lot of languages, Swift does not require semicolons at the end of statements. Therefore, we should not use them. Let's look at the following code:

```
//Preferred Method var name = "Jon"
print(name)

//Non-preferred Method var name = "Jon";
print(name);
```

Do not use parentheses for conditional statements

Unlike a lot of languages, parentheses are not required around conditional statements; therefore, we should avoid using them unless they are needed for clarification. Let's look at the following code:

```
//Preferred Method
if speed == 300_000_000 {
  print("Speed of light")
}

//Non-Preferred Method
if (speed == 300_000_000) {
  print("Speed of light")
}
```

Naming

We should always use descriptive names with CamelCase for customer types, methods, variables, constants, and so on. Let's look at some general naming rules.

Custom types

Custom types should have a descriptive name that describes what the type is for. The name should be in PascalCase. Here are examples of proper names and non-proper names based on our style guide:

```
// Proper Naming Convention BaseballTeam
LaptopComputer

//Non-Proper Naming Convention
baseballTeam  //Starts with a lowercase letter
Laptop_Computer //Uses an underscore
```

Functions and methods

Function names should be descriptive, describing the function or method. They should be in CamelCase. Here are some examples of proper and non-proper names:

```
//Proper Naming Convention getCityName
playSound

//Non-Proper Naming Convention
get_city_name  //All lowercase and has an underscore
PlaySound  //Begins with an upper case letter
```

Constants and variables

Constants and variables should have a descriptive name. They should begin with a lowercase letter and be in CamelCase. The only exception is when the constant is global; in that case, the name of the constant should contain all uppercase characters with the words separated by underscores. I have seen numerous guides that frown upon having all uppercase names, but I personally like them for constants in the global scope because it stands out that they are globally, not locally, scoped. Here are some examples of proper and non-proper names:

```
//Proper Names
playerName
driveSize
//Non-Proper Names
PlayerName  //Starts with uppercase letter
drive_size  //Has underscore in name
```

Indenting

Indenting width in Xcode, by default, is defined as four spaces, and tab width is also defined as four spaces. We should leave this as the default. The following screenshot shows the indentation setting in Xcode:

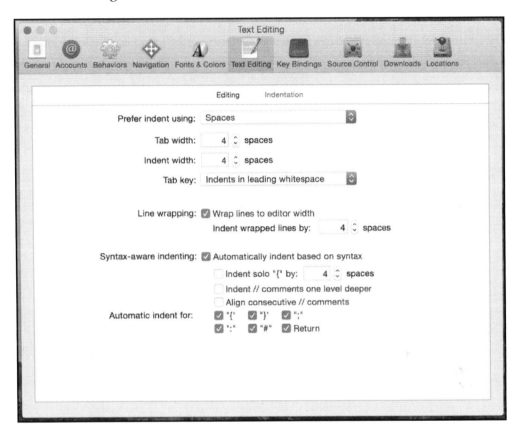

We should add an extra blank line between functions/methods. We should also use a blank line to separate functionality within a function or method. That being said, using many blank lines within a function or method might signify that we should break the function into multiple functions.

Comments

We should use comments as needed to explain how and why our code is written. We should use block comments before custom types and functions. We should use double slashes to comment our code in one line. Here is an example of how comments should be written:

```
///
/// This is a block comment that should be used
/// to explain a class or function
///
public class EmployeeClass {
  // This is an inline comment with double slashes
  var firstName = ""
  var lastName = ""

  ///
  /// Use Block comments for functions
  ///
  /// parameter paramName:  use this tag for parameters
  /// returns:     explain what is returned
  /// throws:    Error thrown
  ///
  func getFullName() -> String {
    return firstName + " " + lastName
  }
}
```

When we are commenting methods, we should also use the documentation tags, which will generate documentation in Xcode, as shown in the preceding example. At a minimum, we should use the following tags if they apply to our method:

- **parameter**: This is used for parameters
- **returns**: This is used for what is returned
- **throws**: This is used to document errors that may be thrown

Using the self keyword

Since Swift does not require us to use the self keyword when accessing properties or invoking methods of an object, we should avoid using it unless we need to distinguish between an instance property and local variables. Here is an example of when you should use the `self` keyword:

```
public class EmployeeClass {
  var firstName = ""
  var lastName = ""
  func setName(firstName: String, lastName: String) {
    self.firstName = firstName
    self.lastName = lastName
  }
}
```

Here is an example of when not to use the `self` keyword:

```
public class EmployeeClass {
  var firstName = ""
  var lastName = ""
  func getFullName() -> String {
    return self.firstName + " " + self.lastName
  }
}
```

Constants and variables

The difference between constants and variables is that the value of a constant never changes, whereas the value of a variable may change. Wherever possible, we should define constants rather than variables.

One of the easiest ways of doing this is by defining everything as a constant by default, and then changing the definition to a variable only after you reach a point in your code that requires you to change it. In Swift, you will get a warning if you define a variable and then never change the value within your code.

Optional types

Only use optional types when absolutely necessary. If there is no absolute need for a nil value to be assigned to a variable, we should not define it as an optional.

Using optional binding

We should avoid forced unwrapping of optionals as there is rarely any need to do this. We should prefer optional binding or optional chaining over forced unwrapping.

The following examples show the preferred and non-preferred methods where the myOptional variable is defined as an optional:

```
//Preferred Method Optional Binding
 if let value = myOptional {
  // code if myOptional is not nil
} else {
  // code if myOptional is nil
}

//Non-Preferred Method
if myOptional != nil {
  // code if myOptional is not nil
} else {
  //  code if myOptional is nil
}
```

If there is more than one optional that we need to unwrap, we should include them in the same if-let or guard statement, rather than unwrapping them on separate lines. There are times, however, when our business logic may require us to handle nil values differently and this may require us to unwrap the optionals on separate lines. The following examples show the preferred and non-preferred methods:

```
//Preferred Method Optional Binding
if let value1 = myOptional1, let value2 = myOptional2 {
  // code if myOptional1 and myOptional2 is not nil
} else {
  // code if myOptional1 and myOptional2 is nil
}

//Non-Preferred Method Optional Binding
if let value1 = myOptional1 {
  if let value2 = myOptional2 {
    // code if myOptional is not nil
  } else {
    // code if myOptional2 is nil
  }
} else {
  // code if myOptional1 is nil
}
```

Using optional chaining instead of optional binding for multiple unwrapping

When we need to unwrap multiple layers, we should use optional chaining over multiple optional binding statements. The following example shows the preferred and non-preferred methods:

```
//Preferred Method
if let color = jon.pet?.collar?.color {
  print("The color of the collar is \(color)")
} else {
  print("Cannot retrieve color")
}

//Non-Preferred Method
if let tmpPet = jon.pet, let tmpCollar = tmpPet.collar{
  print("The color of the collar is \(tmpCollar.color)")
} else {
  print("Cannot retrieve color")
}
```

Using type inference

Rather than defining variable types, we should let Swift infer the type. The only time we should define the variable or constant type is when we are not giving it a value while defining it. Let's look at the following code:

```
//Preferred method
var myVar = "String Type"  //Infers a String type
var myNum = 2.25  //Infers a Double type

//Non-Preferred method
var myVar: String = "String Type"
var myNum: Double = 2.25
```

Using shorthand declaration for collections

When declaring native Swift collection types, we should use the shorthand syntax, and, unless absolutely necessary, we should initialize the collection. The following example shows the preferred and non-preferred methods:

```
//Preferred Method
var myDictionary: [String: String] = [:]
var strArray: [String] = []
var strOptional: String?

//
//Non-Preferred Method
var myDictionary: Dictionary<String,String>
var strArray: Array<String>
var strOptional: Optional<String>
```

Using switch rather than multiple if statements

Wherever possible, we should prefer to use a single `switch` statement over multiple `if` statements. The following example shows the preferred and non-preferred methods:

```
//Preferred Method let speed = 300_000_000
switch speed {
  case 300_000_000:
    print("Speed of light")
  case 340:
    print("Speed of sound")
  default:
    print("Unknown speed")
}

//Non-preferred Method let speed = 300_000_000
if speed == 300_000_000 {
  print("Speed of light")
} else if speed == 340 {
  print("Speed of sound")
} else {
  print("Unknown speed")
}
```

Don't leave commented-out code in your application

If we comment out a block of code while we attempt to replace it, once we are comfortable with the changes we should remove the code that we commented out. Having large blocks of code commented out can make the code base look messy and harder to follow.

Summary

When we are developing an application in a team environment, it is important to have a well-defined coding style that is adhered to by everyone on the team. This allows us to have a code base that is easy to read and maintain.

If a style guide remains static for too long, it means that it is probably not keeping up with the latest changes within the language. What is too long is different for each language. For example, with the C language, too long will be defined in years, since the language is very stable; however, with Swift, the language is new, and changes are coming pretty often, so too long can probably be defined as a couple of months.

It is recommended that we keep our style guides in a versioning control system so that we can refer to the older versions if need be. This allows us to pull the older versions of the style guide and refer back to them when we are looking at older code.

It is recommended, not only with Swift but other languages as well, that you use a Lint tool to check and enforce good coding practices. For Swift there is a great tool called SwiftLint (`https://github.com/realm/SwiftLint`) that has a command-line tool and an Xcode plugin as well as integration with other IDEs.

In the next chapter, we will look at some of the Swift core libraries.

16

Swift Core Libraries

When Apple first announced Swift, it was great; however, I was only able to use it for my macOS and iOS development. Then Apple announced that they were going to release a version of Swift for Linux and I really got excited because now I could use Swift for my Linux and embedded projects. When the first Linux version was released I was a little disappointed because I could not read/write files, access network services, or use libdispatch (GCD) on Linux like I could on Apple's platforms. With the release of Swift 3, Apple corrected this issue by releasing the Swift core libraries.

In this chapter, you will learn about the following topics:

- What are the Swift Core Libraries?
- How to use Apple's URL loading system?
- How to use the Formatter classes?
- How to use the FileManager class?
- How to serialize and deserialize JSON data?

The Swift Core Libraries are written to provide a rich set of APIs that are consistent across the various platforms that Swift supports. By using these libraries, developers are able to write code that will be portable to all platforms that Swift supports. These libraries provide a higher level of functionality as compared to the Swift standard library.

The Core Libraries provide functionality in several areas, such as the following:

- Networking
- Unit testing
- Scheduling and execution of work (libdispatch)
- Property lists, JSON parsing, and XML parsing
- Support for dates, times, and calendar calculations

- Abstraction of OS-specific behavior
- Interaction with the filesystem
- User preferences

We are unable to cover all of the Core Libraries in this single chapter; however, we will look at some of the more useful ones. We will start off by looking at Apple's URL loading system, which is used for network development.

Apple's URL loading system

Apple's URL loading system is a framework of classes available to interact with URLs. We generally use these classes to communicate with services that use standard internet protocols. The classes that we will be using in this section are as follows:

- URLSession: This is the main session object.
- URLSessionConfiguration: This is used to configure the behavior of the URLSession object.
- URLSessionTask: This is a base class to handle the data being retrieved from the URL. Apple provides three concrete subclasses of the URLSessionTask class.
- URL: This is an object that represents the URL to connect to.
- URL6Request: This class contains information about the request that we are making and is used by the URLSessionTask service to make the request.
- HTTPURLResponse: This class contains the response to our request.

Now, let's look at each of these classes in slightly more depth so that we have a basic understanding of what each does.

URLSession

A URLSession object provides an API for interacting with various protocols such as HTTP and HTTPS. The session object, which is an instance of the URLSession, manages this interaction. These session objects are highly configurable, which allows us to control how our requests are made and how we handle the data that is returned.

Like most networking APIs, URLSession is asynchronous. This means that we have to provide a way to return the response from the service back to the code that needs it. The most popular way to return the results from a session is to pass a completion handler block (closure) to the session. This completion handler is then called when the service successfully responds or we receive an error. All of the examples in this chapter use completion handlers to process the data that is returned from the services.

URLSessionConfiguration

The URLSessionConfiguration class defines the behavior and policies to use when using the URLSession object to connect to a URL. When using the URLSession object, we usually create a URLSessionConfiguration instance first, because an instance of this class is required when we create an instance of the URLSession class.

The URLSessionConfiguration class defines three session types:

- **Default session configuration**: This manages the upload and download tasks with default configurations
- **Ephemeral session configuration**: This configuration behaves similarly to the default session configuration, except that it does not cache anything to disk
- **Background session configuration**: This session allows for uploads and downloads to be performed, even when the app is running in the background

It is important to note that we should make sure that we configure the URLSessionConfiguration object appropriately before we use it to create an instance of the URLSession class. When the session object is created, it creates a copy of the configuration object that we provide. Any changes made to the configuration object once the session object is created are ignored by the session. If we need to make changes to the configuration, we must create another instance of the URLSession class.

URLSessionTask

The URLSession service uses an instance of the URLSessionTask class to make the call to the service that we are connecting to. The URLSessionTask class is a base class, and Apple has provided three concrete subclasses that we can use:

- URLSessionDataTask: This returns the response, in memory, directly to the application as one or more data objects. This is the task that we generally use most often.
- URLSessionDownloadTask: This writes the response directly to a temporary file.
- URLSessionUploadTask: This is used for making requests that require a request body, such as a POST or PUT request.

It is important to note that a task will not send the request to the service until we call the resume() method.

URL

The URL object represents the URL that we are going to connect to. The URL class is not limited to URLs that represent remote servers, but can also be used to represent a local file on disk. In this chapter, we will be using the URL class exclusively to represent the URL of the remote service that we are connecting to.

URLRequest

We use the URLRequest class to encapsulate our URL and the request properties. It is important to understand that the URLRequest class is used to encapsulate the necessary information to make our request, but it does not make the actual request. To make the request, we use instances of the URLSession and URLSessionTask classes.

HTTPURLResponse

The HTTPURLResponse class is a subclass of the URLResponse class, which encapsulates the metadata associated with the response to a URL request. The HTTPURLResponse class provides methods for accessing specific information associated with an HTTP response. Specifically, this class allows us to access the HTTP header fields and the response status codes.

We briefly covered several classes in this section and it may not be clear how they all actually fit together; however, once we explore the examples a little further in this chapter, it will become much clearer. Before we go into our examples, let's take a quick look at the type of service that we will be connecting to.

REST web services

REST has become one of the most important technologies for stateless communications between devices. Due to the lightweight and stateless nature of the REST-based services, its importance is likely to continue to grow as more devices are connected to the internet.

REST is an architecture style for designing networked applications. The idea behind REST is that, instead of using complex mechanisms, such as SOAP or CORBA to communicate between devices, we use simple HTTP requests for the communication. While, in theory, REST is not dependent on internet protocols, it is almost always implemented using them. Therefore, when we are accessing REST services, we are almost always interacting with web servers in the same way that our web browsers interact with these servers.

REST web services use the HTTP POST, GET, PUT, or DELETE methods. If we think about a standard **Create, Read, Update, Delete** (**CRUD**) application, we would use a POST request to create or update data, a GET request to read data, and a DELETE request to delete data.

When we type a URL into our browser's address bar and hit Enter, we are generally making a GET request to the server and asking it to send us the web page associated with that URL. When we fill out a web form and click the **Submit** button, we are generally making a POST request to the server. We then include the parameters from the web form in the body of our POST request.

Now, let's look at how to make an HTTP GET request using Apple's networking API.

Making an HTTP GET Request

In this example, we will make a GET request to Apple's iTunes search API to get a list of items related to the search term Jimmy Buffett. Since we are retrieving data from the service, by REST standards, we should use a GET request to retrieve the data.

While the REST standard is to use GET requests to retrieve data from a service, depending on the framework used, the developer of a web service may use a GET request to also create or update a data object. It is not recommended to use a GET request in this manner, but just be aware that there are services out there that do not adhere to the REST standards.

The following code makes a request to Apple's iTunes search API and then prints the results to the console:

```
public typealias dataFromURLCompletionClosure = (URLResponse?, Data?)
-> Void

  public func sendGetRequest (
    handler: @escaping dataFromURLCompletionClosure) {

    let sessionConfiguration = URLSessionConfiguration.default

    var url = URLComponents()
    url.scheme = "https"
    url.host = "itunes.apple.com"
    url.path = "/search"
    url.queryItems = [
      URLQueryItem(name: "term", value: "jimmy+buffett"),
    ]
    if let queryUrl = url.url {
      var request = URLRequest(url:queryUrl)
      request.httpMethod = "GET"
      let urlSession = URLSession(configuration:sessionConfiguration,
                                delegate: nil, delegateQueue: nil)

      let sessionTask = urlSession.dataTask(with: request) {
        (data, response, error) in
        handler(response, data)
      }

      sessionTask.resume()
    }
  }
```

We start off by creating a type alias named DataFromURLCompletionClosure. The type alias will be used for both GET and POST examples of this chapter. If you are not familiar with using a typealias object to define a closure type, please refer to Chapter 12, *Working with Closures*, for more information.

We then create a function named sendGetRequest(), which will be used to make the GET request to Apple's iTunes API. This function accepts one argument, named handler, which is a closure that conforms to the DataFromURLCompletionClosure type. The handler closure will be used to return the results from the request.

The default for closure arguments to functions is not escaping, which means that, by default, the closure argument cannot escape the function body. A closure is considered to escape a function when that closure, which is passed as an argument to the function, is called after the function returns. Since the closure will be called after the function returns, we use the `@escaping` attribute before the parameter type to indicate that it is allowed to escape.

Within our `sendGetRequest()` method, we begin by creating an instance of the `URLSessionConfiguration` class using the default settings. If we need to, we can modify the session configuration properties after we create it, but in this example, the default configuration is what we want.

After we create our session configuration, we create an instance of the `URLComponents` type. `URLComponents` are used to create a URL string. With the GET request, the parameters become part of the URL string itself; therefore, the parameters are added to the URL using the `queryItems` array within the `URLComponents` instance.

After the `URLComponents` instance is configured we use optional binding to create an instance of the URL type from this instance. We create an instance of the `URLRequest` class using the `queryUrl` instance that we just created. In this example, we only set the `HTTPMethod` property; however, we can also set other properties, such as the timeout interval, or add items to our HTTP header.

Now, we use the `sessionConfiguration` constant that we created at the beginning of the `sendGetRequest()` function to create an instance of the `URLSession` class. The `URLSession` class provides the API that we will use to connect to Apple's iTunes search API. In this example, we use the `dataTask(with:)` method of the `URLSession` instance to return an instance of the `URLSessionDataTask` type named `sessionTask`.

The `sessionTask` instance is what makes the request to the iTunes search API. When we receive the response from the service, we use the `handler` callback to return both the `URLResponse` object and the `data` object. The `URLResponse` object contains information about the response, and the `data` instance contains the body of the response.

Finally, we call the `resume()` method of the `URLSessionDataTask` instance to make the request to the web service. Remember, as we mentioned earlier, a `URLSessionTask` instance will not send the request to the service until we call the `resume()` method.

Now, let's look at how we would call the `sendGetRequest()` function. The first thing we need to do is to create a closure that will be passed to the `sendGetRequest()` function and called when the response from the web service is received. In this example, we will simply print the response to the console. Here is the code:

```
let printResultsClosure: dataFromURLCompletionClosure = {

    if let data = $1 {
        let sString = String(data: data, encoding: String.Encoding(rawValue:
                            String.Encoding.utf8.rawValue))
        print(sString)
    } else {
        print("Data is nil")
    }
}
```

We define this closure, named `printResultsClosure`, to be an instance of the `DataFromURLCompletionClosure` type. Within the closure, we unwrap the first parameter and set the value to a constant named `data`. If the first parameter is not `nil`, we convert the data constant to an instance of the `String` class, which is then printed to the console.

Now, let's call the `sendGetRequest()` method with the following code:

```
let aConnect = HttpConnect()
aConnect.sendGetRequest(printResultsClosure)
```

This code creates an instance of the `HttpConnect` class and then calls the `sendGetRequest()` method, passing the `printResultsClosure` closure as the only parameter. If we run this code while we are connected to the internet, we will receive a JSON response that contains a list of items related to Jimmy Buffett on iTunes.

Now that we have seen how to make a simple HTTP GET request, let's look at how we would make an HTTP POST request to a web service.

Making an HTTP POST request

Since Apple's iTunes, APIs use GET requests to retrieve data. In this section, we will use the free `http://httpbin.org` service to show you how to make a POST request. The POST service that `http://httpbin.org` provides can be found at `http://httpbin.org/post`. This service will echo back the parameters that it receives so that we can verify that our request was made properly.

When we make a POST request, we generally have some data that we want to send or post to the server. This data takes the form of key/value pairs. These pairs are separated by an ampersand (&) symbol, and each key is separated from its value by an equals sign (=). As an example, let's say that we want to submit the following data to our service:

```
firstname: Jon
lastname: Hoffman
age: 47 years
```

The body of the POST request takes the following format:

```
firstname=Jon&lastname=Hoffman&age=47
```

Once we have the data in the proper format, we will then use the dataUsingEncoding() method, as we did with the GET request, to properly encode the POST data.

Since the data going to the server is in the key/value format, the most appropriate way to store this data, prior to sending it to the service, is with a Dictionary object. With this in mind, we will need to create a method that will take a Dictionary object and return a string object that can be used for the POST request. The following code will do that:

```
private func dictionaryToQueryString(_ dict: [String : String]) -> String {
  var parts = [String]()
  for (key, value) in dict {
    let part : String = key + "=" + value
    parts.append(part)
  }
  return parts.joined(separator: "&")

}
```

This function loops through each key/value pair of the Dictionary object and creates a String object that contains the key and the value separated by the equals sign (=). We then use the joinWithSeperator() function to join each item in the array, separated by the specified sting. In our case, we want to separate each string with the ampersand symbol (&). We then return this newly created string to the code that called it.

Now, let's create the `sendPostRequest()` function that will send the POST request to the `http://httpbin.org` post service. We will see a lot of similarities between this `sendPostRequest()` function and the `sendGetRequest()` function, which we showed you in the Making an HTTP GET request section. Let's look at the following code:

```
public func sendPostRequest(_ handler: @escaping
dataFromURLCompletionClosure) {

    let sessionConfiguration = URLSessionConfiguration.default

    var url = URLComponents()
    url.scheme = "https"
    url.host = "httpbin.org"
    url.path = "/post"

    if let queryUrl = url.url {
      var request = URLRequest(url:queryUrl)
      request.httpMethod = "POST"
      let params = dictionaryToQueryString(["One":"1 and 1", "Two":"2
                                            and 2"])
      request.httpBody = params.data(using: String.Encoding.utf8,
                                     allowLossyConversion: true)

      let urlSession = URLSession(configuration:sessionConfiguration,
                                  delegate: nil, delegateQueue: nil)

      let sessionTask = urlSession.dataTask(with: request) {
        (data, response, error) in

        handler(response, data)
      }
      sessionTask.resume()
    }
}
```

This code is very similar to the `sendGetRequest()` function that we saw earlier in this section. The two main differences are that the `httpMethod` of the `URLRequest` is set to POST rather than GET and how we set the parameters. In this function, we set the `httpBody` property of the `URLRequest` instance to the parameters we are submitting.

Now that we have seen how to use the URL loading system, let's look at how we can use Formatter.

Formatter

Formatter is an abstract class that declares an interface for an object that creates, converts, or validates a human-readable form of data. The types that subclass the `Formatter` class are generally used when we want to take a particular object, such as an instance of the `Date` class, and present the value in a form that the user of our application can understand.

Apple has provided several concrete implementations of the `Formatter` class, and in this section we will look at two of them. It is important to remember that the formatters that Apple provides will provide the proper format for the default locale of the device the application is running on.

We will start off by looking at the `DateFormatter` type.

DateFormatter

The `DateFormatter` class is a subclass of the Formatter abstract class that can be used to convert a `Date` object into a human-readable string. It can also be used to convert a `String` representation of a date into a `Date` object. We will look at both use cases in this section. Let's begin by seeing how we could convert a `Date` object into a human-readable string.

The `DateFormatter` type has five predefined styles that we can use when we are converting a `Date` object to a human-readable string. The following chart shows what the five styles look like for an en-US locale:

DateFormatter Style	Date	Time
.none	No format	No format
.short	12/25/16	6:00 AM
.medium	Dec 25, 2016	6:00:00 AM
.long	December 25, 2016	6:00:00 AM EST
.full	Sunday December 25, 2016	6:00:00 AM Eastern Standard Time

The following code shows how we would use the predefined `DateFormatter` styles:

```
let now = Date()

let formatter = DateFormatter()
formatter.dateStyle = .short
formatter.timeStyle = .medium

let dateStr = formatter.string(from: now)
```

We use the `string(from:)` method to convert the `now` date to a human-readable string. In this example, for the en-US locale, the `dateStr` constant would contain text similar to `Aug 19, 2016, 6:40 PM`.

There are numerous occasions when the predefined styles do not meet our needs. For those times, we can define our own styles using a custom format string. This string is a series of characters that the `DateFormatter` type knows are stand-ins for the values we want to show. The `DateFormatter` instance will replace these stand-ins with the appropriate values. The following table shows some of the formatting values that we can use to format our `Date` objects:

Stand-in Format	Description	Example output
yy	Two-digit year	16, 14, 04
yyyy	Four-digit year	2016, 2014, 2004
MM	Two-digit month	06, 08, 12
MMM	Three-letter month	Jul, Aug, Dec
MMMM	Full month name	July, August
dd	Two-digit day	10, 11, 30
EEE	Three-letter day	Mon, Sat, Sun
EEEE	Full day	Monday, Sunday
a	Period of day	AM, PM
hh	Two-digit hour	02, 03, 04
HH	Two-digit hour for 24-hour clock	11, 14, 16
mm	Two-digit minute	30, 35, 45
ss	Two-digit seconds	30, 35, 45

The following code shows how we would use these custom formatters:

```
let now = Date()
let formatter2 = DateFormatter()
formatter2.dateFormat = "YYYY-MM-dd HH:mm:ss"

let dateStr2 = formatter2.string(from: now)
```

We use the `string(from:)` method to convert the now date to a human-readable string. In this example, for the en-US locale, the `dateStr2` constant will contain text similar to `2016-08-19 19:03:23`.

Now let's look at how we would take a formatted date string and convert it to a `Date` object. We will use the same format string that we used in our last example:

```
formatter2.dateFormat = "YYYY-MM-dd HH:mm:ss"

let dateStr3 = "2016-08-19 16:32:02"
let date = formatter2.date(from: dateStr3)
```

In this example, we took the human-readable date string and converted it to a `Date` object using the `date(from:)` method. If the format of the human-readable date string does not match the format specified in the `DateFormatter` instance, then the conversion will fail and return `nil`.

If we are working with dates that need to adhere to the ISO 8601 standard, we will want to use the `ISO8601DateFormatter` type. This type can be used as follows:

```
let isoFormatter = ISO8601DateFormatter()
var isoDateString = isoFormatter.string(from: now)
let isoDate = isoFormatter.date(from: isoDateString)
```

In the first line of code we create an instance of the `ISO8601DateFormatter` type. We then covert an instance of the `Date` type to a `String` type using the `String(from:)` method. The last line will convert an ISO8601-formatted date string to an instance of the `Date` type.

Now let's look at the `NumberFormatter` type.

NumberFormatter

The `NumberFormatter` class is a subclass of the Formatter abstract class that can be used to convert a number into a human-readable string with a specified format. This formatter is especially useful when we want to display a currency string since it will convert the number to the proper currency for the current locale.

Let's begin by looking at how we would convert a number into a currency string:

```
let formatter1 = NumberFormatter()
formatter1.numberStyle = .currency
let num1 = formatter1.string(from: 23.99)
```

In the previous code, we define our number style to be `.currency`, which tells our formatter that we want to convert our number to a currency string. We then use the `string(from:)` method to convert the number to a string. In this example, for the en-US locale, the num1 constant will contain the string $23.99.

Now let's see how we would round a number using the `NumberFormatter` type. The following code will round the number to two decimal points:

```
let formatter2 = NumberFormatter()
formatter2.numberStyle = .decimal
formatter2.maximumFractionDigits = 2
let num2 = formatter2.string(from: 23.2357)
```

In this example, we set the `numberStyle` property to the `.decimal` style and we also define the maximum number of decimal digits to be 2 using the `maximumFractionDigits` property. We use the `string(from:)` method to convert the number to a string. In this example, the num2 constant will contain the string 23.24.

Now let's see how we can spell out a number using the `NumberFormatter` type. The following code will take a number and spell it out:

```
let formatter3 = NumberFormatter()
formatter3.numberStyle = .spellOut
let num3 = formatter3.string(from: 2015)
```

In this example, we set the `numberStyle` property to the `.spellout` style. This style will spell out the number. For this example, the num3 constant will contain the string *two thousand fifteen*.

Now let's look at how we can manipulate the filesystem using the `FileManager` class.

FileManager

The filesystem is a complex topic and how we manipulate it within our applications is generally specific to the operating system that our application is running on. This can be an issue when we are trying to port code from one operating system to another. Apple has addressed this issue by putting the FileManager object in the Core Libraries. The FileManager object lets us examine and make changes to the filesystem in a uniform manner across all operating systems that Swift supports.

The FileManager class provides us with a shared instance that we can use. This instance should be suitable for most of our filesystem-related tasks. We can access this shared instance using the default property.

When we use the FileManager object we can provide paths as an instance of either the URL or String types. In this section, all of our paths will be String types for consistency purposes.

Let's start off by seeing how we could list the contents of a directory using the FileManager object. The following code shows how to do this:

```
let fileManager = FileManager.default

do {
  let path = "/Users/jonhoffman/"
  let dirContents = try fileManager.contentsOfDirectory(atPath: path)
  for item in dirContents {
    print(item)
  }
} catch let error {
  print("Failed reading contents of directory: \(error)")
}
```

We start off by getting the shared instance of the FileManager object using the default property. We will use this same shared instance for all of our examples in this section rather than redefining it for each example. Next, we define our path and use it with the contentsOfDirectory(atPath:) method. This method returns an array of String types that contains the names of the items in the path. We use a for loop to list these items.

Next, let's look at how we would create a directory using `fileManager`. The following code shows how to do this:

```
do {
  let path = "/Users/jonhoffman/masteringswift/test/dir"
  try fileManager.createDirectory(atPath: path,
                    withIntermediateDirectories: true)
} catch let error {
  print("Failed creating directory, \(error) ")
}
```

In this example, we use the `createDirectory(atPath: withIntermediateDirectories:)` method to create the directory. When we set the `withIntermediateDirectories` parameter to true, this method will create any parent directories that are missing. When this parameter is set to `false`, if any parent directories are missing the operation will fail. Now let's look at how we copy an item from one location to another:

```
do {
  let pathOrig = "/Users/jonhoffman/masteringswift/"
  let pathNew = "/Users/jonhoffman/masteringswift2/"
  try fileManager.copyItem(atPath: pathOrig, toPath: pathNew)
} catch let error {
  print("Failed copying directory, \(error) ")
}
```

In this example, we use the `copyItem(atPath:toPath:)` method to copy one item to another location. This method can be used to copy either directories or files. If it is used for directories, the entire path structure below the directory specified by the path is copied. The `fileManager` also has a method that will let us move an item rather than copying it. Let's see how to do this:

```
do {
  let pathOrig = "/Users/jonhoffman/masteringswift2/"
  let pathNew = "/Users/jonhoffman/masteringswift3/"
  try fileManager.moveItem(atPath: pathOrig, toPath: pathNew)
} catch let error {
  print("Failed moving directory, \(error) ")
}
```

To move an item, we use the `moveItem(atPath: toPath:)` method. Just like the copy example we just saw, the move method can be used for either files or directories. If the path specifies a directory, then the entire directory structure below that path will be moved. Now let's see how we can delete an item from the filesystem:

```
do {
  let path = "/Users/jonhoffman/masteringswift/"
  try fileManager.removeItem(atPath: path)
} catch let error {
  print("Failed Removing directory, \(error) ")
}
```

In this example, we use the `removeItem(atPath:)` method to remove the item from the filesystem. A word of warning: once you delete something, it is gone and there is no getting it back.

Next, let's look at how we can read permissions for items in our filesystem. For this, we will need to create a file named `test.file`, which our path will point to:

```
let path = "/Users/jonhoffman/masteringswift3/test.file"
if fileManager.fileExists(atPath: path) {
  let isReadable = fileManager.isReadableFile(atPath: path)
  let isWriteable = fileManager.isWritableFile(atPath: path)
  let isExecutable = fileManager.isExecutableFile(atPath: path)
  let isDeleteable = fileManager.isDeletableFile(atPath: path)
  print("can read \(isReadable)")
  print("can write \(isWriteable)")
  print("can execute \(isExecutable)")
  print("can delete \(isDeleteable)")
}
```

In this example, we use four different methods to read the filesystem permissions for the filesystem item. These methods are as follows:

- `isReadableFile(atPath:)` - `true` if the file is readable
- `isWritableFile(atPath:)` - `true` if the file is writable
- `isExecutableFile(atPath:)` - `true` if the file is executable
- `isDeletableFile(atPath:)` - `true` if the file is deletable

If we wanted to read or write text files, we could use methods provided by the `String` type, rather than the `FileManager` type. Even though we do not use the `FileManager` class for this example, we wanted to show how to read and write text files. Let's see how we would write some text to a file:

```
let filePath = "/Users/jonhoffman/Documents/test.file"
let outString = "Write this text to the file"
do {
  try outString.write(toFile: filePath, atomically: true, encoding: .utf8)
} catch let error {
  print("Failed writing to path: \(error)")
}
```

In this example, we start off by defining our path as a `String` type just as we did in the previous examples. We then create another instance of the `String` type that contains the text we want to put in our file. To write the text to the file, we use the `write(toFile: atomically: encoding:)` method of the `String` instance. This method will create the file if needed and write the contents of the `String` instance to the file. It is just as easy to read a text file using the `String` type. The following example shows how to do this:

```
let filePath = "/Users/jonhoffman/Documents/test.file"
var inString = ""
do {
  inString = try String(contentsOfFile: filePath)
} catch let error {
  print("Failed reading from path: \(error)")
}
print("Text Read: \(inString)")
```

In this example, we use the `contentsOfFile:` initiator to create an instance of the `String` type that contains the contents of the file specified by the file path. Now that we have seen how to use the `FileManager` type, let's look at how to serialize and deserialize JSON documents using encoding and decoding.

Encoding and Decoding JSON Data

Before we see how to encode and decode JSON data we will need to create a structure that will define the data we wish to encode from or decode to. In the examples for this section, we will create and parse a JSON document that contains a list of books. Let's define the `Book` structure like this:

```
struct Book {
  var name: String
```

```
      var author: String
      var publisher: String
}
```

This structure contains three properties, which are the name, author, and publisher of the book. To use this structure with the encoder and decoder types, it will need to conform to the Codable typealias. Codable is a typealias for the Decodable and Encodable protocols. To make this type conform to Codable, we need to add it to the type definition like this:

```
struct Book: Codable {
   var name: String
   var author: String
   var publisher: String
}
```

Now that the Book type conforms to the Codable typealias, we can use it with the Encoder and Decoder types. In this section, we will be using the JSONEncoder and JSONDecoder types.

Using JSONEncoder

JSONEncoder will encode instances of types that conform to the Codable typealias, as JSON objects. The following code illustrates how to do this:

```
let book1 = Book(name: "Mastering Swift 3", author: "Jon Hoffman",
publisher: "Packt Publishing")

let encoder = JSONEncoder()
let data = try? encoder.encode(book1)
```

This code starts off by creating an instance of the Book and JSONEncoder() types. Next the encode method of the JSONEncoder is used to encode the Book instance to a JSON object. If the encode method fails it will return nil; otherwise it will return an instance of a Data object. We can convert this object to an instance of the string type as shown in the following code:

```
if let data = data, let dataString = String(data: data, encoding: .utf8) {
   print(dataString)
}
```

This code uses optional binding to JSON data to a string type and then prints it to the console. The default format for this `JSONEncoder` is to compact the JSON object; therefore, the output would look like this:

```
{"name":"Mastering Swift 3","author":"Jon Hoffman","publisher":"Packt
Publishing"}
```

If we would like this output to be formatted, automatically, into a format that displays better, we can set the `outputFormatting` property of the `JSONEncoder` instance like this:

```
encoder.outputFormatting = .prettyPrinted
```

With this property set the output now looks like this:

```
{
  "name" : "Mastering Swift 3",
  "author" : "Jon Hoffman",
  "publisher" : "Packt Publishing"
}
```

We would encode an array of `Book` instances exactly like the previous example except that, instead of passing an instance of a `Book` type to the encoder; we pass an array of `Book` types. The following code illustrates this:

```
let book1 = Book(name: "Mastering Swift 3", author: "Jon Hoffman",
publisher: "Packt Publishing")
let book2 = Book(name: "Mastering Swift 4", author: "Jon Hoffman",
publisher: "Packt Publishing")

let books = [book1, book2]
let encoder = JSONEncoder()
let dataEncoder = try? encoder.encode(books)
if let data = dataEncoder, let dataString = String(data: data, encoding:
.utf8) {
  print(dataString)
}
```

Now that we have seen how to encode JSON objects with the `JSONEncoder` type, let's look at how we can decode JSON objects with the `JSONDecoder` type.

Using JSONDecoder

The JSONDecoder type will decode instances of the data type from JSON objects to types that conform to the Codable typealias. The following code illustrates how to do this:

```
var jsonString = """
{
  "name" : "Mastering Swift 3",
  "author" : "Jon Hoffman",
  "publisher" : "Packt Publishing"
}
"""
if let jsonData = jsonString.data(using: .utf8) {
  let decoder = JSONDecoder()
  let objs = try decoder.decode(Book.self, from: jsonData)
  print(objs)
}
```

This code starts off by defining a string instance that represents the JSON data for a Book type. The string instance is then converted to an instance of the Data type using the data(using:) method. If the conversion is successful, an instance of the JSONDecoder type is created.

The decode() method of the JSONDecoder object is then used to decode the jsonData object. The first property of this method (Book.self) is the object type that we are decoding to. The second method is the Data object that we are converting from. If the decode() method fails it will return nil. If everything was successful the output of this code will look like this:

```
Book(name: "Mastering Swift 3", author: "Jon Hoffman", publisher: "Packt
Publishing")
```

Decoding an array of Book instances is very similar. The only difference is that we change the type of object we are decoding to, from Book.self to [Book].self. The following code shows how to do this:

```
var jsonString2 = """
[{
  "name" : "Mastering Swift 3",
  "author" : "Jon Hoffman",
  "publisher" : "Packt Publishing"
},
{
  "name" : "Mastering Swift 4",
  "author" : "Jon Hoffman",
  "publisher" : "Packt Publishing"
```

```
}]
"""
if let jsonData = jsonString2.data(using: .utf8) {
  let decoder = JSONDecoder()
  let objs = try decoder.decode([Book].self, from: jsonData)
  for obj in objs {
    print(obj)
  }
}
```

Using the Encoder and Decoder types makes it very simple to convert to/from JSON objects. Starting with Swift 4 this is the preferred way to do these conversions.

Summary

In this chapter, we looked at some of the libraries that make up the Swift Core Libraries. While these libraries are only a small portion of the libraries that make up the Swift Core Libraries they are arguably some of the most useful libraries. To explore the other libraries, you can refer to Apple's GitHub page:
`https://github.com/apple/swift-corelibs-foundation`.

Now let's look at how to adapt some of the more useful design patterns with Swift.

17

Adopting Design Patterns in Swift

While the first publication of the Gang of Four's *Design Patterns: Elements of Reusable Object-Oriented Software* was released in October of 1994, I have only been paying attention to design patterns for the last 12 years. Like most experienced developers, when I first started reading about design patterns, I recognized a lot of the patterns because I had already been using them without realizing what they were. I would have to say that in the past 12 years since I first read about design patterns, I have not written a serious application without using at least one of the Gang of Four's design patterns. I will tell you that I am definitely not a design pattern zealot, and if I get into a conversation about design patterns, there are usually only a couple of them that I can name without having to look them up. But one thing that I do remember is the concepts behind the major patterns and the problems they are designed to solve. This way, when I encounter one of these problems, I can look up the appropriate pattern and apply it. So, remember, as you go through this chapter, to take the time to understand the major concepts behind design patterns rather than trying to memorize the patterns themselves.

In this chapter, you will learn about the following topics:

- What are design patterns?
- What types of pattern make up the creational, structural, and behavioral categories of design patterns?
- How to implement the builder and singleton creational patterns in Swift?
- How to implement the bridge, façade, and proxy structural patterns in Swift?
- How to implement the strategy and command behavioral patterns in Swift?

What are design patterns?

Every experienced developer has a set of informal strategies that shape how they design and write applications. These strategies are shaped by their past experiences and the obstacles that they have had to overcome in previous projects. While these developers might swear by their own strategies, it does not mean that their strategies have been fully vetted. The use of these strategies can also introduce inconsistent implementations between different projects and developers.

While the concept of design patterns dates back to the mid 80s, they did not gain popularity until the Gang of Four released their *Design Patterns: Elements of Reusable Object-Oriented Software* book, published in 1994. The book's authors, *Erich Gamma, Richard Helm, Ralph Johnson,* and *John Vlissides* (also known as the Gang of Four), discuss the pitfalls of object-oriented programming and describe 23 classic software design patterns. These 23 patterns are broken up into three categories: creational, structural, and behavioral.

A design pattern identifies common software development problems and provides a strategy to deal with them. These strategies have been proven, over the years, to be an effective solution for the problems they are intended to solve. Using these patterns can greatly speed up the development process because they provide us with solutions that have already been proven to solve several common software development problems.

Another advantage that we get when we use design patterns is consistent code that is easy to maintain because, months or years from now, when we look at the code we will recognize the patterns and understand what the code does. If we properly document the code and document the design pattern we are implementing, it will also help other developers to understand what the code is doing.

The two main philosophies behind design patterns are code reuse and flexibility. As a software architect, it is essential that we build reusability and flexibility into the code. This allows us to easily maintain the code in the future and also makes it easier for the applications to expand to meet future requirements, because we all know how quickly requirements change.

While there is a lot to like about design patterns, and they are extremely beneficial for developers and architects, they are not the solution for world hunger that some developers make them out to be. Sometime in your development career, you will probably meet a developer or an architect who thinks that design patterns are immutable laws. These developers usually try to force the use of design patterns even when they are not necessary. A good rule of thumb is to make sure that you have a problem that needs to be fixed before you try to fix it.

Design patterns are starting points for avoiding and solving common programming problems. We can think of each design pattern as a recipe for a food dish. Just like a good recipe, we can tinker and adjust it to meet the particular tastes. But we usually do not want to stray too far from the original recipe because we may mess it up.

There are also times when we do not have a recipe for a certain dish that we want to make, just like there are times when there isn't a design pattern to solve the problem we face. In cases like this, we can use the knowledge of design patterns and their underlying philosophy to come up with an effective solution for the problem.

Design patterns are generally split into three categories. These are as follows:

- **Creational patterns**: Creational patterns support the creation of objects
- **Structural patterns**: Structural patterns concern types and object compositions
- **Behavioral patterns**: Behavioral patterns communicate between types

While the Gang of Four defined over 20 design patterns, we are only going to look at examples of some of the more popular patterns in this chapter. Let's start off by looking at creational patterns.

Design patterns were originally defined for object-oriented programming. In this chapter, where possible, we will focus on implementing patterns in a more protocol-oriented way. Therefore, the examples in this chapter may look a little different from examples in other design pattern books, but the underlying philosophy of the solutions will be the same.

Creational patterns

Creational patterns are design patterns that deal with how an object is created. These patterns create objects in a manner suitable for a particular situation.

There are two basic ideas behind creational patterns. The first is encapsulating the knowledge of which concrete types should be created and the second is hiding how the instances of these types are created.

There are five well-known patterns that are a part of the creational pattern category. They are as follows:

- **Abstract factory pattern**: This provides an interface for creating related objects without specifying the concrete type
- **Builder pattern**: This separates the construction of a complex object from its representation, so the same process can be used to create similar types
- **Factory method pattern**: This creates objects without exposing the underlying logic of how the object (or which type of object) is created
- **Prototype pattern**: This creates an object by cloning an existing one
- **Singleton pattern**: This allows one (and only one) instance of a class for the lifetime of an applications

In this chapter, we are going to show examples of how to implement the singleton and builder patterns in Swift. Let's start off by looking at one of the most controversial and possibly overused design patterns, the singleton pattern.

The singleton design pattern

The use of the singleton pattern is a fairly controversial subject among certain corners of the development community. One of the main reasons for this is that the singleton pattern is probably the most overused and misused pattern. Another reason this pattern is controversial is because the singleton pattern introduces a global state into an application, which provides the ability to change the object at any point within the application. The singleton pattern can also introduce hidden dependencies and tight compiling. My personal opinion is that, if the singleton pattern is used correctly, there is nothing wrong with using it. However, we do need to be careful not to misuse it.

The singleton pattern restricts the instantiation of a class to a single instance for the lifetime of an application. This pattern is very effective when we need exactly one object to coordinate actions within the application. An example of a good use of a singleton is if the application communicates with a remote device over Bluetooth and we also want to maintain that connection throughout the application. Some would say that we could pass the instance of the connection class from one page to the next, which is essentially what a singleton is. In my opinion, the singleton pattern, in this instance, is a much cleaner solution, because with the singleton pattern any page that needs the connection can get it without forcing every page to maintain the instance. This also allows us to maintain the connection without having to reconnect each time we go to another page.

Understanding the problem

The problem that the singleton pattern is designed to address is when we need one and only one instance of a type for the lifetime of the application. The singleton pattern is usually used when we need centralized management of an internal or external resource, and a single global point of access. Another popular use of the singleton pattern is when we want to consolidate a set of related activities needed throughout the application that do not maintain a state in one place.

In `Chapter 5`, *Classes and Structures*, we used the singleton pattern in the text validation example because we only needed one instance of the text validation types throughout the lifetime of the application. In this example, we used the singleton pattern for the text validation types because we wanted to create a single instance of the types that could then be used by all the components of the application without requiring us to create new instances of the types. These text validation types did not have a state that could be changed. They only had methods that performed the validation on the text and constants that defined how to validate the text. While some may disagree with me, I believe types like these are excellent candidates for the singleton pattern because there is no reason to create multiple instances of these types.

Understanding the solution

There are several ways to implement the singleton pattern in Swift. With this method, a single instance of the class is created the first time we access the class constant. We will then use the class constant to gain access to this instance throughout the lifetime of the application. We will also create a private initializer that will prevent external code from creating additional instances of the class.

Note that we use the word class in this description and not type. The reason for this is that the singleton pattern can only be implemented with reference types.

Implementing the singleton pattern

Let's look at how we implement the singleton pattern with Swift. The following code example shows how to create a singleton class:

```
class MySingleton {
   static let sharedInstance = MySingleton()
   var number = 0
   private init() {}
}
```

We can see that, within the `MySingleton` class, we created a static constant named `sharedInstance`, which contains an instance of the `MySingleton` class. A static constant can be called without having to instantiate the class. Since we declared the `sharedInstance` constant static, only one instance will exist throughout the lifecycle of the application, thereby creating the singleton pattern.

We also created the private initiator that will restrict other code from creating another instance of the `MySingleton` class.

Now, let's see how this pattern works. The `MySingleton` pattern has another property, named `number`, which is an integer. We will monitor how this property changes as we use the `sharedInstance` property to create multiple variables of the `MySingleton` type, as shown in the following code:

```
var singleA = MySingleton.sharedInstance
var singleB = MySingleton.sharedInstance
var singleC = MySingleton.sharedInstance
singleB.number = 2
print(singleA.number)
print(singleB.number)
print(singleC.number)
singleC.number = 3
print(singleA.number)
print(singleB.number)
print(singleC.number)
```

In this example, we used the `sharedInstance` property to create three variables of the `MySingleton` type. We initially set the `number` property of the second `MySingleton` variable (`singleB`) to the number 2. When we printed out the value of the number property for the `singleA`, `singleB`, and `singleC` instances we saw that the `number` property for all three equals 2. We then changed the value of the number property of the third `MySingleton` instance (`singleC`) to the number 3.

When we printed out the value of the `number` property again, we saw that all three now have the value of 3. Therefore, when we change the value of the `number` property in any of the instances, the values of all three changes because each variable is pointed to the same instance.

In this example, we implemented the singleton pattern using a reference (class) type because we wanted to ensure that only one instance of the type existed throughout the application. If we implemented this pattern with a value type, such as a structure or an enumeration, we would run the risk of there being multiple instances of the type. If you recall, each time we pass an instance of a value type, we are actually passing a copy of that instance, which means that, if we implemented the singleton pattern with a value type, each time we called the `sharedInstance` property we would receive a new copy, which would effectively break the singleton pattern.

The singleton pattern can be very useful when we need to maintain the state of an object throughout the application; however, be careful not to overuse it. The singleton pattern should not be used unless there is a specific requirement (**requirement** is the keyword here) for having one, and only one, instance of the class throughout the lifecycle of the application. If we are using the singleton pattern simply for convenience, then we are probably misusing it.

Keep in mind that, while Apple recommends that we prefer value types to reference types, there are still plenty of examples, such as the singleton pattern, where we need to use reference types. When we continuously tell ourselves to prefer value types to reference types, it can be very easy to forget that there are times where a reference type is needed. Don't forget to use reference types with this pattern.

Now, let's look at the builder design pattern.

The builder design pattern

The builder pattern helps us with the creation of complex objects and enforces the process of how these objects are created. With this pattern, we generally separate the creation logic from the complex type and put it in another type. This allows us to use the same construction process to create different representations of the type.

Understanding the problem

The problem that the builder pattern is designed to address is when an instance of a type requires a large number of configurable values. We could set the configuration options when we create instances of the class, but that can cause issues if the options are not set correctly or we do not know the proper values for all the options. Another issue is the amount of code that may be needed to set all the configurable options each time we create an instance of the types.

Understanding the solution

The builder pattern solves this problem by introducing an intermediary known as a *builder* type. This builder type contains most, if not all, of the information necessary to create an instance of the original complex type.

There are two methods that we can use to implement the builder pattern. The first method is to have multiple builder types where each of the types contains the information to configure the original complex object in a specific way. In the second method, we implement the builder pattern with a single builder type that sets all the configurable options to a default value and then we would change the values as needed.

In this section, we will look at both ways to use the builder pattern, because it is important to understand how each works.

Implementing the builder pattern

Before we show how we would use the builder pattern, let's look at how to create a complex structure without the builder pattern and the problems we run into.

The following code creates a structure named `BurgerOld`, and does not use the builder pattern:

```
struct BurgerOld {
  var name: String
  var patties: Int
  var bacon: Bool
  var cheese: Bool
  var pickles: Bool
  var ketchup: Bool
  var mustard: Bool
  var lettuce: Bool
  var tomato: Bool
```

```
init(name: String, patties: Int, bacon: Bool, cheese: Bool,
     pickles:Bool,ketchup: Bool,mustard: Bool,lettuce: Bool,
     tomato: Bool) {
  self.name = name
  self.patties = patties
  self.bacon = bacon
  self.cheese = cheese
  self.pickles = pickles
  self.ketchup = ketchup
  self.mustard = mustard
  self.lettuce = lettuce
  self.tomato = tomato
  }
}
```

In the BurgerOld structure, we have several properties that define which condiments are on the burger and the name of the burger. Since we need to know which items are on the burgers and which items aren't, when we create an instance of the BurgerOld structure the initializer requires us to define each item. This can lead to some complex initializations throughout the application, not to mention that, if we had more than one standard burger (bacon cheeseburger, cheeseburger, hamburger, and so on), we would need to make sure that each is defined correctly. Let's see how to create instances of the BurgerOld class:

```
// Create Hamburger
var hamburger = BurgerOld(name:  "Hamburger", patties: 1, bacon: false,
                  cheese:  false, pickles:  false, ketchup: false,
                  mustard: false, lettuce: false, tomato: false)

// Create Cheeseburger
var cheeseburger = BurgerOld(name:  "Cheeseburger", patties: 1 ,
                  bacon: false, cheese: false, pickles: false,
                  ketchup: false, mustard: false,
                  lettuce: false, tomato: false)
```

As we can see, creating instances of the BurgerOld type requires a lot of code. Now, let's look at a better way to do this. In this example, we will show how to use multiple builder types where each type will define the condiments that are on a particular burger. We will begin by creating a BurgerBuilder protocol that will have the following code in it:

```
protocol BurgerBuilder {
  var name: String { get }
  var patties: Int { get }
  var bacon: Bool { get }
  var cheese: Bool { get }
  var pickles: Bool { get }
  var ketchup: Bool { get }
  var mustard: Bool { get }
```

```
    var lettuce: Bool { get }
    var tomato: Bool { get }
}
```

This protocol simply defines the nine properties that will be required for any type that implements this protocol. Now, let's create two structures that implement this protocol: the HamburgerBuilder and the CheeseBurgerBuilder structures:

```
struct HamburgerBuilder: BurgerBuilder {
    let name = "Burger"
    let patties = 1
    let bacon = false
    let cheese = false
    let pickles = true
    let ketchup = true
    let mustard = true
    let lettuce = false
    let tomato = false
}

struct CheeseBurgerBuilder: BurgerBuilder {
    let name = "CheeseBurger"
    let patties = 1
    let bacon = false
    let cheese = true
    let pickles = true
    let ketchup = true
    let mustard = true
    let lettuce = false
    let tomato = false
}
```

In both the HamburgerBuilder and the CheeseBurgerBuilder structures, all we are doing is defining the values for each of the required properties. In more complex types, we might need to initialize additional resources.

Now, let's look at the Burger structure, which will use instances of the BurgerBuilder protocol to create instances of itself. The following code shows this new Burger type:

```
struct Burger {
    var name: String
    var patties: Int
    var bacon: Bool
    var cheese: Bool
    var pickles: Bool
    var ketchup: Bool
    var mustard: Bool
```

```
  var lettuce: Bool
  var tomato: Bool

  init(builder: BurgerBuilder) {
    self.name = builder.name
    self.patties = builder.patties
    self.bacon = builder.bacon
    self.cheese = builder.cheese
    self.pickles = builder.pickles
    self.ketchup = builder.ketchup
    self.mustard = builder.mustard
    self.lettuce = builder.lettuce
    self.tomato = builder.tomato
  }

  func showBurger() {
    print("Name:\(name)")
    print("Patties: \(patties)")
    print("Bacon: \(bacon)")
    print("Cheese: \(cheese)")
    print("Pickles: \(pickles)")
    print("Ketchup: \(ketchup)")
    print("Mustard: \(mustard)")
    print("Lettuce: \(lettuce)")
    print("Tomato: \(tomato)")
  }
}
```

The difference between this `Burger` structure and the `BurgerOld` structure shown earlier is the initializer. In the previous `BurgerOld` structure, the initializer took nine arguments-one for each constant defined in the structure. In the new `Burger` structure, the initializer takes one argument, which is an instance of a type that conforms to the `BurgerBuilder` protocol. This new initializer allows us to create instances of the `Burger` class as follows:

```
// Create Hamburger
var myBurger = Burger(builder: HamburgerBuilder())
myBurger.showBurger()

// Create Cheeseburger with tomatoes
var myCheeseBurger = Burger(builder: CheeseBurgerBuilder())
// Lets hold the tomatoes
myCheeseBurger.tomato = false
myCheeseBurger.showBurger()
```

If we compare how we create instances of the new `Burger` structure to the earlier `BurgerOld` structure, we can see that it is much easier to create instances of the `Burger` structure. We also know that we are correctly setting the property values for each type of burger because the values are set directly in the builder classes.

As we mentioned earlier, there is a second method that we can use to implement the builder pattern. Rather than having multiple builder types, we can have a single builder type that sets all the configurable options to a default value; then we change the values as needed. I use this implementation method a lot when I am updating older code because it is easy to integrate it with preexisting code.

For this implementation, we will create a single `BurgerBuilder` structure. This structure will be used to create instances of the `BurgerOld` structure and will, by default, set all the ingredients to their default values. The `BurgerBuilder` structure also gives us the ability to change which ingredients will go on the burger prior to creating instances of the `BurgerOld` structure. We create the `BurgerBuilder` structure as follows:

```swift
struct BurgerBuilder {
  var name = "Burger"
  var patties = 1
  var bacon = false
  var cheese = false
  var pickles = true
  var ketchup = true
  var mustard = true
  var lettuce = false
  var tomato = false

  mutating func setPatties(choice: Int) {self.patties = choice}
  mutating func setBacon(choice: Bool) {self.bacon = choice}
  mutating func setCheese(choice: Bool) {self.cheese = choice}
  mutating func setPickles(choice: Bool) {self.pickles = choice}
  mutating func setKetchup(choice: Bool) {self.ketchup = choice}
  mutating func setMustard(choice: Bool) {self.mustard = choice}
  mutating func setLettuce(choice: Bool) {self.lettuce = choice}
  mutating func setTomato(choice: Bool) {self.tomato = choice}
  func buildBurgerOld(name: String) -> BurgerOld {
    return BurgerOld(name: name, patties: self.patties,bacon: self.bacon,
            cheese: self.cheese,pickles: self.pickles,
            ketchup: self.ketchup,mustard: self.mustard,
            lettuce: self.lettuce,tomato: self.tomato)
  }
}
```

In the `BurgerBuilder` structure, we define the nine properties (ingredients) for the burger and then create a setter method for each of the properties except for the `name` property. We also create one method named `buildBurgerOld()`, which will create an instance of the `BurgerOld` structure based on the values of the properties for the `BurgerBuilder` instance. We use the `BurgerBuilder` structure as follows:

```
var burgerBuilder = BurgerBuilder()
burgerBuilder.setCheese(choice: true)
burgerBuilder.setBacon(choice: true)
var jonBurger = burgerBuilder.buildBurgerOld(name: "Jon's Burger")
```

In this example, we create an instance of the `BurgerBuilder` structure. We then use the `setCheese()` and `setBacon()` methods to add cheese and bacon to the burger. Finally, we call the `buildBurgerOld()` method to create the instance of the `burgerOld` structure.

As we can see, both methods that were used to implement the builder pattern greatly simplify the creation of the complex type. Both methods also ensured that the instances were properly configured with default values. If you find yourself creating instances of types with very long and complex initialization commands, I recommend that you look at the builder pattern to see if you can use it to simplify the initialization.

Now, let's look at structural design patterns.

Structural design patterns

Structural design patterns describe how types can be combined to form larger structures. These larger structures can generally be easier to work with and hide a lot of the complexity of the individual types. Most patterns in the structural pattern category involve connections between objects.

There are seven well-known patterns that are part of the structural design pattern type. These are as follows:

- **Adapter**: This allows types with incompatible interfaces to work together
- **Bridge**: This is used to separate the abstract elements of a type from the implementation so the two can vary
- **Composite**: This allows us to treat a group of objects as a single object
- **Decorator**: This lets us add or override behavior in an existing method of an object

- **Façade**: This provides a simplified interface for a larger and more complex body of code
- **Flyweight**: This allows us to reduce the resources needed to create and use a large number of similar objects
- **Proxy**: This is a type acting as an interface for another class or classes

In this chapter, we are going to give examples of how to use the bridge, façade, and proxy patterns in Swift. Let's start off by looking at the bridge pattern.

The bridge pattern

The bridge pattern decouples the abstraction from the implementation so that they can both vary independently. The bridge pattern can also be thought of as a two-layer abstraction.

Understanding the problem

The bridge pattern is designed to solve a couple of problems, but the one we are going to focus on here tends to arise over time as new requirements come in with new features. At some point as these new requirements and features come in, we will need to change how the features interact. Usually, this will eventually require us to refactor the code.

In object-oriented programming, this is known as an **exploding class hierarchy**, but it can also happen in protocol-oriented programming.

Understanding the solution

The bridge pattern solves this problem by taking the interacting features and separating the functionality that is specific to each feature from the functionality that is shared between them. A bridge type can then be created, which will encapsulate the shared functionality, bringing them together.

Implementing the bridge pattern

To demonstrate how we would use the bridge pattern, we will create two features. The first feature is a message feature that will store and prepare a message that we wish to send out. The second feature is the sender feature that will send the message through a specific channel, such as email or SMS messaging.

Let's start off by creating two protocols named `Message` and `Sender`. The `Message` protocol will define the requirements for types that are used to create messages. The `Sender` protocol will be used to define the requirements for types that are used to send the messages through the specific channels. The following code shows how we define these two protocols:

```
protocol Message {
  var messageString: String { get set }
  init(messageString: String)
  func prepareMessage()
}

protocol Sender {
  func sendMessage(message: Message)
}
```

The `Message` protocol defines a single property named `messageString` of the String type. This property will contain the text of the message and cannot be nil. We also define one initiator and a method named `prepareMessage()`. The initializer will be used to set the `messageString` property and anything else required by the message type. The `prepareMessage()` method will be used to prepare the message prior to sending it. This method can be used to encrypt the message, add formatting, or do anything else to the message prior to sending it.

The `Sender` protocol defines a method named `sendMessage()`. This method will send the message through the channel defined by conforming types. In this function, we will need to ensure that the `prepareMessage()` method from the `message` type is called prior to sending the message.

Now let's see how we define two types that conform to the `Message` protocol:

```
class PlainTextMessage: Message {
  var messageString: String
  required init(messageString: String) {
    self.messageString = messageString
  }
  func prepareMessage() {
    //Nothing to do
  }
}

class DESEncryptedMessage: Message {
  var messageString: String
  required init(messageString: String) {
    self.messageString = messageString
```

```
  }
  func prepareMessage() {
    // Encrypt message here
    self.messageString = "DES: " + self.messageString
  }
}
```

Each of these types contains the required functionality to conform to the `Message` protocol. The only real difference between these types is in the `prepareMessage()` methods. In the `PlainTextMessage` class, the `prepareMessage()` method is empty because we do not need to do anything to the message prior to sending it. The `prepareMessage()` method of the `DESEncryptionMessage` class would normally contain the logic to encrypt the message, but for the example we will just prepend a `DES` tag to the beginning of the message, letting us know that this method was called.

Now let's create two types that will conform to the `Sender` protocol. These types would typically handle sending the message through a specific channel; however, in the example, we will simply print a message to the console:

```
class EmailSender: Sender {
  func sendMessage(message: Message) {
    print("Sending through E-Mail:")
    print("\(message.messageString)")
  }
}

class SMSSender: Sender {
  func sendMessage(message: Message) {
    print("Sending through SMS:")
    print("\(message.messageString)")

  }
}
```

Both the `EmailSender` and the `SMSSender` types conform to the `Sender` protocol by implementing the `sendMessage()` function.

We can now use these two features, as shown in the following code:

```
var myMessage = PlainTextMessage(messageString: "Plain Text Message")
myMessage.prepareMessage()
var sender = SMSSender()
sender.sendMessage(message: myMessage)
```

This will work well, and we could add code similar to this anywhere we need to create and send a message. Now let's say that, one day in the near future, we get a requirement to add a new functionality to verify the message prior to sending it to make sure it meets the requirements of the channel we are sending the message through. To do this, we would start off by changing the `Sender` protocol to add the verify functionality. The new sender protocol would look as follows:

```swift
protocol Sender {
  var message: Message? { get set }
  func sendMessage()
  func verifyMessage()
}
```

To the `Sender` protocol, we added a method named `verifyMessage()` and added a property named `message`. We also changed the definition of the `sendMessage()` method. The original `Sender` protocol was designed to simply send the message, but now we need to verify the message prior to calling the `sendMessage()` function; therefore, we couldn't simply pass the message to it, as we did in the previous definition.

Now we will need to change the types that conform to the `Sender` protocol to make them conform to this new protocol. The following code shows how we would make these changes:

```swift
class EmailSender: Sender {
  var message: Message?
  func sendMessage() {
    print("Sending through E-Mail:")
    print("\(message!.messageString)")
  }
  func verifyMessage() {
    print("Verifying E-Mail message")
  }
}

class SMSSender: Sender {
  var message: Message?
  func sendMessage() {
    print("Sending through SMS:")
    print("\(message!.messageString)")
  }
  func verifyMessage() {
    print("Verifying SMS message")
  }
}
```

With the changes that we made to the types that conform to the `Sender` protocol, we will need to change how the code uses these types. The following example shows how we can now use them:

```
var myMessage = PlainTextMessage(messageString: "Plain Text Message")
myMessage.prepareMessage()

var sender = SMSSender()
sender.message = myMessage

sender.verifyMessage()
sender.sendMessage()
```

These changes are not that hard to make; however, without the bridge pattern, we would need to refactor the entire code base and make the change everywhere that, we are sending messages. The bridge pattern tells us that when we have two hierarchies that closely interact together like this, we should put this interaction logic into a bridge type that will encapsulate the logic in one spot. This way, when we receive new requirements or enhancements, we can make the change in one spot, thereby limiting the refactoring that we must do. We could make a bridge type for the message and sender hierarchies, as shown in the following example:

```
struct MessageingBridge {
    static func sendMessage(message: Message, sender: Sender) {
        var sender = sender
        message.prepareMessage()
        sender.message = message
        sender.verifyMessage()
        sender.sendMessage()
    }
}
```

The logic of how the messaging and sender hierarchies interact is now encapsulated into the `MessagingBridge` structure. Now, when the logic needs to change we only need to make the change to this one structure rather than having to refactor the entire code base.

The bridge pattern is a very good pattern to remember and use. There have been (and still are) times that I have regretted not using the bridge pattern in my code because, as we all know, requirements change frequently, and being able to make the changes in one spot rather than throughout the code base can save us a lot of time in the future.

Now, let's look at the next pattern in the structural category: the façade pattern.

The façade pattern

The façade pattern provides a simplified interface to a larger and more complex body of code. This allows us to make the libraries easier to use and understand by hiding some of the complexities. It also allows us to combine multiple APIs into a single, easier to use API, which is what we will see in the example.

Understanding the problem

The façade pattern is often used when we have a complex system that has a large number of independent APIs that are designed to work together. Sometimes it is hard to tell where we should use the façade pattern during the initial application design. The reason for this is that we normally try to simplify the initial API design; however, over time, and as requirements change and new features are added, the APIs become more and more complex, and then it becomes pretty evident where we should have used the façade pattern.

Understanding the solution

The main idea of the façade pattern is to hide the complexity of the APIs behind a simple interface. This offers us several advantages, with the most obvious being that it simplifies how we interact with the APIs. It also promotes loose coupling, which allows the APIs to change, as requirements change, without the need to refactor all the code that uses them.

Implementing the façade pattern

To demonstrate the façade pattern, we will create three APIs: `HotelBooking`, `FlightBooking`, and `RentalCarBookings`. These APIs will be used to search for and book hotels, flights, and rental cars for trips. While we could very easily call each of the APIs individually in the code, we are going to create a `TravelFacade` structure that will allow us to access the functionality of the APIs in single calls.

We will begin by defining the three APIs. Each of the APIs will need a data storage class that will store the information about the hotel, flight, or rental car. We will start off by implementing the hotel API:

```
struct Hotel {
  //Information about hotel room
}

struct HotelBooking {
  static func getHotelNameForDates(to: Date, from: Date) ->[Hotel]? {
    let hotels = [Hotel]()
    //logic to get hotels
    return hotels
  }

  static func bookHotel(hotel: Hotel) {
    // logic to reserve hotel room
  }
}
```

The hotel API consists of the `Hotel` and `HotelBooking` structures. The `Hotel` structure will be used to store the information about a hotel room and the `HotelBooking` structure will be used to search for a hotel room and to book the room for the trip. The flight and rental car APIs are very similar to the hotel API. The following code shows both of these APIs:

```
struct Flight {
  //Information about flights
}

struct FlightBooking {
  static func getFlightNameForDates(to: Date, from: Date) ->[Flight]? {
    let flights = [Flight]()
    //logic to get flights
    return flights
  }
  static func bookFlight(flight: Flight) {
    // logic to reserve flight
  }
}

struct RentalCar {
  //Information about rental cars
}

struct RentalCarBooking {
  static func getRentalCarNameForDates(to: Date, from: Date)-> [RentalCar]?
```

```
{
    let cars = [RentalCar]()
    //logic to get flights
    return cars
}

static func bookRentalCar(rentalCar: RentalCar) {
    // logic to reserve rental car
}
}
```

In each of these APIs, we have a structure that is used to store information and a structure that is used to provide the search/booking functionality. In the initial design, it would be very easy to call these individual APIs within the application; however, as we all know, requirements tend to change, which causes the APIs to change over time. By using the façade pattern here, we are able to hide how we implement the APIs; therefore, if we need to change how the APIs work in the future, we will only need to update the façade type rather than refactoring all of the code. This makes the code easier to maintain and update in the future. Now let's look at how we will implement the façade pattern by creating a `TravelFacade` class:

```
class TravelFacade {
    var hotels: [Hotel]?
    var flights: [Flight]?
    var cars: [RentalCar]?

    init(to: Date, from: Date) {
        hotels = HotelBooking.getHotelNameForDates(to: to, from: from)
        flights = FlightBooking.getFlightNameForDates(to: to, from:from)
        cars = RentalCarBooking.getRentalCarNameForDates(to: to, from:from)
    }

    func bookTrip(hotel: Hotel, flight: Flight, rentalCar: RentalCar) {
        HotelBooking.bookHotel(hotel: hotel)
        FlightBooking.bookFlight(flight: flight)
        RentalCarBooking.bookRentalCar(rentalCar: rentalCar)
    }
}
```

The `TravelFacade` class contains the functionality to search the three APIs and book a hotel, flight, and rental car. We can now use the `TravelFacade` class to search for hotels, flights, and rental cars without having to directly access the individual APIs. We can also use the `TravelFacade` class to book the hotel, flights, and rental cars without having to access the individual APIs.

As we mentioned at the start of this chapter, it is not always obvious when we should use the façade pattern in the initial design.

A good rule to follow is: if we have several APIs that are working together to perform a task, we should think about using the façade pattern.

Now, let's look at the last structural pattern, which is the proxy design pattern.

The proxy design pattern

In the proxy design pattern, there is one type acting as an interface for another type or API. This wrapper class, which is the proxy, can then add functionality to the object, make the object available over a network, or restrict access to the object.

Understanding the problem

We can use the proxy pattern to solve several problems, but I find that I mainly use this pattern to solve two problems.

The first problem that I use the proxy pattern to solve is when I want to create a layer of abstraction between a single API and my code. The API could be a local or remote API, but I usually use this pattern to put an abstraction layer between my code and a remote service. This will allow changes to the remote API without the need to refactor large portions of the code.

The second problem that I use the proxy pattern to solve is when I need to make changes to an API, but I do not have the code or there is already a dependency on the API elsewhere in the application.

Understanding the solution

To solve these problems, the proxy pattern tells us that we should create a type that will act as an interface for interacting with the other type or API. In the example, we will show how to use the proxy pattern to add functionality to an existing type.

Implementing the proxy pattern

In this section, we will demonstrate the proxy pattern by creating a house class that we can add multiple floor plans to, where each floor plan represents a different story of the house. Let's begin by creating a FloorPlan protocol:

```
protocol FloorPlan {
    var bedRooms: Int { get set }
    var utilityRooms: Int { get set }
    var bathRooms: Int { get set }
    var kitchen: Int { get set }
    var livingRooms: Int { get set }
}
```

In the FloorPlan protocol, we define five properties that will represent the number of rooms contained in each floor plan. Now, let's create an implementation of the FloorPlan protocol named HouseFloorPlan, which is as follows:

```
struct HouseFloorPlan: FloorPlan {
    var bedRooms = 0
    var utilityRooms = 0
    var bathRooms = 0
    var kitchen = 0
    var livingRooms = 0
}
```

The HouseFloorPlan structure implements all five properties required from the FloorPlan protocol and assigns default values to them. Next, we will create the House class, which will represent a house:

```
class House {
    var stories = [FloorPlan]()
    func addStory(floorPlan: FloorPlan) {
        stories.append(floorPlan)
    }
}
```

Within the House class, we have an array of instances that conforms to the FloorPlan protocol where each floor plan will represent one story of the house. We also have a function named addStory(), which accepts an instance of a type that conforms to the FloorPlan protocol. This function will add the floor plan to the array of FloorPlan protocols.

If we think about the logic of this class, there is one problem that we might encounter; we are allowed to add as many floor plans as we want, which may lead to houses that are 60 or 70 stories high. This would be great if we were building skyscrapers, but we just want to build basic single-family houses. If we want to limit the number of floor plans without changing the House class (either we cannot change it or we simply do not want to), we can implement the proxy pattern. The following example shows how to implement the HouseProxy class, where we limit the number of floor plans we can add to the house, as follows:

```swift
struct HouseProxy {
  var house = House()

  mutating func addStory(floorPlan: FloorPlan) -> Bool {
    if house.stories.count < 3 {
      house.addStory(floorPlan: floorPlan)
      return true
    } else {
      return false
    }
  }
}
```

We begin the HouseProxy class by creating an instance of the House class. We then create a method named addStory(), which lets us add a new floor plan to the house. In the addStory() method, we check to see if the number of stories in the house is fewer than three; if so, we add the floor plan to the house and return true. If the number of stories is equal to or greater than three, then we do not add the floor plan to the house and return false. Let's see how we can use this proxy:

```swift
var ourHouse = HouseProxy()

var basement = HouseFloorPlan(bedRooms: 0, utilityRooms: 1,
bathRooms:1,kitchen: 0, livingRooms: 1)
var firstStory = HouseFloorPlan (bedRooms: 1, utilityRooms: 0,bathRooms:
2,kitchen: 1, livingRooms: 1)
var secondStory = HouseFloorPlan (bedRooms: 2, utilityRooms: 0,bathRooms:
1,kitchen: 0, livingRooms: 1)
var additionalStory = HouseFloorPlan (bedRooms: 1, utilityRooms:
0,bathRooms:1, kitchen: 1, livingRooms: 1)

ourHouse.addStory(floorPlan: basement)
ourHouse.addStory(floorPlan: firstStory)
ourHouse.addStory(floorPlan: secondStory)
ourHouse.addStory(floorPlan: additionalStory)
```

In the example code, we start off by creating an instance of the `HouseProxy` class named `ourHouse`. We then create four instances of the `HouseFloorPlan` type, each with a different number of rooms. Finally, we attempt to add each of the floor plans to the `ourHouse` instance. If we run this code, we will see that the first three instances of the `floorplans` class were added to the house successfully, but the last one wasn't because we are only allowed to add three floors.

The proxy pattern is very useful when we want to add some additional functionality or error checking to a type, but we do not want to change the actual type itself. We can also use it to add a layer of abstraction between a remote or local API.

Now, let's look at behavioral design patterns.

Behavioral design patterns

Behavioral design patterns explain how types interact with each other. These patterns describe how different instances of types send messages to each other to make things happen.

There are nine well-known patterns that are part of the behavioral design pattern type. They are as follows:

- **Chain of responsibility**: This is used to process a variety of requests, each of which may be delegated to a different handler.
- **Command**: This creates objects that can encapsulate actions or parameters so that they can be invoked later or by a different component.
- **Iterator**: This allows us to access the elements of an object sequentially without exposing the underlying structure.
- **Mediator**: This is used to reduce coupling between types that communicate with each other.
- **Memento**: This is used to capture the current state of an object and store it in a manner that can be restored later.
- **Observer**: This allows an object to publish changes to an object's state. Other objects can then subscribe so they can be notified of any changes.
- **State**: This is used to alter the behavior of an object when its internal state changes.
- **Strategy**: This allows one out of a family of algorithms to be chosen at runtime.
- **Visitor**: This is a way of separating an algorithm from an object structure.

In this section, we are going to give examples of how to use strategy and command patterns in Swift. Let's start off by looking at the command pattern.

The command design pattern

The command design pattern lets us define actions that we can execute later. This pattern generally encapsulates all the information needed to call or trigger the actions at a later time.

Understanding the problem

There are times in the applications when we need to separate the execution of a command from its invoker. Typically, this is when we have a type that needs to perform one of several actions; however, the choice of which action to use needs to be made at runtime.

Understanding the solution

The command pattern tells us that we should encapsulate the logic for the actions into a type that conforms to a command protocol. We can then provide instances of the command types for use by the invoker. The invoker will use the interface provided by the protocol to invoke the necessary actions.

Implementing the command pattern

In this section, we will demonstrate how to use the command pattern by creating a `Light` type. In this type, we will define the `lightOnCommand` and `lightOffCommand` commands and will use the `turnOnLight()` and `turnOffLight()` methods to invoke these commands. We will begin by creating a protocol named `Command`, which all of the command types will conform to. Here is the command protocol:

```
protocol Command {
   func execute()
}
```

This protocol contains a method named execute(), which will be used to execute the command. Now, let's look at the command types that the Light type will use to turn the light on and off. They are as follows:

```swift
struct RockerSwitchLightOnCommand: Command {
  func execute() {
    print("Rocker Switch:Turning Light On")
  }
}

struct RockerSwitchLightOffCommand: Command {
  func execute() {
    print("Rocker Switch:Turning Light Off")
  }
}
struct PullSwitchLightOnCommand: Command {
  func execute() {
    print("Pull Switch:Turning Light On")
  }
}

struct PullSwitchLightOffCommand: Command {
  func execute() {
    print("Pull Switch:Turning Light Off")
  }
}
```

The RockerSwitchLightOffCommand, RockerSwitchLightOnCommand, PullSwitchLightOnCommand, and PullSwitchLightOffCommand commands all conform to the Command protocol by implementing the execute() method; therefore, we will be able to use them in the Light type. Now, let's look at how to implement the Light type:

```swift
class Light {
  var lightOnCommand: Command
  var lightOffCommand: Command

  init(lightOnCommand: Command, lightOffCommand: Command) {
    self.lightOnCommand = lightOnCommand
    self.lightOffCommand = lightOffCommand
  }

  func turnOnLight() {
    self.lightOnCommand.execute()
  }
```

```
    func turnOffLight() {
      self.lightOffCommand.execute()
    }
  }
```

In the `Light` type, we start off by creating two variables, named `lightOnCommand` and `lightOffCommand`, which will contain instances of types that conform to the `Command` protocol. We then create an initiator that lets us set both of the commands when we initiate the type. Finally, we create the `turnOnLight()` and `turnOffLight()` methods that we will use to turn the light on and off. In these methods, we call the appropriate command to turn the light on or off.

We would then use the `Light` type as follows:

```
var on = PullSwitchLightOnCommand()
var off = PullSwitchLightOffCommand()

var light = Light(lightOnCommand: on, lightOffCommand: off)

light.turnOnLight()
light.turnOffLight()

light.lightOnCommand = RockerSwitchLightOnCommand()
light.turnOnLight()
```

In this example, we begin by creating an instance of the `PullSwitchLightOnCommand` type named `on` and an instance of the `PullSwitchLightOffCommand` type named `off`. We then create an instance of the `Light` type using the two commands that we just created and call the `turnOnLight()` and `turnOffLight()` methods of the `Light` instance to turn the light on and off. In the last two lines, we change the `lightOnCommand` method, which was originally set to an instance of the `PullSwitchLightOnCommand` class, to an instance of the `RockerSwitchLightOnCommand` type. The `Light` instance will now use the `RockerSwitchLightOnCommand` type whenever we turn the light on. This allows us to change the functionality of the `Light` type during runtime.

There are several benefits from using the command pattern. One of the main benefits is that we are able to set which command to invoke at runtime, which also lets us swap the commands out with different implementations that conform to the `Command` protocol as needed throughout the life of the application. Another advantage of the command pattern is that we encapsulate the details of command implementations within the command types themselves rather than in the container type.

Now, let's look at the last design pattern, which is the strategy pattern.

The strategy pattern

The strategy pattern is pretty similar to the command pattern in that they both allow us to decouple implementation details from the calling type and also allow us to switch the implementation out at runtime. The big difference is that the strategy pattern is intended to encapsulate algorithms. By swapping out an algorithm, we are expecting the object to perform the same functionality, but in a different way. In the command pattern, when we swap out the commands, we are expecting the object to change the functionality.

Understanding the problem

There are times in the applications when we need to change the backend algorithm that is used to perform an operation. Typically, this is when we have a type that has several different algorithms that can be used to perform the same task; however, the choice of which algorithm to use needs to be made at runtime.

Understanding the solution

The strategy pattern tells us that we should encapsulate the algorithm in a type that conforms to a strategy protocol. We can then provide instances of the strategy types for use by the invoker. The invoker will use the interface provided by the protocol to invoke the algorithm.

Implementing the strategy pattern

In this section, we will demonstrate the strategy pattern by showing you how we could swap out compression algorithms at runtime. Let's begin this example by creating a `CompressionStrategy` protocol that each one of the compression types will conform to. Let's look at the following code:

```
protocol CompressionStrategy {
  func compressFiles(filePaths: [String])
}
```

This protocol defines a method named `compressFiles()` that accepts a single parameter, which is an array of strings that contain the paths to the files we want to compress. We will now create two structures that conform to this protocol. These are the `ZipCompressionStrategy` and the `RarCompressionStrategy` structures, which are as follows:

```
struct ZipCompressionStrategy: CompressionStrategy {
  func compressFiles(filePaths: [String]) {
    print("Using Zip Compression")
  }
}
struct RarCompressionStrategy: CompressionStrategy {
  func compressFiles(filePaths: [String]) {
    print("Using RAR Compression")
  }
}
```

Both of these structures implement the `CompressionStrategy` protocol by using a method named `compressFiles()`, which accepts an array of strings. Within these methods, we simply print out the name of the compression that we are using. Normally, we would implement the compression logic in these methods.

Now, let's look at the `CompressContent` class, which will be used to compress the files:

```
class CompressContent {
  var strategy: CompressionStrategy
  init(strategy: CompressionStrategy) {
    self.strategy = strategy
  }
  func compressFiles(filePaths: [String]) {
    self.strategy.compressFiles(filePaths: filePaths)
  }
}
```

In this class, we start off by defining a variable, named `strategy`, which will contain an instance of a type that conforms to the `CompressStrategy` protocol. We then create an initiator that will be used to set the compression type when the class is initiated. Finally, we create a method named `compressFiles()`, which accepts an array of strings that contain the paths to the list of files that we wish to compress. In this method, we compress the files using the compression strategy that is set in the strategy variable.

We will use the `CompressContent` class as follows:

```
var filePaths = ["file1.txt", "file2.txt"]
var zip = ZipCompressionStrategy()
var rar = RarCompressionStrategy()

var compress = CompressContent(strategy: zip)
compress.compressFiles(filePaths: filePaths)

compress.strategy = rar
compress.compressFiles(filePaths: filePaths)
```

We begin by creating an array of strings that contains the files we wish to compress. We also create an instance of both the `ZipCompressionStrategy` and the `RarCompressionStrategy` types. We then create an instance of the `CompressContent` class, setting the compression strategy to the `ZipCompressionStrategy` instance, and call the `compressFiles()` method, which will print the `Using zip compression` message to the console. We then set the compression strategy to the `RarCompressionStrategy` instance and call the `compressFiles()` method again, which will print the `Using rar compression` message to the console.

The strategy pattern is really good for setting the algorithms to use at runtime, which also lets us swap the algorithms out with different implementations as needed by the application. Another advantage of the strategy pattern is that we encapsulate the details of the algorithm within the strategy types themselves and not in the main implementation type.

This concludes the tour of design patterns in Swift.

Summary

Design patterns are solutions to software design problems that we tend to see over and over again in real-world application design. These patterns are designed to help us create reusable and flexible code. Design patterns can also make the code easier to read and understand for other developers and also for ourselves when we look back at the code months/years later.

If we look at the examples in this chapter carefully, we will notice that one of the backbones of design patterns is the protocol. Almost all design patterns (the singleton design pattern is an exception) use protocols to help us create very flexible and reusable code.

If this was the first time that you really looked at design patterns, you probably noticed some strategies that you have used in the past in your own code. This is expected when experienced developers are first introduced to design patterns. I would also encourage you to read more about design patterns because they will definitely help you to create more flexible and reusable code.

Swift is a language that is rapidly changing and it is important to keep up to date. Since Swift is an open source project there are plenty of resources that will help you. I would definitely recommend bookmarking `http://swiftdoc.org` in your favorite browser. It has auto-generated documentation for the Swift language and is a great resource.

Another site to bookmark is `https://swift.org`. This is the main open source Swift site. On this site, you will find links to the Swift source code, blog posts, getting started pages, and information on how to install Swift.

I would also recommend signing up for some of the mailing lists on the swift.org site. The lists are located in the community section. The swift-users mailing list is an excellent list to ask questions on and is the list that Apple monitors. If you want to stay up-to-date with the changes to Swift then I would recommend the swift-evolution-announce list.

I hope you have enjoyed reading this book as much as I have enjoyed writing it.

Index

A

ABI (Application Binary Interface) 8
access controls
  about 137
  fileprivate 138
  internal 138
  open 137
  private 138
  public 137
algorithms for arrays
  about 73
  filter 74
  forEach 76
  map 75
  sort 73
  sorted 74
Animal class 176
animal types
  requirements 176
Apple's GitHub page
  reference 8
arguments, availability attribute
  iOS 202
  iOSApplicationExtension 202
  OSX 202
  OSXApplicationExtension 202
  tvOS 202
  watchOS 202
arithmetic operator 59
array algorithms, Swift
  closures, using 250
arrays
  about 65
  algorithms 73
  appending 69
  bulk changes, making 72
  creating 65
  elements, accessing 67
  elements, counting 68
  elements, removing 70
  elements, replacing 70
  emptiness, checking 69
  initializing 65
  iterating over 76
  merging 71
  structure 190
  subarray, retrieving 71
  value, inserting 70
assignment operator 58
associated types 241
Automatic Reference Counting (ARC)
  about 150
  working 150
availability attribute 202

B

behavioral design pattern
  chain of responsibility 359
  command design pattern 360
  command pattern 359
  iterator pattern 359
  mediator pattern 359
  memento pattern 359
  observer pattern 359
  state pattern 359
  strategy pattern 359, 363
  visitor pattern 359
Boolean type 43
bridge pattern
  implementing 348
  issues 348
  solution 348
builder design pattern

about 341
implementing 342
issues 342
solution 342

C

calculated subscripts 209
calculation type
about 287
async, versus sync 292
asyncAfter, using 293
code, executing from main queue function 292
queues, creating 287
classes
about 122
creating 124
differences, with structures 122
features 122
value, versus reference types 123
closures
about 243
based on results, selecting 259
shorthand syntax 247, 250
strong reference cycles 264
strong reference cycles, creating 261
style guidelines 254
using, with Swift's array algorithms 250
collection types 64
command design pattern
about 360
implementing 360
issues 360
solution 360
comparison operator 59
compound assignment operator 60
computed properties 127
concurrency 284
concurrent queues (global dispatch queue)
about 286
creating 288
using 288
conditional statements
case statements, using 102
conditional code execution, if...else statement
used 92

guard statement 93
if statements 91
where statements, using 102
constants
about 34
defining 35
control flow
about 91
conditional statements 91
for-in loop 95
switch statement 98
while loop 96
control transfer statements
about 107
break statement 108
continue statement 107
fallthrough statement 108
Create, Read, Update, Delete (CRUD) 317
creational patterns
about 337
abstract factory pattern 338
builder design pattern 341
builder pattern 338
factory method pattern 338
prototype pattern 338
singleton design pattern 338
singleton pattern 338
curly brackets 90
custom initializers
about 133
failable initializers 136
internal and external parameter names 135
custom subscripts
creating 207
using 207, 213

D

DateFormatter class 323
design patterns
about 336
behavioral patterns 337
creational patterns 337
structural patterns 337
dictionaries
about 77

creating 78
emptiness, checking 79
initializing 78
key or values, counting 79
values, accessing 78
DispatchQueue
attributes parameter 288
label parameter 288
do's, style guide
shorthand declaration, using for collections 310
switch, using rather than multiple if statements 310
type inference, using 309
don'ts, style guides
commented-out code, avoiding in application 311
comments 306
constants and variables 307
naming 303
optional types 307
parentheses for conditional statements, avoiding 303
self keyword, using 307
semicolons at end of statements, avoiding 303

E

enumerations 54
explicit types 38
exploding class hierarchy 348
extensions 148
external names
for subscripts 210

F

facade pattern
about 353
implementing 353
issues 353
solution 353
FileManager class 327
first-in, first-out (FIFO) 285
formatter
about 323
DateFormatter 323
FileManager 327
JSONDecoder, using 333

JSONEncoder, using 331
NumberFormatter 326
function
about 109
example 118
external parameter names, adding 115
inout parameters 117
multi-parameter function, using 111
multiple values, returning 113
optional values, returning 114
parameter's default values, defining 112
single parameter function, suing 109
variadic parameters, using 116
functionality
modifying 257

G

generic functions 234
generic subscripts 238
generic types 234, 237
generics 229
Grand Central Dispatch (GCD)
about 283, 285
concurrent queues 286
main dispatch queue 286
serial queues 286

H

Hashable protocol 81
Hello World applications
about 30
separator parameter 31
terminator parameter 31

I

inheritance 139, 173
Internet Protocol (IP) 118
iOS Playground 15

J

JSONDecoder
using 333
JSONEncoder
using 331

K

key value
 updating 79
key-value pair
 adding 80
 removing 80

L

logical NOT operator 61
logical OR Operator 62

M

macOS playgrounds 16
main dispatch queue 286
main queue 294
markup functionality
 reference 25
memory management
 about 150
 Automatic Reference Counting (ARC), working 151
 strong reference cycles 152
methods
 about 131
 overriding 141, 142
mix and match
 about 267
 using 268
multidimensional subscripts 211, 213
mutability 64

N

naming rules
 about 303
 constants and variables 304
 custom types 304
 functions and methods 304
 indenting 305
native error handling
 about 194
 errors, catching 198, 201
 errors, representing 194
 errors, throwing 195
nil coalescing operator

using 226
NumberFormatter class 326
numeric types
 about 39
 double values 42
 floating-point number 42
 integer types 39

O

object-oriented design
 about 176, 181
 protocol composition 184
 protocol inheritance 183
 protocol-oriented design 182, 185
 where statement, using with protocols 188
object-oriented programming (OOP) 159
Objective-C code
 accessing, from Swift 280
Objective-C project
 creating 269
 file, adding 276
 header file, bridging 275, 280
 MessageBuilder Swift class 280
 Messages Objective-C Class 279
 Swift class, accessing 281
 Swift files, adding 272
 Swift, adding 269
Operation class
 subclassing 297
Operation
 addOperation() method, using 296
 BlockOperation, using 294
 using 293
OperationQueue types
 using 293
operators
 about 58
 arithmetic operators 59
 assignment operators 58
 comparison operators 59
 compound assignment operators 60
 logical AND operator 61
 logical NOT operator 61
 logical OR operator 62
 Remainder operator 60

ternary conditional operator 61
optional binding
  about 51, 219
  guard statement, using 223
  using 308
optional chaining
  about 52, 224
  nil coalescing operator, using 226
  using, instead of optional binding for multiple
    unwrapping 309
optional type
  defining 218
  forced unwrapping 219
  need for 217
  optional binding 220
  returning, from functions and methods 221
  using 218
  using, as parameter in function or method 222
  using, with tuples 223
optional variables 49
optionals 215, 216
overrides
  preventing 144

P

parallelism 284
parentheses 90
Playgrounds
  about 11
  Assignment Operator, not returning value 29
  avoiding 22
  comments 23
  curly brackets 28
  Debug Area 12
  graphs, creating 21
  graphs, displaying 21
  images, displaying 16, 20
  optional spaces, in conditional and assignment
    statements 30
  parentheses 27
  Results Sidebar 12
  semicolons 26
  Swift language syntax 23
polymorphism
  with protocols 162

POST request
  reference 320
programming style guide 301
properties, classes
  computed properties 124
  stored properties 124
properties, structures
  computed properties 124
  stored properties 124
properties
  overriding 141, 144
property observers 130
protocol composition 187
protocol-oriented programming (POP) 159, 175
protocol
  about 145
  extensions 164, 169, 172
  method requirements 147
  polymorphism 162
  property requirements 146
  syntax 145
  type casting 162
  using, as types 160
  using, need for 173
proxy design pattern
  about 356
  implementing 357
  issues 356
  solution 356

R

read-only custom subscripts 208
remainder operator 60
REPL (Read-Evaluate-Print-Loop) 11

S

serial queues (private queue)
  about 286
  creating 290
  using 290
session types, URLSessionConfiguration
  background session configuration 315
  default session configuration 315
  ephemeral session configuration 315
set operations

intersection and fromIntersection 84
subtracting and subtract 84
symmetricDifference and
  fromSymmetricDifference 84
union and formUnion 84
set
  about 81
  initializing 81
  item count, determining 82
  item, checking 83
  items, inserting 82
  items, removing 83
  iterating 83
  operations 84
shorthand syntax
  for closures 247, 250
simple closures 244
singleton design pattern
  implementing 340
  issue 339
  solution 339
standalone closures 254
stored properties 125
strategy pattern
  about 363
  implementing 363
  issues 363
  solution 363
string type 44
strong reference cycles
  creating, with closures 261, 264
structural design patterns
  about 347
  adapter pattern 347
  bridge pattern 347, 348
  composite pattern 347
  decorator pattern 347
  facade pattern 348, 353
  flyweight 348
  proxy design pattern 356
structures
  about 122
  creating 124
  similarities 122
  value, versus reference types 123

versus classes 189
style guide 302
subscript values 209
subscripts
  about 205
  external names 210
  using, with Swift arrays 206
Swift API design
  guidelines, reference 168
Swift arrays
  subscripts, using 206
Swift standard library
  about 173
  reference 173
Swift
  explicit types 38
  features 9
  optional types 217
  reference 8
  source compatibility, reference 8
  type inference 38
  type-safe language 37

T

ternary conditional operator 61
tuples 86
tvOS Playgrounds 15
two-sided range operator 72
type inference 38

U

unwrapping 218
URL loading system, Apple
  about 314
  HTTP POST request, making 320
  HTTPURLResponse 316
  REST web services 317
  URL 316
  URL Session 314
  URLRequest 316
  URLSessionConfiguration 315
  URLSessionTask 316

V

variables
  about 34
  defining 35

W

where statement

filtering, with for-case statement 103
if-case statement, using 106
used, for filtering 103
while loop
  about 97
  repeat-while loop, using 97
World Wide Developers Conference (WWDC) 7,
  175

Printed in Great Britain
by Amazon